Beyond the Killing Fields

Voices of Nine Cambodian Survivors in America

ASIAN AMERICA

A Series Edited by Gordon H. Chang

The increasing size and diversity of the Asian American population, its growing significance in American society and culture, and the expanded appreciation, both popular and scholarly, of the importance of Asian Americans in the country's present and past—all these developments have converged to stimulate wide interest in scholarly work on topics related to the Asian American experience. The general recognition of the pivotal role that race and ethnicity have played in American life, and in relations between the United States and other countries, has also fostered this heightened attention.

Although Asian Americans were a subject of serious inquiry in the late nineteenth and early twentieth centuries, they were subsequently ignored by the mainstream scholarly community for several decades. In recent years, however, this neglect has ended, with an increasing number of writers examining a good many aspects of Asian American life and culture. Moreover, many students of American society are recognizing that the study of issues related to Asian America speak to, and may be essential for, many current discussions on the part of the informed public and various scholarly communities.

The Stanford series on Asian America seeks to address these interests. The series will include work from the humanities and social sciences, including history, anthropology, political science, American studies, law, literary criticism, sociology, and interdisciplinary and policy studies.

Beyond the Killing Fields

Voices of Nine Cambodian Survivors in America

Usha Welaratna

STANFORD UNIVERSITY PRESS

STANFORD, CALIFORNIA   1993

Stanford University Press
Stanford, California

© 1993 by the Board of Trustees
of the Leland Stanford Junior University

Printed in the United States of America

CIP data are at the end of the book

*I dedicate this book to
Look Tha, Bopha, Pu Ma, Bun Thab, Mum, Niseth,
Nya Srey, Apsara, and Koun Srey, and to their loved ones
who perished under the Khmer Rouge.*

Acknowledgments

This book came into being only because of Look Tha, Bopha, Pu Ma, Bun Thab, Mum, Niseth, Nya Srey, Apsara, and Koun Srey, who, despite the pain and suffering they had endured, had the courage to share their experiences and thoughts with me. They received me into their families and community with warmth and hospitality, and extended friendship and trust without reservation. My gratitude to them is immeasurable; and as one small gesture, I will donate a portion of the royalties earned from the sale of this book to a Cambodian refugee cause in memory of their loved ones who perished under the Khmer Rouge.

My heartfelt thanks go to Sitha Sao, the Khmer artist who drew the beautiful illustrations.

I also thank other members of the Cambodian community for their friendship, and for teaching me many facets of the Cambodian experience and culture.

I remember with love my grandmother, Mrs. Nancy Rodrigo, who first instilled in me a love for reading, hearing, and relating stories; I believe the seeds for this book were planted then, at least 35 years ago. I also acknowledge, with love and gratitude, my parents, Mr. and Mrs. C. O. L. Bandaratilaka, who nurtured those early beginnings by providing me with the best possible education in Sri Lanka, and my family, who continue to encourage my academic and professional efforts in every letter they write from home.

I thank the San Jose State University Foundation for partially funding my early research. I am also deeply grateful to several professors at San Jose State University who encouraged and guided my research. Mira Zussman sparked my initial interest in anthropology, and then ensured my success by initiating my career as a graduate student. I thank her sincerely.

I also thank Richard Keady and Lou Lewandowski of San Jose State for their encouragement, and Denise Murray for her critical evaluation of my early research.

I returned to the academic world when our children were older only because of the wisdom of my husband, Ramya. Not only has he given me continuous moral support throughout my career as a student, he also spent countless hours reading the manuscript at every stage of its development. His questions and observations often provoked new thoughts and insights, and his commitment to excellence in his own work influenced me deeply to do my best in writing this book. I will always be indebted to him.

I thank our children, Ruwan, Sumudu, and Deepthi, who forfeited many planned activities to enable me to finish this book, and showed me ways to make it livelier. It gives me enormous pride to acknowledge in particular the mature critiques made by Sumudu, who read the complete manuscript with such care and dedication.

The penetrating criticisms, comments, and suggestions made by Gordon H. Chang of Stanford University enabled me to improve this work 100 percent, and I thank him sincerely. I also thank my editor, Muriel Bell, for her encouragement and her enthusiastic response to my work.

James M. Freeman, my major advisor at San Jose State University, exceeded my expectations in every way. From the beginning, he encouraged and assisted me to seek knowledge at my own pace. His insights and understanding of diverse cultures inspired me to discover the Cambodian people and their culture, and his patience and compassion helped me to overcome many misgivings and mishaps I had during the course of my research. The research and data-collection methods he used in his award-winning book *Hearts of Sorrow: Vietnamese-American Lives* influenced my own approach to collecting the narratives for this book, which was completed only because of his generous encouragement and support. I thank him most sincerely for all that he has done, and for writing the foreword.

U.W.

Contents

FIGURES

Foreword

James M. Freeman

In the spring of 1987, Mrs. Usha Welaratna came to my office in the department of anthropology at San Jose State University. She expressed an interest in doing a master's degree research project on immigrants. I suggested that she consider one of the many refugee groups that resided in San Jose.

Several days later, she returned to say that she would focus on Cambodian refugees. She intended to collect life histories to portray a humanistic understanding of Cambodians in the United States. The Cambodians interested her because, as a native of Sri Lanka, she shared with them the traditions of Theravada Buddhism. She hoped that this common ground would help her gain rapport among Cambodians and provide a bridge to understanding their culture.

Usha Welaratna spent several months establishing contacts in the Cambodian community and familiarizing herself with background sources. She also began her two-year study of the Khmer language, which eventually she used for most of the interviews she conducted.

Almost from the start, her project yielded a wealth of information and insights that broke new ground in studies of Cambodians and Cambodian refugees. Although several autobiographies and oral histories described the period of the Khmer Rouge massacres, hardly any recounted the experiences of refugees after they arrived in the United States. Conversely, studies of refugees in the United States generally overlooked the lives and culture of these refugees in their homeland of Cambodia. By contrast, Usha Welaratna's account set out to emphasize both life in Cambodia and in America, demonstrating the importance of understanding the former to make sense of subsequent refugee adjustments. By presenting the life stories of several people with different historical experiences and backgrounds, she has called attention both to the diversity of the Cambodians as well as some of the common cultural threads that they share.

In my view, *Beyond the Killing Fields,* which is a revised version of her prize-winning master's thesis, is especially significant for two reasons. First, it presents, in a compelling and moving manner, a detailed documentation of the lives of Cambodian refugees, from their own points of view. These details are unprecedented. Clearly, many Cambodians felt comfortable enough with the author to share with her many of the intimate and often painful memories of their lives, and also their rather blunt appraisals of life in America. The Cambodians in this book emerge first and foremost as distinct individuals. Through their stories, I came to know and like them; my heart ached as I read of their terrible sufferings; I marveled at their resilience and courage as they described how they survived and kept going against impossible odds. And I was both moved and enormously impressed by the conscious and sophisticated choices that they made in deciding how to live in America. Despite the terrible things that happened to them, the narrators in this book did not give up; their message is a positive one, not of forgiveness, but of compassion, and hope for the future.

Second and equally significant is the perspective the author uses to weave the narratives together. This book could not have been written by a Westerner. Although she is a Western-trained anthropologist, Usha Welaratna is also a Sri Lankan Theravada Buddhist. She combines these backgrounds to present a truly unique book. Her role as a female interviewer has enabled her to gain rapport with female as well as male narrators in ways that probably could not be duplicated by males. Her cultural grounding as an Asian and a Theravada Buddhist leads her to interpret the Cambodian refugee experience in ways overlooked by other investigators, but apparently widely accepted by Cambodians. A striking example is found in her observations on differing notions of "success" among Cambodian refugees and mainstream Americans. A second example is her discussion, using Cambodian points of view, of why the Khmer Rouge period was so traumatic for so many people. What is well known is that the Khmer Rouge murdered well over one million of their own citizens; what has received less attention is that the Khmer Rouge also deliberately desecrated Cambodian culture. The author provides the cultural and historical background to enable the reader to comprehend the magnitude of this auto-ethnocide. A third example is the author's discussion of the attitudes of Cambodian refugees toward the Khmer Rouge. Why is it that so many of the narrators, despite the horrors inflicted on them, do not wish to take revenge on their torturers? Usha Welaratna's analysis of this highlights ways of thinking that might easily be overlooked or misunderstood by writers who lack her thorough understanding of Theravada Buddhism. Furthermore, these distinctive points of view might prompt Americans to reassess their own cultural values in ways they might not previously have considered.

While Usha Welaratna presents a sympathetic portrait of Cambodian refugees, she is not their apologist. She elicits with great skill narratives that reveal an insider's point of view, but she also steps back from the data collected to analyze the material in a dispassionate manner.

The result, then, is quite a remarkable document: it is a testimony to the courage and determination of Cambodian refugees who have endured horrendous traumas and great stress; it is a sensitive and insightful presentation of how Cambodian refugees look upon their lives, their culture, and their adjustment in America; it calls attention to some cherished American values and practices that look very different through Cambodian eyes; finally, it presents a pathbreaking perspective for interpretation that calls into question many of the assumptions and stereotypes about Cambodians that are perpetuated by Westerners.

Usha Welaratna's book should be an indispensable source of information for teachers, for scholars, and for any reader who wishes to understand Cambodian culture and society, the refugee experience, and the effects of Americanization on newly arrived refugees. It also holds up a mirror to American society from a perspective that might enable Americans to see themselves in a new light. But above all, it is a document that inspires; it celebrates a triumph of the human spirit, humaneness, and compassion that remained steadfast through one of the darkest hours of humankind's troubled history.

Preface

Beyond the Killing Fields is an account of the Cambodian refugee experience. In the following pages, nine refugees reflect on three distinct phases of their lives: first, their experiences in pre-Communist Cambodia, in a largely non-Western, Indianized, Theravada Buddhist culture; second, their traumatic survival of the Khmer Rouge holocaust while many of their loved ones were brutally killed, or left to die of starvation and sickness; third, their hazardous escapes in search of freedom, and their experiences of adjusting as refugees to their new country, the United States.

When I first met Cambodians at a Cambodian Buddhist temple in northern California in January 1987, I had no plans to write a book about them. My husband and I, immigrants from Sri Lanka, had gone to the temple with our three children to visit a newly arrived Sri Lankan monk. Unlike the ancient, beautifully constructed temples standing in large compounds in our countries, this temple was situated in a small house in a run-down residential area primarily occupied by Cambodian refugees. From the outside, I could not distinguish the temple from the other houses. Even the footwear that people left outside the front door did not look unusual, since many houses nearby displayed a similar sight; Cambodians, like most other Asians, prefer to leave footwear outside so they don't carry the dust and dirt inside. Once we entered the front room of the house, however, we saw an unmistakably Buddhist shrine. A golden statue of the Buddha, serene and elegant, reposed on a small platform. In front of the statue lay flowers and incense offered by other devotees. Woven mats covered the floor of the shrine room, and three sitting cushions for monks lay against one wall.

In keeping with our tradition, we had taken alms (food) for the monks for their noon meal, and so had the two Cambodian families we met there. As we all offered food to the monks, I was struck by the similarities in our religious traditions that enabled us to act almost as one, even though we had originally come from two different countries and were meeting each other for the first time. Of the four adult Cambodians, only one man spoke a few words of English.

After the monks finished their meal, I began to pack our empty utensils to return home, for Sri Lankans do not customarily eat in the temple. By contrast, the Cambodians sat in a circle on the floor of the shrine room, preparing to have their meal. When they realized that we had not brought food for ourselves, the man who spoke English turned to us and asked haltingly, "You eat my food?" We accepted his kind invitation.

While we ate, the monk told us that our hosts were refugees who had recently arrived in the United States after suffering unspeakable atrocities under Pol Pot and the Khmer Rouge. I was both horrified and fascinated by the monk's accounts, particularly because neither the refugees' faces nor their behavior betrayed any of the traumas they had suffered, even though almsgiving is traditionally an occasion for remembering the dead (see Chapter 2). The women, dressed in traditional sarongs, were unable to respond to my questions, but they smiled often and shared the food generously throughout the meal. The men were dressed in Western-style clothing. But when one of them laughed, covering his mouth with his hand and looking down at the floor, he reminded me of village folk back home.

Once the mightiest kingdom of Southeast Asia, Cambodia has been in more recent times an agrarian country where over 80 percent of the people lived in rural areas. From the beginning of the Christian era, Cambodia's history and ideology evolved around Indian cultural concepts and Buddhist religious teachings. Despite French colonization spanning almost a hundred years, Western culture and thought had a strong impact on urban areas only; life changed little in rural areas, where much of the social activity revolved around the village temple. Even after independence in 1954, successive governments continued to instill pride in the national culture and customs.

After independence, Cambodia became relatively peaceful and prosperous under the leadership of Prince Norodom Sihanouk. But the war in neighboring Vietnam, the American bombing of the Cambodian countryside, other interventions in Cambodia by the Chinese and the Vietnamese, and local political corruption and social conflicts led to Cambodia's destruction.

On April 17, 1975, after five years of devastation and upheaval caused by civil war, the Cambodians, or the Khmer, as the people are known, welcomed the victorious Communist Khmer Rouge led by Pol Pot. The people were relieved that the war was over and they expected the Khmer Rouge to lead their country to peace and prosperity. Upon their ascent to power, the Khmer Rouge closed Cambodia's doors to the outside world for the next three years and eight months. Cambodia remained relatively unknown to most Americans until the Vietnamese Communists invaded it in 1979, and defeated their enemies, the Khmer Rouge. Soon after, the world learned that during their control, the Khmer Rouge had initiated a social, economic, and cultural revolution by completely desecrating Cambodia's ancient culture, and by turning the country into one of the most horrifying death camps ever known. Of an estimated 7 million people, about 1.5 million, mostly the wealthy and the educated, had been killed, or had died of starvation and sickness.

After the Vietnamese liberation, thousands of starved, tortured, and abused survivors of the Khmer Rouge, fearful of continuing war and a new Communist regime, fled their homeland amid great risks in search of refuge in any country that would take them. Since 1979, America has received approximately 150,000 Khmer refugees, the vast majority of whom came from rural backgrounds. The refugees I met at the temple were just two families of about 80,000 Cambodians who now live in the state of California.

About six months after I met the Cambodians, I attended a conference on Southeast Asian refugees at the University of California, Berkeley. I was a graduate student in anthropology and linguistics at San Jose State University at the time, and had decided to study a group of Southeast Asian refugees. Most of the other conference participants were schoolteachers who had newly arrived refugee students in their classrooms. They had many questions and concerns about the refugees, but the one that attracted my immediate attention was this remark: "I just don't understand Cambodians! They have come to the United States, but they don't seem to try to change their ways and become like us."

As an Asian immigrant, I have always been acutely aware of the choices newcomers have to make in adjusting to a new society, and also of the fact that many of these choices are influenced by our past cultural experiences and beliefs. Comparing my voluntary immigrant experiences to that of refugees, such as the Cambodians, who fled their country with no prior emotional or physical preparation, I felt they must experience even more disharmony between cultures. When I expressed these views to the teacher at that conference, however, her response was that because Cambodians now live here, they should get rid of the "cultural baggage" they had brought with them, and become Americanized as quickly as possible. Other conference participants also appeared to hold the view that regardless of backgrounds or circumstances leading to their arrival here, newcomers to America should take on American values and behaviors, and, in particular, become economically successful as quickly as possible.

I was both disturbed and intrigued by the teacher's views. I had never perceived the cultural heritage of refugees or immigrants as "cultural baggage," or thought that newcomers could or should completely abandon their past and assimilate overnight, as it were, to a new culture. Soon after the conference, I asked a forty-five-year-old refugee widow with six children if she saw any connections between her Cambodian background and her adjustments in America. She replied:

> The important thing for us is not to lose our heritage, our culture. We feel we have a unique culture that is right for us. We were born and raised from generation to generation in that culture. We cannot assimilate totally. We want to compare both Cambodian and American cultures, and be careful to pick the good things from the American culture and mix with ours.

Implicit in her reply was the refugee's strong sense of ethnic identity. I decided then to do an ethnographic study of this one ethnic group, Cambodian refugees, with particular emphasis on their adjustments to the United States. This book is the result of that research. (The attributes used by social scientists to define ethnic groups include a common national and geographic origin, culture, customs, religion, language, values, and ethos [Isajiw 1974]. All of these attributes are central to Cambodian ethnic identity.)

While this book has obvious relevance and implications for students of anthropology, ethnicity, religion, Asian Americans, history, biography, and psychology, I have decided to present my findings in a manner that might also appeal to a wider audience, including general readers, teachers of Cambodian students, other classmates and colleagues of Cambodian refugees, and new generations of Cambodian Americans. Two important factors influenced my decision. First, the study was conducted partly in response to teachers' need to understand Cambodian refugees. Second, while conducting my research, I discovered many characteristics of the Cambodian people that I would like to convey to the larger American public. I was particularly touched by the courage and humanity the refugees have displayed amid all the indignities, traumas, and tragedies that have beset their lives. They have affected me deeply, and caused me to reexamine my own actions and perceptions.

Since a discussion of ethnic identity involves not only how one perceives and creates one's self, but also how one is perceived and labeled by others, I have discussed the observations and findings of some researchers and refugee service providers about Cambodian refugee adjustments in the final part of this book. Policies affecting refugees are formulated on the basis of various research studies conducted by social scientists; therefore an important issue raised here is the extent to which American views of refugee adjustments differ from those of Cambodian refugees, who are expected to meet American goals. This book, however, is mainly an attempt to convey something of the lives and ethos of the Cambodians themselves; it presents not only the views of the nine narrators whose stories are presented here but also those of other refugees in the larger community whom I came to know during the course of my work.

While my intent has been to let the Khmer people speak for themselves, many questions I sought to answer have resulted from my own immigrant experience. I believe that my background and experiences as an Asian Theravada Buddhist female immigrant give me some insights about the Cambodian refugee experience that Western-born researchers may have missed. I hope that through this work, Cambodian refugee views and needs will become known to teachers, other refugee service providers, and policy makers, and that it will lead to a better understanding of Cambodians, who are now an integral part of America's pluralistic society.

Beyond the Killing Fields

*Voices of Nine Cambodian
Survivors in America*

Creating *Beyond the Killing Fields*

The Narrators

Although several biographies and autobiographies have been written about or by Cambodian refugees, these accounts focus primarily on childhood and the terrible experiences of the Pol Pot era. Furthermore, they are generally the stories of educated, urbanized, ethnic Cambodians. In contrast, *Beyond the Killing Fields* represents a wider spectrum of Cambodian society. While all nine narrators in this book grew up in Cambodia as Theravada Buddhists, they vary in age, sex, ethnic heritage, and socioeconomic background. The narratives in this book also differ from others in their detailed accounts of the narrators' adjustments in America.

Seven women and only two men appear in this book; this reflects the present disparity of Cambodian males to females in the United States. Patrick Cooke (*New York Times Magazine*, June 23, 1991) writes that of the estimated 1.5 million people who died under the Khmer Rouge, 80 percent were men between the ages of 20 and 50. One consequence of this is that most Cambodian refugee households in America are headed by women. This is similar to the situation in Cambodia, where women constitute 64 percent of the adult population and head some 35 percent of the households (UNICEF 1990).

To protect their identities, I have changed the real names of the narrators whose stories appear in this book. Their pseudonyms highlight some distinctive characteristic of each narrator; these are explained in the introduction to each life history.

In recent years, several different regimes have ruled Cambodia. Frequently, each new regime changed the official name of the country. In this book, I follow the preference and usage of the narrators in referring to their country as Cambodia, and their usage of Mother, Father, Mom, and Dad interchangeably.

When the Khmer Rouge gained control of Cambodia, Bun Thab, an ethnic Cambodian, was a poor, uneducated fourteen-year-old farm boy, cultivating rice fields in a remote village, while thirty-year-old Chinese Cambodian Nya Srey, the educated daughter of a rice field owner, lived in Phnom Penh as the wife of a successful lawyer. Mum is Nya Srey's only daughter. She was a happy, spoiled eight-year-old when the Communists came. Eighteen-year-old Vietnamese Cambodian Bopha had just been admitted to medical school, and Pu Ma, an ethnic Cambodian who was an unskilled factory worker, was also eighteen, but already married and the mother of two children. Koun Srey, her younger child, was a two-year-old toddler. Fifty-year-old Look Tha, formerly a Buddhist monk, was also a farmer, but unlike Bun Thab, he was married, and economically self-sufficient. Niseth, an ethnic Cambodian, was a twelve-year-old elementary-school girl and the daughter of a well-to-do veterinarian, while Apsara, an ethnic Cambodian of fifteen, was training to become a professional dancer.

The life histories in *Beyond the Killing Fields* add a wealth of information to existing accounts of the Cambodian refugee experience. The Khmer Rouge forced Niseth and her family, along with others of her social background, to live among one of the tribes of Cambodia. This tribe helped Niseth's group to survive under extreme hardship, sharing what little food they had with the newcomers. Niseth's account contrasts with Vickery's observations that Khmer Rouge atrocities were partly perpetrated by tribal people taking revenge on mainstream Cambodians (1984). Bopha's experiences of the Khmer Rouge period differ from other available accounts because, as a Vietnamese Cambodian, she was repatriated by the Khmer Rouge to Vietnam, although her siblings and relatives were trapped, and some perished in Cambodia. Koun Srey, a mere toddler when the Khmer Rouge took over, may be the youngest victim of the Communist regime to relate her memories. Mum provides a detailed account of childhood under the regime. Nya Srey and Pu Ma reflect the hardships and loneliness experienced by almost all wives widowed by the Communist regime. The descriptions of peasant life by Bun Thab and Look Tha, as well as Look Tha's description of his youth as a monk, reflect the experiences of many other refugees who came from rural Cambodia. The recounting of Buddhist traditions by all narrators, and of folk tales by two narrators, brings to life the very essence of Cambodian culture. Their strategies of coping with the memories and experiences of the holocaust provide insights into the strengths and weaknesses of human nature.

Even with the varied backgrounds and experiences of these narrators, which reflect divergent views and strategies of adjustment, the narrators may not represent all varieties of Khmer refugees and their experiences. I have interviewed only nine persons, all of whom live in northern California. My choice was to focus on a few lives, rather than include more narrators from different locations with less detail.

The refugees in this book express their joys and fears, hopes and frustrations about the past, present, and future. Their stories are culturally distinctive, but also open out to broader human experiences. I hope that the telling of their stories will help other Americans to understand and appreciate the Cambodian experience, and that it will enhance the development of friendships with Cambodian refugees.

The Interviews

I began this study in 1987; although I completed recording the narratives for this book in 1990, my research and friendship continue, both with the narrators and with other Cambodian refugees. Since I plan to publish a technical monograph with portions of the full texts as dialogues along with discussion of the editing process, I will describe only some of the conditions under which the interviews took place in this book.

My aim in this project was to understand and convey Khmer refugee views of life, using life-history and participant-observation methods as the main tools of research. Before I embarked on my mission, however, I first learned the Khmer language, since the vast majority of Khmer refugees spoke only minimal English. Because I believed that refugee perspectives and their adjustments to the United States would be influenced by the larger historical and cultural events and experiences in their lives, I also read extensively on the history and culture of the Khmer people. The works of Chandler, Chhim, Ebihara, Grant et al., Kiernan and Boua, Ngor, Shawcross, and Yathay were very helpful.

Once I had an understanding of the language, historical background, and cultural roots of the refugees, I immersed myself in the Cambodian refugee community as an active participant and observer. Through this process, I both secured their trust and gained access to possible narrators; I also came to understand the continuities and discontinuities between their past experiences and their present existence in the United States as refugees.

I met five of the narrators during my fieldwork, and the other four were referred to me by Cambodian and American acquaintances. While I shared some traits with Cambodians because I am Asian and Buddhist, as an academic from a middle-class background I represented more power and authority than my informants. I was sensitive to the disparities of our positions. Also, I realized that the recollection of memories of the holocaust would be particularly painful to the narrators. Consequently, before I began to collect their life histories, I informed each narrator in writing (in Khmer and/or English) about the exact nature of the project and gave them complete freedom to withhold any information they did not wish to disclose. They were also free to withdraw from the project at any stage, which three people did. Each narrator also retained complete editorial discretion for his or her story, although I did the final editing of all the narratives.

The interviews ranged from 24 to over 100 hours, and participants received copies of the narratives they contributed. The interviews were conducted in Khmer and English (depending on the narrators' wishes and ability to communicate in English), and all but one took place in the narrators' homes. I requested the narrators to relate those incidents and experiences that were particularly significant in their lives, especially if they were important for their adjustment to America. My questions were open-ended, and I generally let the narrators relate their stories in the order and manner they found comfortable. On occasion, I departed from this procedure when I sought information about their adjustments to the United States. My questions frequently were prompted by my own immigrant experience; my understanding of Theravada Buddhist teachings and traditions; my knowledge of Cambodian history and Cambodian and other Asian cultural values; views of American teachers, researchers, and refugee service providers about Cambodians; the voluntary service I provided as an English instructor; and events I had witnessed taking place in the refugee community.

I explored, for instance, how events in Cambodia's lengthy and ancient history affected the refugees' current adjustments. I investigated their perceptions of why Cambodia fell to a Communist regime, and how their unplanned move from their cooperative society to individualistic competitive American society influenced their lives. I was also interested in learning how Cambodia's relative isolation from the West, and the Khmer people's historic animosity toward the Vietnamese, affected Cambodian refugee adjustments to Western, multicultural America, now also the home of a large number of Vietnamese refugees.

Some researchers and refugee service providers view Cambodian refugees as generally socially and economically unsuccessful in the United States (see Chapter 15). In many respects I have come to doubt this. As I explored Cambodian views about life-cycle events such as birth, marriage, childrearing, education, employment, freedom and success, old age and death, and investigated their perceptions of American views of such events and experiences, I discovered that their ideas of "success" differed from the American concept frequently used by researchers and service providers. My Asian ethnicity was particularly helpful in eliciting frank and candid responses to these questions.

Memories of my early frustration at not knowing how to speak in the "American" way, even though I was conversant in English when I came to America, led me to investigate how English-language acquisition affected the Cambodians, most of whom had never heard English until they came to refugee camps. I learned English as a second language in Sri Lanka; later I taught English to Asian and Middle Eastern immigrant students in two American public schools. I used this background to teach English to adult Cambodian refugees in their own homes. I am convinced that successful social adjustment is largely the result of learning not only the language of the host country but also the manner of its use, such as speaking directly rather than indirectly (see Chapter 15). Because of this, I investigated refugee views on this subject and then paid close attention to refugee interactions with mainstream Americans. My students were receiving public assistance, and their homes were located in economically and socially depressed areas. By teaching and observing my students in their home environment, I gained invaluable insights into and understanding of their special learning problems that I would not have gained had I taught them in a regular classroom.

The Khmer Rouge killings and other atrocities prompt strong reactions from Americans as well as Cambodians. The way questions are asked influences how Cambodians respond in telling about and interpreting these terrible events. My knowledge of Buddhist teachings, particularly about reverence for all life, abstinence from killing, karma (kamma), and rebirth (see Chapter 2), enabled me to ask painful, yet important questions about how the refugees cope with the aftermath of the holocaust. Because of my own Theravada Buddhist background, I was able to ask questions of particular significance to Cambodians, and to do it in a manner that might not occur to a researcher unfamiliar with the traditions of these people; and I found that Cambodian coping strategies differ significantly from what many Westerners might expect.

I attended many religious ceremonies both in the Buddhist temple and in refugee homes. While my active participation and understanding of Buddhist traditions and customs enabled me to gain the trust of the community, I discovered through these activities that Cambodian Buddhist beliefs are heavily intertwined with folk beliefs that are not a part of the Sri Lankan Buddhism with which I am familiar. This was particularly interesting to me, because it was the Sinhalese or Sri Lankan form of Buddhism that spread to Cambodia. The differences that I discovered here added a new dimension to my understanding of the holocaust experience and the symbolic actions I witnessed at religious ceremonies.

During my research, I witnessed Christian missionary attempts to convert Cambodian refugees using coercive methods, and to recruit them to their churches. (See *San Jose Mercury News* of Aug. 18, 1991, for similar missionary attempts among the Hmong people.) Because of the important role Buddhism plays in helping refugees cope with the Pol Pot tragedies (see Chapters 2 and 14), I investigated refugee views of Christian beliefs and the missionary recruitment activities. I interpret narrators' responses to my questions in Part IV of this book.

The Arrangement of the Narratives

In their narratives, the refugees describe three distinctly different phases of their lives. First, they give us a glimpse of their close-knit, cooperative families and communities in pre–Khmer Rouge Cambodia, and the distinct way of life that had evolved from Indian and Buddhist traditions.

Second, the refugees relive the physical and emotional devastation and suffering they and their people endured under the Khmer Rouge. They analyze how their cultural norms and religious practices helped them to survive the holocaust, and how these norms continue to help them in their adjustments to its aftermath.

Third, the narrators open for us the world of closed refugee camps, which few outsiders are permitted to visit. The narrators fled to these camps when their historical enemies, the Vietnamese, liberated them in 1979. They then talk candidly about their experiences in adjusting to the United States, faced with the challenge that they are culturally, religiously, and linguistically non-Western.

The narratives appear in Parts I, II, and III of this book, and are placed according to the phase they describe most fully or compellingly. At the same time, a full life history is included so that the reader can grasp the continuity of the life of each narrator, and the wider context in which to view his or her life in America.

Each of the above parts opens with an introductory section that provides a background for understanding the narratives. Part I, covering Cambodia before the Communist era, begins with an overview of pre–Khmer Rouge Cambodian history and culture, and Theravada Buddhist teachings and practices.

Part II covers the Khmer Rouge revolution. The life histories included here illustrate some of the worst horrors of this tragic era. Because my aim in this book is to further the understanding of Khmer refugees' adjustments to the United States, I do not focus on the political aspects of the rise of the Khmer Rouge in my introduction. (This has been covered widely by other authors.) Instead, I describe the Khmer Rouge desecration of Cambodian cultural values and Buddhist ideology, which has had a strong impact on the refugees.

Part III covers the adjustments of Cambodian refugees to America, and the introduction to this section gives an overview of refugee camps in Southeast Asia, the American reception of and response to these refugees at the time of their arrival, and subsequent developments.

Part IV contains my interpretations of the life histories. These cover the aftermath of the holocaust and Cambodian and American views of Khmer refugees. Refugee views in this section have been presented in relation to the larger historical and cultural background of the Cambodian people; this enables the reader to understand why, in evaluating their adjustments, the Cambodians trace the threads that connect them to their historic past.

Part IV also provides some views of the concept of "freedom" from a Cambodian refugee perspective. These views provide an alternative and challenge to conventional American views of freedom.

PART I

Pre-Khmer Rouge
Cambodia

CHAPTER ONE

Historical Background

Origins of the Cambodian People

This chapter presents those Cambodian historical events that have been formative in the lives of the narrators or that have been described by them as an integral part of their identities.

Historians assert that Cambodia, at one time the dominant kingdom of Southeast Asia, has many elements that connect the present-day Cambodians, or Khmer, to their ancestors. Prehistoric human skulls and bones found in the northern region of the country show resemblances to modern Cambodians; methods of pottery production in Cambodia date back six thousand years; and the Khmer language evolved from languages spoken at the beginning of the Christian era. Other links to their ancient culture include the consumption of large amounts of fish, domestication of pigs and buffalo, pile dwellings, village games played at the lunar new year, slash-

and-burn cultivation, and animistic beliefs and ancestor worship (Chandler 1983).

With the exception of the three years and eight months when the Khmer Rouge severed the people's connections to their historic past, this thread of continuity runs through the many eras of Cambodian history up to the present time. Although continuity does not mean that Cambodians are averse to change, it has been an important element in the ways they accommodate new social and cultural ideas through the centuries.

Indianization

The first major transformations in the region that is Cambodia came at the beginning of the Christian era, when Indian culture and thought arrived. India never colonized Cambodia, and Indian influences were not imposed by force. Instead, Indianization spread through the exchange of ideas via traders and travelers between the two countries, intermarriage between Khmer and Indians, and brahman advisers to Khmer rulers. The Indian monarchic system, with its strict social hierarchy, replaced the egalitarian social system of the Cambodian tribal cultures of the time, and the Khmer acquired from India a vocabulary for the social hierarchy, a system of codified law, a writing system, meters for poetry, a pantheon, Buddhism, architecture, iconography, and astronomy. While these changes continued for over a thousand years, the Khmer did not embrace every aspect of Indian culture, but developed their own distinctive culture by choosing only those aspects they wanted from the Indian model. For instance, the caste system, an important feature of Indian social structure, never became a part of Khmer society.

Early Cambodian kingdoms also traded and had diplomatic relations with China, the other great power at this time. A number of Khmer dynasties paid token tribute to Chinese rulers, and there was some Chinese cultural influence on Cambodian art and certain forms of dress. However, Cambodia remained essentially Indianized rather than Sinicized. Because Indianization was not imposed by force it did not produce the identity crisis among Cambodians that Sinicization produced among the Vietnamese (Chandler 1983: 12). Indianization was so pervasive, however, that the structure and worldview it provided united the society and gave it a national identity, until the Khmer Rouge attempted by force to eradicate the past. As this book shows, they did not fully succeed in their attempt.

The Angkor Empire

From the ninth century to about the fifteenth, Cambodia ascended to a period of political and cultural brilliance with the Angkor empire, founded by King Jayavarman II, and extending over parts of today's Thailand, Vietnam, Laos, and Burma. Angkorian kings, known as *Devarajas*, or god-kings, were believed to be the earthly incarnations of divinity, and in theory had absolute power over all subjects and land. Their subjects were stratified into aristocracy, priests, administrators, free peasants, and slaves. Both the higher and lower levels of society were marked by hierarchical vocabulary and various rights and symbols; for example, Brahmanism was the religion of the royal court, while Mahayana Buddhism, ancestor worship, and animistic beliefs formed the religion of the masses. During the thirteenth century, however, most of the population converted to Theravada Buddhism, proclaimed as the national religion.

By the fifteenth century, the Angkor empire began to decline politically and economically, and principalities that were former vassals of Angkor declared their independence. The Thai became a major invading force, and in 1430–31 their final sack of Angkor brought the empire to an end. But the high cultural development of the period is evident even today in the famous ruins of Angkor Wat and its complex of magnificent temples, palaces, libraries, and irrigation works. These monuments are a source of pride and provide a strong sense of ethnic identity to Khmer refugees.

Decline of Cambodia

With the downfall of Angkor, Thailand and Vietnam became increasingly powerful, and gradually usurped much of what was formerly Cambodian territory. During their control, the Vietnamese removed large portions of territory and thousands of ethnic Cambodians from Cambodian control, and stories about their mistreatment of Khmer people became legends passed on through generations. In addition to exercising military control, Vietnam also tried to dominate Cambodian culture by colonizing the region with Vietnamese, and by attempting to reform every aspect of Cambodian lifestyle: language, dress, eating habits, patterns of measurement, land holdings, tax payments, irrigation works, and agricultural methods. These actions were bound to fail: "The two peoples lived on different sides of a deep cultural divide, perhaps the most sharply defined of those in effect in nineteenth-century Southeast Asia" (Chandler 1983: 127). Vietnamese activities caused deep resentment; these anti-Vietnamese feelings persisted through the centuries, and are present among Cambodian refugees even today.

When Vietnam, Thailand, and other Southeast Asian countries were opening trading posts to Spanish and Portuguese traders, the Vietnamese closed Phnom Penh to foreigners. A few Christian missionaries gained entry into Cambodia, but were unsuccessful in their missions because Theravada Buddhism was especially strong. Thus, when Western culture and thought began to spread to other Asian countries, Cambodia was not exposed to them. Sporadic rebellions against the Vietnamese escalated to a wide-ranging but unsuccessful rebellion in 1840. In 1847, Vietnam withdrew her forces because of Thai intervention.

Although the Khmer rebelled against the Thai invaders as well, there was less resentment against the Thais because, as Theravada Buddhists, they were culturally and religiously similar to the Khmer. The Thais, moreover, never attempted to impose cultural changes; they governed Cambodian territory at most levels with ethnic Khmer. In 1848 King Duang, a Khmer king, ascended the throne under the auspices of Thai and Cambodian brahmans.

In the mid-1850's, King Duang, plagued by Thais and Vietnamese, sought support from the French, but a French diplomatic mission sent in 1856 failed to reach the king owing to Thai intervention. King Duang's successor, King Norodom, started secret negotiations with the French to eliminate Thai control, and in 1863 the French signed a secret treaty with Norodom, offering him the protection of a French resident in exchange for timber concessions and mineral exploration rights. In 1864 the Thai and the French agreed to co-sponsor his coronation, and for the first time in Cambodian history a Cambodian king accepted his crown from a European power. Thus France gained control of Cambodia not through military power, but through Cambodia's need for protection.

Cambodia Under the French

At the time the French arrived in Cambodia, kingship had changed little since the time of Angkor; theoretically, the king still had supreme power over legislative, judicial, and religious matters, as well as over land and people. This autocratic system was contrary to French ideas of rational, centralized control. The French saw their role in Cambodia as a "civilizing mission," and in 1884, Charles Thomson, governor general of Cochin China, proposed reforms to replace Cambodian officials with French residents or local governors in provincial cities, abolish slavery, and institutionalize the ownership of land. The king was coerced into agreement with these reforms even though they struck at the heart of traditional Cambodian politics, built on entourages, exploitation of labor, and the taxation of harvests rather than land. They also made the Khmer elite paid civil servants of the French, which enraged them. In 1885, a nationwide rebellion, which lasted a year and a half, demonstrated that the Cambodian status quo was too important to be tampered with by the French, and that the regional elites could effectively organize substantial guerrilla forces against them. The king, to whom the French turned, quelled the rebellion by proclaiming that traditional Cambodian laws and customs would be upheld.

By 1897, King Norodom was failing in health, and Paris granted the resident executive authority to issue royal decrees, appoint officials, and collect taxes. In Phnom Penh, land became available for purchase by French citizens, and slavery was abolished.

King Norodom died in 1904, and in the succeeding years, Cambodia became a relatively important revenue-producing source for the French. They obtained Battambang and Siem Riep provinces from the Thais through negotiations, and with advanced agricultural technology, Battambang became the most prosperous province in the country, with the highest rice exports. But these improvements were limited to the northwestern part of the kingdom. In the rest of the country, expanding populations cultivated rice in traditional ways.

Even though the French colonization of Cambodia spanned nearly 100 years, French administrators did not as a rule speak Khmer, nor did they make attempts to educate Cambodians either in the French language or in French ideals. Instead, to govern the Cambodians they imported Vietnamese who were proficient in French and familiar with the French administrative system. By 1945, more than half the inhabitants of Phnom Penh were ethnic Vietnamese, as were nearly all the workers on Cambodia's rubber plantations. The Cambodian officials of high rank played a subordinate and ceremonial role, and those at the lower levels were underpaid colonial servants.

The French financed almost all their expenses in Cambodia, including public works and the salaries of their officials, by taxing salt, rice and other crops, alcohol, opium, exports, and imports, by levying high fees for government services, and by requiring corvée labor. The harshness of life during this period has been documented by Bunchan Mul, who later joined the Khmer Issaraks, the resistance fighters against the French (see Kiernan and Boua 1982: 115–16).

Despite the high level of taxation, French spending on Cambodia was almost negligible. May Ebihara, the first American anthropologist to study a Khmer village, observes that while a number of services to augment and improve agriculture, forestry, and animal husbandry were created, there was little actual or widespread effect at the local level. As a result, much of the peasant culture was not exposed to French influences, but remained largely and fundamentally unmodified (Ebihara 1971: 43–46). The French kept Cambodia an agricultural colony, to be used as a source for various natural products, and as a market for French manufactured goods. Thus industrialization was not encouraged, and running water and electricity were almost unknown outside Phnom Penh. In 1922, a French official called French efforts in the fields of education and medical services "a mere facade."

Taxation was increased during the First World War. This led overburdened villagers to murder a French resident named Bardez. There were also unprecedented massive peasant protests. However, the populace sought justice from the king, and not from the French; French control was not directly challenged and the protests did not become political. But the high salaries of French officials and their preference for Vietnamese civil servants over Cambodians had important effects on the development of Cambodian nationalism and communism.

The 1920's brought an economic boom in Indochina, but life changed little for Cambodians. Near the end of the decade, paved and gravel roads were built throughout the country and a 500-kilometer stretch of railroad was constructed between Phnom Penh and Battambang and later extended to the Thai border. While these developments led to an expansion of transportation and communication, they also increased the exploitation of the rural economy by Chinese and Vietnamese immigrants, who generally controlled the rice exports and rubber plantations.

Development of Cambodian Nationalism and Communism

The first French lycée was established in Cambodia in 1936. Until then, Cambodian students received a traditional education in *wats* (Buddhist temples) and community-supported schools, except for a privileged few who were sent to France or to French schools in Vietnam. Among them was Prince Norodom Sihanouk. In 1941, at nineteen years of age, Sihanouk was crowned by the French; they believed he would be more malleable than Prince Sisowath, the rightful heir.

After the 1930's, a new nationalist consciousness began to develop among a young generation of students who had acquired the democratic and nationalist ideals of the French revolution. They became concerned about colonialism, the Vietnamese domination of the Cambodian civil service, and the Chinese domination of Cambodian commerce. An association of graduates, the first of its kind, was formed with a membership of more than five hundred, and the first Khmer newspaper, *Nagara Vatta,* was begun. Its mission was the political awakening of the Khmer people. When one of its founders, Son Ngoc Thanh, was arrested by the French in 1941, his followers fled to Thai-controlled Cambodian territory in the north, where they formed themselves into bands called Khmer Issaraks, or Free Cambodians. Their purpose was to fight for independence.

Through all these developments, one group that worried the French more than others was the Buddhist clergy, or the *Sangha,* who commanded great respect and obedience from the people. The French saw them as a group who offered the people a value system other than the colonial one. In fact, the Sangha did prove to be a considerable force when they organized the first Cambodian nationalist demonstration in 1942, which provided impetus to Cambodian anticolonial ideas. In 1943, the French resident forcibly changed the Khmer alphabet to a romanized system in the belief that a change in the status quo of Khmer society would improve the natives' thinking about the outside world. But many people, especially the Sangha, saw the reforms as an attack on traditional education and the high status accorded to traditional educators in Cambodia, and thus an attack on an essential character of their civilization passed down since Angkorean times.

The Japanese disarmament of the French administrators during the Second World War gave the Khmer the immediate strength to fight for independence. Supported by the Japanese, the Thais also waged war against the French and recaptured Battambang and Siem Riep, the northwestern territories of Cambodia. The Japanese ordered Sihanouk to declare independence in 1945, and to appoint Son Ngoc Thanh as prime minister. The new government changed the name of the country to Kampuchea and reinstated the Khmer alphabet, stating that for Cambodia to adopt the roman alphabet would be for it to become "a society without history, without value, without mores, and without traditions" (Chandler 1983). This outlook reveals how deeply the Cambodians feel about their history and traditions.

The French returned to power in 1945, exiled Thanh, and tried to recapture their former status. But their weakness in the face of Japanese advances had seriously undermined the confidence of the Cambodians in the colonial regime, and had set the stage for political changes in the postwar period.

Although the first Cambodian Communist activity dates from the early 1930's when a few ethnic Khmer joined Ho Chi Minh's Indochina Communist Party (ICP), left-wing nationalism did not gain momentum until the Japanese occupation of Cambodia. At this time, some Khmer Issarak cadres and ICP members allied themselves with Vietnamese and Laotian Communists and formed formidable forces of resistance fighters. Over the next few years, their bases extended over the northwestern, southwestern, and southeastern regions of Cambodia. As the organization developed, the groups were linked to form a large, united military-political organization. With the formal dissolution of the ICP in 1951, a Khmer People's Revolutionary Party was formed, with an estimated membership of about 1,000 people. This was the forerunner to the Communist Party of Kampuchea, scathingly referred to as the "Khmer Rouge" by Prince Sihanouk in the 1960's.

Sihanouk opened negotiations with the French, with complete independence as the ultimate goal. While he was not allied with the freedom fighters because they were opposed to a monarchy, he nevertheless used their victories to strengthen his negotiations by insisting that all of Cambodia supported them in their demands for independence. The French, however, refused to grant full independence to Cambodia, saying they needed the Cambodian bases to fight the war with the Viet Minh. But by 1949, mostly because of the intensification of the war in Indochina, the French signed a treaty allowing the Cambodians some freedom in foreign affairs and military autonomy in Battambang and Siem Riep, which the Thais had returned.

In 1952, Sihanouk assumed power as prime minister, appointed his own cabinet, and promised to gain independence within three years. In 1953, the French gave Sihanouk powers over the Cambodian armed forces, judiciary, and foreign affairs, but kept their hold on the economy. Finally, in 1954, at the Geneva Conference, Cambodia was granted full independence.

The Issaraks, who contributed much to Sihanouk's success in winning independence from the French, and who then controlled perhaps as much as 40 percent of Cambodia's territory, were not allowed representation at the conference by China and the Western powers. Following independence, thousands of Issaraks fled to Hanoi. When they returned in the early 1970's, almost all were killed by American bombing, Lon Nol's army, or by internal Communist purges under the leadership of Pol Pot. A few survivors hold important positions in the post-1979 Cambodian regime, the People's Republic of Kampuchea.

The Sihanouk Era

In 1955, King Sihanouk abdicated his throne in favor of his father. As prince, he announced he was a politician and formed a new political party, the Sangkum Reastr Niyum (Popular Socialist Community) to compete in the general elections. He won the elections and assumed the title of chief of state, dominating the executive, judicial, and legislative branches of the government. Lon Nol remained in control of military establishments in one post or another throughout the Sihanouk years.

In trying to build up the solidarity of the nation, Sihanouk gave new significance to old symbols. The first of these was the monarchy, representing not only Cambodian history and culture but also the new regime's political conservatism based on neutrality and moderation. To achieve his goal, Sihanouk fostered intimacy with the peasantry by communicating with them in the popular idiom during frequent visits to villages. With his closeness, the monarchy was no longer a remote power indifferent to the needs of the people, but a benevolent paternalistic authority, concerned with the welfare of the nation.

Buddhism was the second symbol used by Sihanouk to connect the people to their historic past, and it acted as a cohesive agent by providing a common philosophy. Among the Buddhist values Sihanouk extolled were the brotherhood of man, self-help, and self-sacrifice for the good of the group. These ideals were also integrated into the newly expanded educational system.

A third concept Sihanouk tried to introduce was that of the nation, but this was less successful than the other symbols. The peasantry had been historically isolated in villages with little connection to the capital; also, they were aware of the social inequality between the elites and the masses. To bring the elites and the peasantry closer, Sihanouk tried to use both groups for the socioeconomic development of the country. He urged the elites to exercise moderation and tried to inculcate in the peasantry the idea of equality under the Buddhist religion and before the law. But Sihanouk, believing that a successful relationship with the masses only was sufficient to assure the stability of the country, never fully succeeded in unifying Cambodia.

Soon after independence, new groups of graduates, including future Khmer Rouge leaders such as Saloth Sar (alias Pol Pot), Ieng Sary, and Khieu Samphan began to return from France with legal, political, and economic educational backgrounds and Marxist leanings. But Sihanouk's Sangkum party remained a loose coalition of powerful families and cliques of different ideologies, and these younger, politically ambitious intellectuals were not allowed to introduce any significant changes. Furthermore, since it was not possible to absorb all of them into government offices, Sihanouk tried to encourage them to return to their provinces, where good teachers and public servants were badly needed. Only those favored by the sovereign became prosperous, and dissatisfaction spread among the new intellectuals.

As time went on, Sihanouk became threatened, first by the American-supported Khmer Serei (a group formed out of the remnants of the Khmer Issarak) based in Thailand and South Vietnam, and second by a CIA coup to overthrow his government with the support of the Serei. In 1962, he terminated American economic and military aid, believing that the Viet Minh would win the war.

After 1962, the money supply shrank, and steps taken by Sihanouk to nationalize the economy were not followed by suitable economic measures. Minor civil servants, for whom bribes had been an essential supplement to meager salaries, joined the unemployed graduates and the officer corps in bitter resentment of the expulsion of the Americans and the socialization of the economy. Toward the latter part of Sihanouk's rule, widespread corruption, especially among those in power, hampered the nation's growth.

As the dissatisfaction of those around him increased, Sihanouk began harassing anyone who opposed him. Following a student demonstration in 1963, he forced some left-wing ministers to resign. From then on, many Paris-trained Communist intellectuals who later emerged as Khmer Rouge leaders disappeared from their jobs and joined the Communist forces in the jungle. Among them were schoolteachers Saloth Sar (later known as Pol Pot) and Ieng Sary; their wives, Khieu Ponnary and Khieu Thirith; government ministers Hu Nim and Khieu Samphan; and Son Sen, a director of curriculum at the National Pedagogical Institute.

The country continued to decline politically and economically, and in

1967 the first large revolt by left-wing rebels against Sihanouk was suppressed with bloodshed. By now the conservatives in the government, including Lon Nol, had started to voice concern about ties between indige-
nous insurgents and Vietnamese Communists, and for the first time Sihanouk also attributed the troubles not to the Khmer Serei, but to outside
Communist leadership, specifically Hanoi. From then on, he became increasingly worried about the Communist infiltration into Cambodia.

Sihanouk was strongly anti-Communist, but he maintained a neutral
foreign policy. By exploiting the ambitions and weaknesses of competing
foreign countries, he obtained the maximum possible aid for Cambodia
without allowing the society to be influenced either by modernizing capitalists or revolutionary socialists. But after the United States began its political and military commitment to the anti-Communist regime in Saigon,
American officials found that Cambodia's neutrality posed many problems
for them. With the outbreak of fighting in Vietnam, the United States and
South Vietnam pressured Sihanouk for support. But because of his fears of
Vietnamese territorial demands on Cambodia, he would not support their
requests. Eventually Saigon and the United States accused Cambodia of
providing refuge for Communist troops. In 1963 Sihanouk terminated relations with the United States. Although he approached the United States for
aid again in 1969, it was more from economic than military need.

While Sihanouk distrusted and disliked the Vietnamese, he recognized
the power of Hanoi. Although he realized that Cambodia would be far
more vulnerable to a united Marxist Vietnam than to a divided nation at
war, he believed that he had no choice but to reach an ambiguous modus
vivendi with the Communists. In 1965 he allowed them to come across the
ill-defined border and build temporary base camps in areas of the eastern
provinces of his country. In 1967 Kissinger and Nixon granted the American General Westmoreland permission to "search and destroy" these Communist strongholds or "sanctuaries," and on March 18, 1969, America started secretly bombing the Cambodian countryside, causing great destruction. The attacks continued over a period of fourteen months. To avoid
them, the North Vietnamese and the Viet Cong pushed their sanctuaries
and supply bases deeper into Cambodia, and the area that the B-52s bom-
barded expanded. The war spread. The Cambodian left accused Sihanouk
of secretly selling out to the United States.

By 1970, although Cambodia was not nearly as impoverished as most
other Asian countries, and was spared the problems of landlessness or ab-
sentee landlordism in general, the stagnant economy and a bad harvest in

1969 created pockets of peasant discontent. Still, the vast majority of peasants continued to consider Sihanouk a modern-day god-king, and the Khmer Rouge remained small and insignificant. But Sihanouk had alienated the upper class, the bourgeoisie, and the army by depriving them of their traditional financial advantages. While he was out of the country, Sihanouk was ousted in a coup orchestrated by the American-backed prime minister, Lon Nol. Allman describes the March 28, 1970, coup as "an upper-class coup, and not a revolution" (Allman 1971: 97). Sihanouk formed a government in exile, the National United Front of Cambodia, and joined his former enemies, the Khmer Rouge. Under Lon Nol, Cambodia became a republic on April 10, 1970.

The Lon Nol Era

The Lon Nol government began by wooing the elites, the urbanites, and the students. They promised economic prosperity, increased incomes, job opportunities through denationalization of the economic structure, encouragement of private enterprise, and foreign investment capital. In addition, the new regime tried to instill a new national spirit by promising to repulse Vietnamese Communists from border regions, which helped to justify an increase for military expenses in the new budget.

By asserting its "active" neutrality through an anti-Communist campaign, the new government hoped to attract American support, which won them the full support of the army. Not only did the officers profess loyalty to Lon Nol as their commanding officer, they were attracted to the possibility of again having the more bountiful days they once had enjoyed, with American aid. United States military aid started secretly in April, with the supply of automatic rifles and several thousand Khmer Krom troops, made up of Khmer minorities living in South Vietnam, who became mercenaries and allies of the United States. Within a year, the Lon Nol army was, at Kissinger's insistence, a force of 220,000 men.

In much of the countryside, Sihanouk was still the god-king to the peasants. Rioting broke out against Lon Nol, and spread to towns as well. Charging that the riots were incited by the Viet Cong, the government suppressed them with brutal force. The aggressive acts of the Lon Nol army against peasants drove them to join the Communists; the Khmer Rouge, who had until then numbered a few hundred, gained in strength.

To compensate for the lack of peasant support, Lon Nol exploited the Khmers' traditional fear of the Vietnamese. Some 40,000 Vietnamese, mostly merchants, had remained in Cambodia after the division of French Indochina. While Sihanouk had deliberately controlled violent racial antipathies that existed between the two nationalities, Lon Nol began to brand all Vietnamese as members of the Viet Cong. Massacres of Vietnamese civilians in the name of anti-Communism marked symbolically the new government's hatred of both the Vietnamese and the Communists, and this led the Khmer Rouge and the Vietnamese Communists to join forces. Previously, they had operated largely in separate areas and with different objectives.

The United States continued massive "sanctuary" invasions. Only when thousands of South Vietnamese troops poured into the major cities, often looting as they came, did the real dimensions of Cambodia's plight become evident to its citizens (Grant 1971: 113). The American invasions drove large numbers of Cambodians, including the current prime minister, Hun Sen, to join the Khmer Rouge (see the interview with Hun Sen, Chou Meng Tarr 1990).

When the American government withdrew its forces on June 30, 1974, the Cambodian government controlled only the larger towns and at best half the countryside. Hopes of economic development had been dashed, trade was at a standstill, 90 percent of the rubber plantations had been destroyed, tourism to the Angkor ruins was halted, and inflation was severe. Communists gained in both popular support and territorial control, and on April 17, 1975, the Khmer Rouge entered Phnom Penh as victors.

Village scene: taking produce to market

CHAPTER TWO

Society and Culture

Social Groups

At the time the Khmer Rouge took over the country in 1975, Cambodia's population was estimated to be 7.3 million. Of this, 90 percent or more were ethnic Khmer, virtually all of whom were Theravada Buddhists (Ross 1987: 83, 112). The remaining people were Vietnamese, Chinese, Cham (Muslim) Khmer, Khmer Loeu or the tribal peoples (generally referred to as Pnongs), Eurasians, and Indians.

Only a very small percentage of ethnic Khmer, perhaps about 10 percent, lived in cities, typically places settled by diverse ethnic groups. They were the aristocracy, government workers, religious personnel, or low-level workers. The rest of the urban population was made up of Vietnamese and Chinese immigrants and their descendants.

Cambodian towns, which usually had a market, a school, and government offices, were also occupied by more than one ethnic group. Villages were occupied predominantly by one ethnic group numbering several hundred, and had an economy with one major focus and little or no occupational diversification beyond part-time specializations. Unlike urban areas, the villages were exposed to little influence from the West, or even from nearby villages, since the people were physically and emotionally secure within the confines of their own village, and were often uneasy about venturing beyond its borders. One's fellow residents were considered to be "good people," while those in other villages were generally considered to be "bad people."

The majority of ethnic Khmer were rural peasants who lived in villages, where they engaged in rice cultivation. Rice, Cambodia's staple diet, was eaten daily, and its importance can be seen in everyday language. The term for eating a meal is literally "to eat rice," while hunger is expressed as "to be hungry for rice."

A few villages specialized in cottage industries such as weaving, carpentry, basketry, pottery-making, and metalwork, but in many they were part-time occupations. Although many ethnic Khmer villages were situated on riverbanks and fish were plentiful in the rivers, farmers usually limited their fishing to family consumption because of Buddhist injunctions against killing.

The second largest ethnic group in Cambodia was the Vietnamese, whom the Khmer held in enmity and mistrust because historically the two nations have been enemies, invading each other's territory. The Vietnamese generally lived in certain sections in Phnom Penh, and worked as clerks or secretaries in government and business, small merchants, professionals, and domestic servants for Europeans, or they lived in clusters in their own villages as farmers, plantation laborers, or fishermen.

As middlemen in Cambodia's economy, the Chinese were primarily large- and small-scale businessmen, rice dealers, bankers, moneylenders, concessionaires in fishing and lumbering, importers and exporters, and hotel and restaurant owners. Like the Vietnamese, they too maintained their linguistic and cultural identities. The Khmer had more amicable social relations with the Chinese, and especially in urban areas, the two groups intermarried.

Of the numerically lesser minorities, the Cham Khmer were Muslims, and lived in their own sections in larger cities. As Muslims, they were not an integral part of mainstream Khmer society, but Cambodian governments traditionally granted them various constitutional rights not given to other minority groups. Though individual ethnic Khmer families raised a few pigs and chickens for sale, large-scale animal husbandry was carried out by the Cham Khmer cattle breeders.

The Khmer Loeu, or the tribal people, practiced slash-and-burn cultivation and lived in the highlands in the northeastern and southwestern areas of the country. The rest of Cambodian society looked down on them as primitives. The Indians and Eurasians, engaged in business and administration, were the smallest in numbers.

Social Structure

Khmer society was hierarchically structured by age and social status, and was roughly divided into three broad groups. At the highest level were the royalty and aristocracy, high-ranking officials in government and religious organizations, and the wealthiest Khmer or Sino-Cambodian businessmen or professionals. In the middle were Khmer, Chinese or Vietnamese professionals such as doctors and teachers, businessmen, lower-ranking government officials, and white-collar workers in the commerce sector. At the bottom were the rural peasantry and the lowest-level workers in urban areas, "who were little removed from their rural origins" (Ebihara 1971: 62).

Among the peasantry, there were five social classes. At the top were the landlords, who possessed land but did not work it themselves. The second level consisted of rich peasants who owned land and also rented land from landlords. They used wage labor, and had fairly substantial agricultural equipment and working capital. The third category consisted of the middle-level peasants who owned from five to ten hectares of land, and often rented part of the land they farmed. They owned adequate agricultural equipment, provided for their existence exclusively or principally by their own personal labor, frequently engaged in mutual aid, and seldom sold their labor. The fourth class was that of poor peasants. It was the most numerous and complex, and included about 80 percent of the rural population. A poor peasant owned 0.1 hectare, and as a general rule rented land, livestock, and farm equipment in order to work. Some also sold their labor as day or seasonal laborers. At the bottom was the semiproletariat class consisting of permanent agricultural workers and those who worked by the day, month, season, or year. They either had no land, no tools, and no financial means, or had only a little plot of land with or without limited farm equipment. They subsisted only by selling their labor and were partial tenants, poor peasants, landless peasants, and debt bondsmen from needy peasant families who had been completely ruined. In the very worst situations, they migrated to cities in search of work and ended up as street porters; pedicab drivers; laborers who worked on building sites, roads, and bridges; shoe-shiners; bicycle repairers; water carriers; cake sellers; and female servants (Kiernan and Boua 1982: 45).

Cultural Values

For over 2,000 years, Cambodian history and ideology evolved around Indian cultural concepts and Buddhist religious teachings, which emphasize reverence for all life, nonviolence, an egalitarian outlook, and guidance in secular and spiritual matters by the priesthood.

Ebihara observed that Buddhist precepts and practices pervade the values and the behavior of the populace, who accept Buddhism sincerely and devoutly (1971: 68), and that even though the peasantry was divided into distinct classes based on economic worth, people were respected not for social class or material wealth but for displaying, both in action and in word, the "good characteristics" advocated in Buddhist teachings. These characteristics included generosity and selfless concern for others, warmth and a good-natured temperament, abhorrence of fighting, drinking, fornication, and other sins, devotion to family, industriousness, religious devotion, cooperation with others, and honesty.

Several narrators in this book refer to "good people" and "bad people." The latter were those who displayed qualities such as selfishness, bad temper, quarrelsomeness, drunkenness, or even worse sins such as thievery, the breaking of Buddhist norms of conduct, disregard for familial obligations, or dishonesty.

Cambodian society also emphasized respect, particularly for monks who were the educators and spiritual leaders, learned people, grandparents and parents, and other elders. Personal or community problems were resolved not by legal means but by monks, other elders, or leaders of the community.

Legal and cultural duties to family members were based on Buddhist precepts and covered such things as parental authority, arrangement of proper marriages for children, provision of support in the event of divorce and in old age, inheritance, adoption, guardianship, and provision of proper funeral arrangements. The ideals were passed down through generations by folklore and by Buddhist Jataka stories depicting the lives of the Buddha in his earlier incarnations.

These ideals were especially strong in the villages because of the subsistence economy, which required cooperation among peasants, and because villagers looked to the monks for guidance in secular as well as in spiritual matters. They were generally upheld in urban areas, too, as can be seen from the narratives of the urban Khmer contained in this book.

Chhim sums up the importance of Buddhism in Khmer life as follows:

> Religion has a deep root in the Khmer traditional society, not only on the artistic and cultural life, but it also shaped the personality and the mentality of the Khmer people entirely. The pagoda (the temple), the supreme and sacred place of Buddhism, is considered the pillar of the Khmer society. Everybody spends one's life around it. The Khmer pagoda is the best example of a social, medical, spiritual and artistic center of the Khmer people. All private or socio-economic problems in the community usually find their satisfactory solution in the pagoda. Therefore, during a three-day New Year celebration, the Khmer go to the pagoda bringing food and some offering to the Buddhist monks. They request that the monks recite and preach the Buddha's doctrines. They, especially on the third day of the New Year, give an annual bath not only to Buddha statues, but also to the monks, the elderly people and the teachers. The monks are invited to chant the Dhamma in order to consecrate good deeds to the dead. (Chhim 1987: 56)

Family Life and Education

In prerevolutionary Cambodian society, "the nuclear family was the glue that held the society together" (Ngor 1987: 105). The mother dealt with child-rearing, family budget, and other household matters, and the prosperity, well-being, and reputation of the household depended mostly on her. The father dealt with the outside world and provided major family support. But even when financial needs were not severe, many women engaged in business ventures. When necessary, children helped their mothers with their businesses, and close interaction between mothers and their offspring led to a strong empathetic bond between them.

After children married and set up their own households, they continued to interact closely with their parents and siblings for mutual physical, emotional, and financial support. In her description of a Cambodian village society, Ebihara writes:

> The nuclear family can be considered the most fundamental social group, bound together by a variety of affective, economic, moral and legal ties. The strongest and most enduring relationships in village life are

found in the bonds between husband and wife, sibling and sibling, and especially parent and child. Even after a family of orientation has split into the various families of procreation of the different offspring, members of the former often retain deep affection for and frequent contact with one another. According to both legal and cultural norms, family members should (and usually do) offer one another daily support, loyalty, and consideration, as well as special assistance in time of trouble. (Ebihara 1971: 110-11)

Children generally received a great deal of affection in the first four or five years of life, not only from parents but also from other adults and adolescents. As they grew older, children were taught and were expected to conform to norms of politeness, cooperation, and obedience. In games, for instance, while some competition was present, the stress was on playing rather than on winning.

The Khmer placed great value on education, and in this regard, the welfare of the individual child came before that of the family. However, when the needs of the family became severe, the children had to stop their formal education until times were better. When possible, boys entered the monkhood for a few months or years to obtain formal education, to learn the proper modes of social behavior, and to bring merit to their parents.

Traditionally, learning was done by rote with emphasis on Khmer history, language and literature, and Buddhist doctrine. Students were expected to obey and show respect to their teachers. In Cambodian villages, unlike the West, education was considered a means of growing up to be "good men and women" who were useful members of society, rather than a means to secure future social and financial advancement.

Although Western ideas spread with the arrival of the French, they were limited to the capital city of Phnom Penh and one or two other larger cities. Mainly because of language barriers, Westernization did not spread to rural areas where the vast majority of the ethnic Khmer lived. Even after independence, when great strides had been made by Sihanouk to expand the number of schools of all levels as well as to improve the adult literacy rate, government schools in both towns and villages continued to guide students in the awareness of their civic duties, because it was personal conduct and service to the community that gained people social recognition (Chhim 1987: 14).

By the age of ten or so, in addition to their formal education, both boys and girls knew basic survival skills, since boys accompanied their fathers to the rice fields from an early age, and girls were trained in cooking, caring for younger siblings, and other chores by their mothers. However, when necessary, sons also helped their mothers around the house, while daughters accompanied them to work in the rice fields at transplanting and harvest times.

During their adolescent years, the two sexes were segregated in school, which was strictly a place for education, and not for entertainment or romance. Premarital sex was deplored and sexual knowledge not considered suitable for children, since it was considered to lead to desire and trouble. While marriages were long-lasting and spouses were generally devoted and respectful to one another, couples did not display physical love publicly even after marriage, ideally arranged by parents. If the potential bride or groom did not agree to the proposed mate, however, they were usually not forced into marriages.

Though divorce could be initiated by the wife or the husband, it was not frequent. When a marriage was dissolved, the children's wishes about which parent they wanted to live with were respected; usually they elected to stay with the mother.

Men and women around 50 or 60 years of age enjoyed relative leisure, devoted themselves increasingly to religious activities, and earned respectful deference from others. When a parent was widowed, or both parents were advanced in age, it was common for one of the children to continue to reside at home after marriage and look after the parents.

Khmer Language

The Khmer language is linguistically classified as belonging to the Austro-Asiatic stock and the Mon-Khmer language family. It has about 30 vowels and 21 consonants. It is nontonal and lacks such things as verb tenses and conjugations, articles, gender, and number, but it has a fairly complex morphology, with prefixation and infixation. Syntax is fairly similar to English sentence structure, although it can become quite different and complicated in longer sentence constructions.

Khmer cultural values are reflected in the language, which contains four different registers denoting social differences in speaking to or about royalty, monks, elderly or respected members of society, and equals. For instance, the verb "eat" may differ according to whether monks, nobility, ordinary people, children, or animals are eating, or whether one speaks formally or casually.

These differences are clearly defined and consciously used by the refugees. The form of address is still of great importance, and older people are called not by their first names, but by kinship terms. Most adults here find the casual form of addressing people by first names rather uncomfortable. They are especially offended when children call them by their first names. When Khmer children use the direct style of American communication, or when they talk back, their parents perceive the children's behavior as disrespect toward them. They refer to such children as being subhuman, without human parentage. These strong feelings about respectful speech are based on cultural values denoting respect for those who are older, or who are socially higher.

Linguistic differences are further distinguished by appropriate body language. A villager speaking to a government official, for example, will use formal Khmer depending on his or her level of education, while also denoting respect through various gestures, such as offering or accepting items with both hands. When talking to a villager of equal age and status, however, he or she will use colloquial speech and will have quite different hand motions, such as slapping the other on the arm or the back to heighten a joke.

Like other Asians, the Khmer summon a person by waving their hand up and down, and not by motioning with a finger, as Americans do. Before they realized this was a common gesture in America, the refugees believed Americans summoned them with a finger because they looked down on the Khmer.

French was the main European language, and the second language, in Cambodia. English was introduced around 1967. Derivatives from the Indian languages Sanskrit and Pali also remained—Sanskrit in the realms of government and literature, and Pali in the Buddhist canon.

Buddhism as a Way of Life

Like all Buddhists, the Khmer look to the "Ratana Thrai" or the Three Jewels for their knowledge. The Three Jewels are Buddha, Dhamma, and Sangha. The Buddha was not a divine god, but a human being. Though he learned from other teachers, he finally attained enlightenment through his own individual effort.

Dhamma are the teachings of the Buddha. The teachings describe a certain way of life, but there are no mandatory rules and regulations such as attending the temple, giving alms, or even following the precepts. Based on the Buddha's own individual achievements, much importance is attached to individual learning, leading to understanding and conviction that the teachings provide the correct lifestyle.

Sangha are the clergy who disseminate Buddha's teachings to laypeople. They reside in temples, and rules of honesty and sobriety are more exacting for the Sangha than for laypeople. Cambodians hold the Sangha in the highest esteem, both as exemplars of Buddhist values and as educators.

Women are not ordained, but many women, especially widows, become nuns in their advanced years. They shave their heads and eyebrows, wear white robes, and may live in the temple or in their own homes. They generally follow the same precepts as monks and play an important role in the everyday life of the temple.

On a secular level, Buddhist teachings try to promote a sense of both individual and social responsibility; the aim is to avoid causing harm or fear to others through one's conduct. As such, a Buddhist way of life for laypeople starts at a young age with the first five precepts of the code of conduct: one should not kill any living being; one should not steal; one should not commit adultery; one should not lie; one should not consume intoxicants. Causes and effects of these and other concepts about daily life are taught to children by monks, teachers, and elders. Children are guided to develop nonviolent, nonaggressive, cooperative, and tolerant habits through an emphasis on "the avoidance of causing suffering, self-discipline and improvement, humility, temperance, non-accumulation of wealth, and harmonious relations with others" (Chhim 1987: 13).

Although social expectations exert a certain pressure on people to live according to the teachings, people vary in their behaviors depending on their individual commitment and their effort in living according to the precepts. This was demonstrated tragically in that gentle Buddhist Cambodia has also been the land of the autogenocidal Khmer Rouge.

On a spiritual level, Buddhist teachings are based on a theory of reincarnation. Buddhists believe that life is a cyclical and recurrent process. Life causes suffering because of its impermanence, and—depending on the results of one's actions, referred to as karma or kamma—an individual may be born in a better or a worse place in the next birth. Karma can be improved by living according to Buddhist precepts and through meritorious actions. The ultimate goal for a Buddhist is to end the cycle of rebirths with the attainment of Nirvana, to be achieved only by individual effort and not through divine intervention.

Merit is acquired by adherence to the Eightfold Path, which embodies all of the precepts mentioned above, and consists of right understanding, right purpose, right speech, right conduct, right vocation, right effort, right thinking, and right meditation. The Eightfold Path primarily develops the mind and not the body, as it is believed that it is the mindfulness, or the wisdom of a person, that is passed on to the next birth. Like all other objects, the physical form is subject to decay. Hence the Khmer, like other Buddhists, are encouraged to develop their inner selves, and to give generously both of themselves and of material things so they can be rid of their worldly desires, which prolong the life cycle.

In advocating nonattachment to material wealth, the Buddha, who was one of the world's greatest and first social workers, did not advocate fatalism, or teach that one should not seek to improve one's standing by actively earning wealth. Rather, what he advocated was not cleaving to wealth, and the use of it for the good of the whole society, and not for purely individual gain (Wijayatilake 1970).

Buddhism and Cambodian Folk Religious Beliefs

An important part of Buddhism is the acquisition of merit not only for oneself but also for its transference to others, especially the dead. Buddhism, with its nonaggressive and nonviolent norms, has characteristically been tolerant toward other religious systems. In Cambodia, it coexisted with folk religious beliefs centering around supernatural beings (of which only house spirits never create trouble), magical rituals, and other practices.

In the context of the Khmer Rouge killings and the refugees' adjustments, ghosts known as *kmauit* (meaning "corpse") are important. These are comparable to ghosts in the Western sense, that is, spirits of dead persons. But in Cambodia, these are especially the spirits of those who commit suicide or are murdered. It is believed that they wander about in either human or animal form. Some live on dirt and excrement, although they eat rice and other food placed in the fields for them. Others inhabit large trees. Kmauit are a source of very real fear for Cambodians.

People try to help these spirits attain a better life by transferring merit to them by acts of kindness or generosity done in their memory. One of the most effective means of achieving this is by offering food or other necessary items in the memory of the dead to monks who spend their time in educational pursuits, or to any hungry person or animal.

When offerings are made to the monks, they consecrate the merit acquired by that act to the dead relatives and friends of the people. However, no one is coerced to give anything, and one may give only as much as one can afford. Very often, donations are given in cooperation with others. When donations are made to monks in particular, the Khmer tend to give the best offerings they can afford. They also display donations by walking around with them outside so that any spirit wandering about may be consoled, knowing they are remembered.

Pchum Ben, an annual ceremony held solely for remembering the dead, is continued by Khmer refugees in America. It was at such a ceremony that I first met Look Tha, whose narrative follows.

CHAPTER THREE

Look Tha: A Former Buddhist Monk

Look Tha and his wife live with their daughter's family in a three-bedroom stucco dwelling situated in a cul-de-sac of unpretentious houses. From the outside, Look Tha's home, with its brown shutters and faded lawn, looks like any other in the neighborhood. But the visitor who peers through the oval glass pane on the front door sees a different world inside. The wall facing the door is lined with a bookshelf, but there are no books on it. Instead, it is adorned with a framed poster of the Buddha placed beside a large painting of the Angkor Wat. A brass container with three sticks of incense stands to the right of the Buddha, and a brass vase with pink and yellow plastic flowers stands on the left. At either end of the painting of the Angkor Wat are deep maroon roses preserved in sealed glass bowls.

I first met Look Tha, which is a polite term for "grandfather," at a Cambodian wat or temple ceremony, where, at 5'2", he was one of the shortest men around. As the day went by, however, I became increasingly aware of his presence; his pleasant, unhurried demeanor projected a certain

A Buddhist temple in Cambodia

dignity, and he was treated with much respect by the community who had gathered that day to offer alms to the monks in memory of their dead relatives and friends. I requested the friend who had invited me to the ceremony to introduce me to him. When he discovered I was a fluent English speaker, Look Tha told me of his great desire to learn English. Delighted, I asked him if he would teach me Khmer in exchange for English lessons, and over the next two years we met a couple of times a week at his house to learn languages from each other.

Every time I step across Look Tha's threshold, I leave American culture behind. After greeting me with hands clasped in the traditional manner, Look Tha carries my bag and books to the coffee table, to indicate his respect for me as his teacher, even though I am twenty years younger than he. We begin our lessons only after he serves me a glass of soda, or a cup of coffee prepared by his wife, sometimes accompanied with homemade sweets or tropical fruits. Although I am accustomed to the warm hospitality Cambodians extend to their visitors, I am particularly touched by Look Tha's thoughtfulness and concern for me because he is an elder.

The first time I visited him, Look Tha's actions took me back to my childhood in Sri Lanka, where we stood up when the teachers entered the classroom, greeted them with clasped hands, and carried their books to the teachers' room at the end of the lesson. At the end of my first lesson with Look Tha, I found myself taking his leave as I would from a teacher in Sri Lanka, and I did so almost unconsciously. I bade him farewell first, with my hands clasped, and allowed him to walk to the door ahead of me; I have done that ever since.

I chose Look Tha as a narrator because he appeared to embody many of the characteristics of traditional Khmer culture. But I soon realized that while he agreed enthusiastically to tell me his life history, he was reluctant to recount the Khmer Rouge atrocities in detail, even though he never said so directly. When I asked him about those experiences, he replied that he could not relate them because his English was not good enough. When I asked him to tell me in Khmer, his answer was that my Khmer was not good enough. Despite my knowledge of the regime's atrocities and the immense pain they cause survivors and my firm intention not to probe for information that the narrators did not wish to convey, I was deeply disappointed at his reticence.

Compassion had to come before knowledge, and I did not press him for information on the Khmer Rouge period. Instead, I talked about his culture, traditions, and Buddhism. Recounting these gave him immense pleasure, but Look Tha was by no means a passive narrator. To be sure that I understood Buddhism and his views and experiences, he once tested my knowledge and understanding of Buddhism by asking me to define a list of 30 Buddhist terms.

Because Look Tha displayed such a deep respect for religious teachings and ideals, I was curious to find out if and how he lived a Buddhist way of life; in this way, Look Tha came to mention some events about the Pol Pot era without any coercion from me. Even more important, I discovered he continues to cope with the Pol Pot trauma largely by following Buddhist teachings and practices. He departed from his ideals, however, when it came to his relations with the Vietnamese; here events in his country's history became much more significant.

Since, in the Buddhist outlook, old age and death are as much a part of life as birth and youth, I felt quite at ease talking with Look Tha about his remaining years in this life. His extension of not only his present life but also the lives of the Khmer Rouge soldiers to future rebirths shows how deeply the belief in karma (kamma) and rebirth is ingrained in the Buddhist worldview.

I have presented Look Tha's narrative first in this book for two reasons. First, his explanations of and insights about Cambodian history, society, culture, and Theravada Buddhist doctrines help to clarify information presented in the other narratives. Second, as an elder and a former monk, Look Tha occupies a primary place in his community. ❖❖❖

Early Years

I was born a child of a farmer in November 1926, and I am now 62 years old. My father was a strong, handsome man. He was tall and big like an American. My mother was just about five feet tall; that is why I am small. Still, when I was younger, I was strong like my father.

When I was growing up, I lived with my parents, two brothers, and three sisters in a village of about five hundred people, in Battambang province. Many of our relatives, including our grandparents, Mother's older brother, and Father's older sister, lived in our village too. Most of the villagers, including my parents, were good people who went to the Buddhist temple every holy day. We call the Buddhist holy days "*Sila* days."

Almost everybody in my village was a farmer. Rich farmers had big fields all together in one place, and a lot of oxen. Poor farmers had no land, and perhaps just two oxen, so they usually worked for other people.

My father came from a very poor family, but after marriage, he worked very hard and became more prosperous. When I was growing up he was a middle-level farmer, neither rich nor poor. His fields were scattered in different places, and he had only six oxen. But he had a big house, two bicycles, and a motorcycle.

In the village, the only people who were not farmers were the twenty or so Vietnamese families that lived on the riverbank. They were fishermen. They spoke to each other in Vietnamese, but they spoke to us in Cambodian. Since Cambodians were not regular fishermen, we never became close friends with them. We did not like to fish for a living because we did not want to kill, but we fished occasionally when people got together to chat, or when rice fields were far away from the market.

When the rainy season started, Father cultivated about 70 ares of rice fields and orange gardens [100 ares = 1 hectare]. He hired labor only during transplanting and harvesting seasons. After harvesting the rice, he grew beans, peanuts, potatoes, mustard, white pepper, cucumber, chili, corn, and pumpkin in the fields. My father sold some of his harvest to people who came to the farm. Mother and I took the rest to sell in the market.

During the dry season, Father went in his ox cart to distant villages in the countryside to sell clothing, food, and medicines to people who lived there. Those people always looked dirty and ragged, and spoke in a different dialect. They also knew Khmer, so they could deal with us; from them, Father bought tobacco and reeds to make chairs, which he sold in Battambang. Mother helped him in the farm, and also went with him to the countryside whenever possible. Sometimes they hired people to help them, and about thirty ox carts trundled toward the countryside for two weeks or more. My older sisters looked after the family then. After my sisters got married and moved to their houses, I took care of my younger sister and brother. When I grew up and accompanied my parents, somebody from the village took care of them.

My mother never had any free time. When she was not working in the farm, she went to the countryside. During the rainy season she made cakes and sold them at a small stand she built near the river. When she returned home in the evenings, she prepared cakes for the next day. Like other women in the village, Mother cooked on a wood fire, and except for the rice pot, which was made of copper, all her cooking pots were made of clay. Later on, however, people used aluminum pots because the clay ones broke so easily.

When I was a child, I liked to play marbles with my friends.

"Now don't play in the sun, it's too hot. Play in the shade," Mother would say, as I ran out. And, "Don't climb those tall trees, you'll fall and break your legs!"

I also loved to play in the clear, fast-flowing river near my home, and my mother constantly worried that I might drown in it, especially when it was swollen after the rains.

"You are not to go near the river while I am gone," she would tell me whenever she had to go somewhere.

Although I obeyed her much of the time, sometimes when she was gone I could not stop myself from going to the river when friends called me. If I got caught, she or Father caned me for disobeying her.

As I grew older, I had to help Mother cook and take care of younger children, so I did not have much time to play. Still, whenever I could, I went to the river with my friends to swim or fish. Sometimes we brought food to share with each other. In Cambodia we had all kinds of fruits—oranges, grapefruits, papayas, mangosteens, pineapples, bananas, and sugar cane—my favorites were mangoes and young green coconuts, which have delicious water in the center.

My aunt and uncle who lived closest to our house had no children. We visited them often, and looked after them. We also frequently visited other neighbors. In Cambodia, unlike in America, we did not keep our doors closed. They were always left open so we could go to each other's home. If a new person came to the village, people talked to him and introduced him to others. People from my village went to other villages too. Even though our villages did not have paved roads, it was easy to go to other places because many of us had Honda motorcycles.

The happiest time for us in the village was during New Year, which we celebrated in mid-April. In the morning everybody took food to the monks in the temple and made merit. In the night, we played lots of different games in the temple grounds, which would be beautifully lit. Even though New Year came in the dry season, we felt cool and comfortable because we celebrated in the night.

My favorite game was called *chung*. To play chung, we first made a ball with a *kramar* [a large multipurpose scarf]. Then, girls and boys about fifteen to twenty years of age divided into two teams, and they threw the chung to each other, singing:

Boys: When I throw the chung,
         The chung will break into four pieces.
         Any girl who gets the chung,
         Can then catch me.

Girls: When I throw the chung,
         The chung will break into five pieces.
         Any boy who has my kamma,
         Can wait to wed with me.

Another festival we celebrated was Pchum Ben, in memory of our dead relatives. We believe that when people die, they are born in different places, and that once a year, the spirits of the dead come to visit all the children. So every November, we made floats with banana-tree trunks, and decorated them with 40 or 50 candles, incense, many kinds of foods, cigarettes, and betel leaves, and sent them down the river, saying, "I send all these good things to release you, every spirit, every living thing. So if you are searching for food, take whatever you can eat and be happy!"

Many people gathered on the riverbank to see the floats go down, and we felt very happy as we watched them go. We believed they also made the spirits happy, so that they could go back to their dwellings.

Schooling in the Temple

There were only two government schools in Battambang when I was little, so most villagers taught their children at home until the children could read and write some, after which the boys continued their education at the temple.

When I was about six years old, my father taught me to read and write Khmer, just as he had taught my sisters. Father did not have a high education because he had not gone to school, and after some months had gone by he said, "It is time for you to go and live in the temple and learn from the monks; there is nothing more I can teach you." I was eight or nine years old when my father took me there.

"You must behave well in the temple and not do anything unreasonable or disrespectful," my mother advised me before I left. "Don't speak harshly to the monks, or to the old men and women who come to the temple. Don't steal anything or harm anyone. Listen to the monks and do as they say."

The temple was across from the river, and Father carried my clothes, a blanket, and a pillow, tied up in a bundle. There were 60 or 70 boys of various ages already living there. I was the youngest. Father handed me over to the monks, and before he left, he too advised me to always obey the monks. After he left, I did not want to stay. I missed my parents, brothers, and sisters terribly, and always asked the monks to go back home. They allowed me to go home about seven or eight times the first year, but after that, the monks did not allow me to return home so often.

In the temple, everyone got up at half-past five. The older boys prepared rice gruel for breakfast, plucked ripe fruits from the many fruit trees in the temple yard, and served the monks their breakfast. The younger boys swept the dry leaves off the temple grounds and watered the plants.

When they finished breakfast, some monks walked from house to house with their bowls, and villagers gave them rice to use at lunchtime. After we finished breakfast, those monks who remained in the temple taught us Sanskrit, using long-leaf books. They also told us stories of the Buddha and other great people in our history.

We studied until about nine-thirty, when the villagers started arriving with different kinds of soups, meat and fish, vegetables, fruits, and sweetmeats to offer the monks at lunchtime. We always had enough left over for dinner as well, but the monks had only two meals a day; after the noon hour, they only drank tea or juices. Sometimes, instead of bringing food to the temple, people invited the monks to their houses.

After lunch, the younger monks went to a nearby temple to study because our temple did not have learned monks. The older monks read Dhamma books, studied Pali and Sanskrit, or rested.

We went swimming in the river, and for the next two hours, the river was filled with screaming, yelling children. When we returned we studied Sanskrit again till five o'clock, when we had dinner. In the evening all of us, the monks and students, washed again at the river. Later on the villagers installed a water machine [spigot] in the temple, so the monks did not go to the river to wash. Because we wanted to play, we continued to go to the river, and after we came back we had some free time.

In the night, the monks taught us Dhamma until ten o'clock. At this time they did not give us any books; we had to listen and memorize everything they taught. When it was time to sleep, the monks slept in the bed-rooms, and the boys slept outside on the verandah.

Although we were fond of the monks, we were also afraid of them because they were strict disciplinarians. When we misbehaved or did something wrong, the monks first advised us using moral proverbs; if we continued to do wrong things, they beat us two or three times with the switch. However, they did so only to scare us, and to teach us good be-havior.

One time a monk beat me too. We went to bathe in the river, and saw some Vietnamese men catching fish. When they finished, the fishermen took with them the big fish, and threw away the little ones, which we picked up and took back to the temple.

"Why did you catch those fish?" asked a monk who saw them.

"We did not catch them, we just picked them up because the Viet-namese threw them out," we told him.

However, the monk did not believe us. Thinking we caught the fish ourselves, he beat us, because in the Buddhist religion we are told not to kill animals.

There were about 30 or 40 monks in my temple, but I liked Sankharaja, the head monk, best. He was 75 years old, and was tall and fair-skinned. Oh, he was handsome! He was also a very good man. When he spoke to the pupils, he always smiled. He never scolded anybody. When he lay down and rested after lunch, he sometimes called me to fan him to keep him cool, or to massage his legs.

When I was fourteen years old, I decided to go back home because I wanted to go to government school. Sankharaja said, "When you go back home, obey your parents just like you did when you were a little boy," and gave me permission to leave. I returned home with my father's approval.

The government school was very different because about 30 percent of the 50 or 60 students in my class were female; but we did not become friends with them. At recess girls played on one side of the schoolyard and boys played on the other side. We talked to each other only if we needed any help with our lessons.

In the classroom, about five students of the same sex sat on a long bench at each table. We learned French as well as Cambodian, but we did not learn English. We used regular books instead of the long-leaf books the monks used in the temple, and since ballpoint pens did not exist in those days we used dip pens for writing. When I came home after school, I con-tinued to help my parents on the farm and with household chores.

When I was about seventeen, my sisters were married, and had left with their husbands to live on their own. Father said to me, "You are a big man and you had your education. Now you must stay at home and look after your younger brother and sister while they go to school."

Although I did not want to stop my schooling I had to obey my father and I remained at home. But whenever I had free time I tried to learn the Thai language from a monk who knew it well, because at that time, Battambang was ruled by the Thai. Two years later I left home again to become a monk.

A Novice Monk

When I was young, it was the tradition for all peasant boys who could do so to become monks. If a boy did not enter monkhood, he would not know the Buddha's teachings and would have wrong thoughts; the villagers did not consider such a person a good man. So when my parents told me to become a monk at age twenty, I returned to the temple in which I had studied, this time to be ordained as a monk, just as my grandfather and father had done.

Five other boys joined the monkhood with me, and this was marked by a big ceremony. A layperson shaved our heads. We were given white kramars to cover our shoulders and special *sarongs* [worn by men and women] to wear, but not the kind that monks wore. When we were ready, musicians, dancers, my parents, and hundreds of other people escorted us into the temple in a procession. There, Sankharaja ordained us as novice monks.

Although I had learned some Dhamma when I lived in the temple before, now I had much more to learn about *dana* [giving], *seela* [disciplinary precepts], and *bhavana* [meditation]. As a monk, I had to strive continually to purify my mind and do good deeds.

The Buddha said:

> Sabbha papassa akaranam
> Kusalassa Upa Sampada
> Sachitta pariyodapanam
> Etam Buddhanu Sasanam.

This means:

> Avoid all evil,
> Do what is good,

> Purify your heart,
> This is the advice of all the Buddhas.

When monks have seela, or are disciplined, they bring happiness to people. The disciplinary precepts taught us how to behave so we could control our thoughts and actions, and not lose our concentration. For instance, when I went to people's houses I could not laugh or speak loudly; and when I walked, I was required to look ahead, and not glance around. If I behaved otherwise, it led to loss of concentration and discipline.

We spent much of our time teaching Dhamma to laypeople, because if people did not know about dana, seela, and bhavana, they would not know about good and bad; then they would be like animals. To teach people about life experiences, we told them Jataka stories, which are about the Buddha's past lives.

In return for our guidance, the people looked after our needs since we had little time to cook, and we lived in the temple without parents or family. They gave us food, robes, bedding, and other items we needed.

In addition to receiving moral guidance, they also received much merit, or good karmic results for their actions. For instance, when someone gave food to us, or to those who were destitute, or to animals, they enabled us to live one more day. We believe that this act of giving to others brings merit to those who gave, and helps them to attain worthy lives in future rebirths. In Buddha's language merit is called *punya*. Even though we believe it is meritorious to give to others and we encouraged people to do so, no one was forced to give anything; it was up to the people to do so if they wished.

In Buddhism, we also believe that we can transfer merit we acquire to those who are deceased, and who may not yet be reborn in a good place. So after lunch, we prayed that those dead relatives of the people who had offered food or other items to us would benefit from those good deeds.

I learned Dhamma at my village temple for three years. There was a great deal to learn, and I wished to study for at least seven years, but after my third year, I was sent to a temple in Phnom Penh to teach for a year. After that I returned to my own temple because it needed a teacher.

I was much happier as a monk than as a layperson, because as a monk, I became a good person. But I was still young and strong, and when I was 26, I decided to return home because I wanted to work. I knew I could return to monkhood when I grew older. I obtained my father's approval to go back home.

Before I left, Sankharaja advised me on how to be a good layperson again. He then blessed me, and sprayed holy water on my head. I removed my robes and put on a normal sarong, and cried as I worshiped Sankharaja and bade him farewell. After returning home, I did what my parents asked me to do, but for a long time, I felt sick in my heart because I wanted to return to the temple.

A few months after I came back, I started working for a Chinese businessman, overseeing about 300 loggers working in the jungles near the Thai-Cambodia border. That work was done in the dry season only. During the rainy season, I supervised coolies building the railway lines in Battambang. Three years later, I got married.

An Arranged Marriage

When I was 16 or 17 I liked a certain girl, but I never told her of my feelings; in those days, boys and girls did not talk about love and romance. She got married when I became a monk, so when I was 29 years old, I got married to a girl chosen for me by my parents, as was our custom.

In Cambodia, when a man's parents found a girl whom they considered a suitable bride for their son, they first asked her neighbors about her character. If those neighbors said, "She never had a boyfriend. She cooks well, and she knows how to look after a house. She will make a good wife!" the groom's parents approached her parents. If the girl's parents found the proposition agreeable, they in turn inquired from the groom's neighbors about his conduct and character. To be considered suitable, a man had to be a good worker who did not drink, gamble, or engage in cockfighting.

When both families were satisfied, the groom's parents came to the girl's house bearing trays with gifts of fruits, a whole head of a pig, two hens, new clothes, and other things. If the young couple agreed to the marriage, a wedding date was set. The night before the wedding monks visited the bride's home and advised the couple to always speak respectfully to each other, not to commit adultery, to take care of one another, and so on, so the two would have a harmonious marriage. Then festivities continued for three days.

I never saw her before my parents arranged my marriage, but everybody who knew the girl that my parents chose for me said she was a very good person. My parents told me she had never had a boyfriend; if it had been otherwise, I would never have married her. I did not worry about how she looked; whether she was beautiful, or whether she was dark or light-skinned, because I trusted my parents' judgment. When I saw her I thought, "That girl is the right person for me."

After the wedding, I went to live with my wife's parents. I had to show my parents-in-law that I would be a good husband to their daughter. I worked with my father-in-law on his farm, and planted mangoes, oranges, grapefruits, coconuts, and many other fruit trees, but because they would not bear fruit for a few years, I also planted vegetables such as cucumber, corn, and eggplant, for faster yields.

After about a year, my wife's parents said, "We see you can do things for yourself, and we think you make a good husband for our daughter. It is time for you to live on your own."

In Cambodia, as people became prosperous, they bought furnishings to decorate the house, or land and other gifts for their children. Parents did not sell things to children as they do in America. When children married, parents gave gold necklaces, earrings, and bracelets to daughters, and rings and necklaces to sons. When newly married couples went to live on their own, their parents gave them land and various household items.

When my wife and I moved from her parents' house, my father-in-law gave me about three ares of land in the countryside and tools for my new farm. It was a very small parcel of land, but sufficient for us to begin our new life. Also, because I had no farm machinery I could not have managed a bigger farm.

Every morning I went to my farm at half-past six, and about an hour later my wife brought me freshly cooked hot rice and grilled fish for breakfast. Sometimes she stayed on and helped me with the work, but I did not think she was strong enough to do farm work. Besides, she had to look after our house and the children. My wife had eleven pregnancies, but she had five miscarriages. Of the other six children, a boy and a girl died just after birth, and a daughter died of disease when she was seven. So we were left with only three children.

After breakfast I worked till about noon, plowing the land with the oxen, or cultivating by hand. Some mornings I drew about 150 buckets of water from the well and watered my plants. When the sun became too hot, I bathed in the river, and went home to eat a full plate of rice, fish, soup, and vegetables my wife cooked for our noon meal. Then I slept for an hour or two, and returned to my fields and worked until five or six in the evening.

Like my parents, I too worked seven days a week. "You work too hard; why don't you take a rest?" some people would say to me, but I did not like to stop working even for a day because things piled up. Besides, I could see the results of my work. We had nice clothes to wear and good food to eat. My family had a good life, and I had a good marriage.

After we had been married for about seven years, the fruit trees I planted in my father-in-law's land started to produce bountiful harvests. Every year, I earned about six or seven thousand *riel* [Cambodian currency] selling fruit, and I gave that money to my parents for safekeeping. All of us in the village kept our savings in our homes. Only the big people [rich people] in the city kept money in the bank. Later, as I became more experienced, I bought more land in other places, but I was careful to buy only as much land as I could manage.

Peasants in Cambodia were different from government people who were born in Phnom Penh. The city people went to good schools and got a high education; they were rich, high-class people. As a child of a farmer, I knew I could never become rich like the people in Phnom Penh, but I did not feel angry that I was poor, because I knew what I could do for myself. I could plant, sell, and do good things for my family, and for other people in the village.

I never fought with anybody in the village; even if someone made me angry I usually kept quiet, not because I feared others or surrendered to them, but because I did not want to lose control of myself. My village was generally a peaceful place, though, because even if two people disagreed about something, a third person would say gentle words to both and help to resolve their problem.

Although I avoided arguments and physical fights, I knew how to defend myself if someone confronted me, because an elder who liked me taught me martial arts; and once I almost fought with some Vietnamese who tried to steal the food from the floats we had sent downstream to honor our dead relatives. When they heard us shouting and running toward them they turned back, so we never went after them.

Another time, I used my wit to fend off two Laotians who tried to accost me in the countryside. I had gone there with a lot of gold to buy some goods from the villagers when two hefty men closed in on me, asking, "Well, what's your business here?" I knew I was strong, and I carried a knife tucked into my sarong, but I did not want to fight two people. So even though I spoke some Laotian, I pretended not to understand what they said. Instead, I smiled broadly and carried on with my journey, and to my relief, they stopped following me.

In 1970, the year my father died, I was struck with a serious illness. My legs became numb, and at harvesttime I had to hire people to gather my crops. My wife and children too had to work hard. For about six months, I had to crawl on the floor, but finally, some medicine made with tree roots helped me to get better.

About the time I was using a cane and walking a little, Lon Nol soldiers and the Khmer Rouge started fighting close to our village. When bombs started to destroy the houses and farms in my village, we were forced to go to live in the town. There, my wife and daughters earned a living by selling cooked food and sweetmeats in the market.

Life and Death Under the Khmer Rouge

On April 17, 1975, Khmer Rouge came to Battambang. Two days later Pol Pot soldiers came to my brother-in-law's house in the night and said, "We want you to come with us to get something to eat." When they reached the store they shot my brother-in-law, right on the sidewalk. The next day the soldiers came and ordered us to bring his body to the temple for cremation. Since I was still unable to walk, my wife and his wife did so. In the next two or three days they also killed my father-in-law, brother, another brother-in-law, and my wife's uncle. The soldiers did not say why they were killed, but all of the victims had worked in the previous regime.

The Pol Pots also killed the head monk of Battambang, who was my relative. He was a very kindhearted man and everybody loved him. He was also very intelligent; he spoke French, Cambodian, Thai, and Vietnamese, and he also knew Sanskrit and Pali. Later, a woman told me that before he was killed, the Pol Pots ordered the monk to dig a big hole. They then bashed his head with a hoe, and pushed him into it. But, she said, they did not even cover his body properly; after the soldiers left, the monk's legs protruded from the grave.

A week after they came to Battambang, the Pol Pots chased all of us from our houses to the countryside. They talked by the gun: Out, out, out. Shoot.

Like other villagers, my family too kept large supplies of rice and dry fish in our home. When the soldiers ordered us to leave, we wanted to take the food with us, but they said, "Take only enough food for three days. You will come back to your houses after three days, when we have cleaned up the city."

However, we did not believe them, and took as much food as we could carry, and all the money and gold we had collected.

The street was packed with thousands of people. Some even took their pigs, cattle, and chickens with them, and those who had to carry young children as well as their goods could barely walk. But the soldiers did not care. They forced us to hurry, with threats and random shootings.

I brought my family back to my farm in the countryside, only to find that my house and land had been taken over by other people. The Pol Pots gave us a small hut nearby, and that night, I hid my gold inside the bamboo steps leading to that hut, and buried the money in the ground.

A few months after evacuation, the Pol Pots took my older daughter and son to live with other young people in youth camps. For the next several months, we did not know where our children were, or if they were alive. My wife and I felt sick with worry, but there was nothing we could do; the soldiers told us our families belonged to Angka. Finally, after about six months my daughter came to visit us, but only for two days. We did not see our son for a whole year.

My younger daughter who lived with us had to look after small babies because their parents, along with my wife, had to work in the rice fields.

Because I still could not walk without using a cane, the soldiers ordered me to sit on the ground and cut grass, or weave baskets. I worked very slowly because I was old and ill, and the Pol Pots often accused me of pretending to be sick. "We will kill you if you lie to us," they would threaten me often. I knew they would do so; I saw many people who were beaten or killed for such crimes.

We worked all day, under the sun and in the rain, with no medicine and hardly any food. I was so hungry that I caught every snail, lizard, frog, and fish I saw, even though I had stopped fishing after I was about 40 years old, because I did not want to kill living beings anymore. Other people did the same, but we were very careful not to let Pol Pots see us when we foraged for food because they would have punished us severely for "stealing."

Once they killed a handicapped person in my village who ate the stem of a cassava that was left on the ground after the cassava was dug up. Another time I saw a man tied up and beaten with hefty bamboo poles because he had plucked an orange. There was a thundering noise every time they beat him, and blood gushed out of his head and back. Oh, it was terrible! I also saw a soldier return an ax he had borrowed from a boy who lived near my hut, and it was covered with blood. I don't know who was killed. At that time, we all lived with great fear; every moment we expected the soldiers would come to take us away to be killed.

I didn't want to die during the Pol Pot time because the Buddha said that humans who did not purify their minds at the time of death would be born in a bad place. But how could I purify my mind then? I was very angry with the Pol Pots; they did not give us enough clothes or food, and forced us to do hard labor. So because I did not have good thoughts, I did not want to die at that time.

Although I was angry with the Pol Pots, I never said or did anything to get revenge; if I did so, I would also be bad like them. The Buddha said, "If someone does wrong to another person and that person takes revenge, the result will never end."

Whenever I was tempted to take revenge on the soldiers, I thought of those words, and also of my past lives. I believed that if I had acted badly in a previous life, something bad will happen to me in this life. But if in a previous life I had not killed, stolen, or done bad things to other people, I would escape being killed by the Pol Pots.

To help me control my anger, I recited Dhamma in my mind every night, and prayed to the Ratana Thrai [the Three Jewels]. I prayed over and over,

> Khadesa, khadesa
> Kang karana khadesa
> Ahang petthang cha na mi

This means, "Even if anybody does me any wrong, I will never take revenge."

That was all I could do. I had so little food or possessions that I could not give dana [alms] to anybody. I had no seela because I killed. The only thing I could do was meditate.

I believe my meditation also helped my son. When he was assigned to a youth camp close to our village, he came over to our hut whenever he could, in the night. One night Pol Pot soldiers saw him and arrested him. A man who saw my son being taken away came and told me what had happened. I was terrified that my son would be killed. So while my hands worked, my mind meditated on Buddha, Dhamma, and Sangha on behalf of my son. My son was not killed. Someone had told the Pol Pot leader that my son was a good worker, and the leader had released my son after warning him not to disobey their orders again.

I believe that when people die, they are reborn, and that those who observed *Panchaseela* [the Five Precepts] and led good lives will be reborn in the heavens or in the universe. Those who did bad things will be born in hell or as animals. Therefore, in the future, the result of kamma (karma) will not bring Pol Pot soldiers to a good place. Someday they too will suffer and be killed, either in this life or in a future life. Already they have had to suffer in this life; I saw them living in the jungle like animals, after the Vietnamese came.

When the Vietnamese Came

After the Vietnamese liberation, my family and I went back to our farm because the people who lived there in the Pol Pot time had gone back to their own place. We planted sweet potatoes, corn, chili, and other vegetables, and we were in control of our lives when the Vietnamese ordered my eighteen-year-old son and the husband of my older daughter, who married during the Pol Pot regime, to join the army. They did not want to do so, because though it was the Cambodian army, it was controlled by the Vietnamese. We heard that those who did not follow orders were forcibly taken away to the army, and we decided then to leave our country because we knew that whether they were Cambodian or Vietnamese, under Communists we had no freedom.

In November 1979 we left our home for the Thai-Cambodia border. We carried very little food and clothing with us because we did not want to attract the attention of Vietnamese soldiers. Because I walked so slowly, my son and son-in-law helped me by carrying me on their backs, but soon my wife too had problems walking: her soles cracked, became bloody, and caused her severe pain. After five days we had made little progress because we were ill, tired, and had little to eat. We had no choice but to pay some gold and hire a motor trailer [a trailer pulled by a motorcyclist] to take us to the border. When we reached the border, we discovered that it was too dangerous to stay there because the Khmer Rouge and the Vietnamese continued to fight close to our camps, and we left for Khao-I-Dang camp in Thailand on December 8, 1979.

The United Nations gave my family a single room in a long shelter, and rations of bean sauce, fish sauce, salt, and rice. Although we ate sparingly, the rations were not sufficient for our family, and I sold gold for *baht* [Thai currency] and bought food from vendors. Still, I felt happy; even though our living conditions were bad and we did not have enough to eat, things were now much better than in the Pol Pot time.

In the camp I studied English using a Thai-English dictionary because I did not have enough money to pay a teacher. I did not know much Thai, but I could speak and read enough to look up English words in the dictionary. I would then write them in Thai, and memorize them. My son-in-law didn't know Thai, but knew a little English and a lot of French, and we helped each other to learn English, using *English for Today, Book III.*

Thousands of new refugees continued to come to Khao-I-Dang, and I met several people from my village. From them I heard that the Vietnamese soldiers had begun to commit many robberies in my village, although they had not done so before I left. One friend said, "You know what happened to your good friend Prov? He went back and forth between the border and the village selling things, and every time he traveled, the Vietnamese soldiers checked his bags and took whatever they wanted. One time because the soldiers did not find anything they liked, they kicked him so badly that they broke three ribs, and he died."

I decided I would not return to Cambodia until the Vietnamese left.

I had not planned to come to America when I left my country; I knew nothing about America then. I went to the refugee camp only to move far away from the fighting. There, however, I discovered that many people, including my mother, brother, and sister, and their children who had also escaped, had gone to America, and I thought I will also come here. My brother sent a letter saying he would sponsor us, but before I applied to come, I received orders from the camp officials to move with my wife to another camp.

When we first went to Khao-I-Dang, the officials told us that we would not be separated from our children; later, they ordered my wife and me to move. We had no choice in the matter. I do not know why we were moved. After twenty months, with no explanation, they sent us back to live with our children. By then, our children had applied to come to America and they left a few months later. We also applied to come, and finally, in 1982, the Americans called us for an interview. We passed the interview, but we lived in Khao-I-Dang for two more years before being moved to a transit camp in the Philippines. In that camp, we went to school to learn English, and how to live in America. We arrived here in 1984.

An Old Man in America

When we came, my daughter and son-in-law were living in a small apartment, and we too lived with them. My son-in-law showed me how to get to the grocery store, to the International Rescue Committee, which helps refugees, to the hospital, and to various other places. During my first year in America, I went to the hospital often because I still had problems with numbness. In this country, I like the hospital best because the receptionists, nurses, and doctors always speak nicely to me, which makes me feel happy.

Sometimes I think Americans don't like refugees. One time a young American man climbed into the bus ahead of me, but instead of moving forward, he stood still. I waited for a while, and climbed up behind him. Suddenly, he shoved me with his elbow; if I had not been holding the handrail I would have fallen on the street. I did not say or do anything. I kept quiet because I am an old man, and I am not American. The driver and many people in the bus saw what happened, but they didn't say anything. I wonder why that young man did that? America is a capitalist country, not a Communist country, so why do people behave like that?

I miss my homeland. I liked living in my village because I had relatives and friends, and the freedom to go about whenever and wherever I liked. Here, I don't even know my neighbors. During the day they go to work, and in the evening, they keep their doors closed. In America, people wait for Saturday or Sunday to talk to others.

I also miss my rice fields and my big garden with all the fruits and vegetables. There, I worked hard and ate a lot more food than I eat here; in Cambodia we didn't have diets. Now, because I don't do any work, I eat only what I need to keep me from starvation. Otherwise I will get fat, and lose my health.

My biggest problem is that I do not know much English. The first time I heard some white people speak English in Cambodia, I knew it was not French, but I did not know what language it was. When I heard it again in the refugee camp, I remembered the sounds of the unknown language that I had heard before, and realized that it was English!

I wish I could go to school to learn English, but because my children have to go to work they don't have too much time to take us around. My ambition now is to learn to drive, buy an old car, and go to school to learn English. Some people say, "You are an old man. Why do you want to go to school?" I tell them I want to be able to speak to American people.

Sometimes I try to learn English by watching television, but usually the man speaks too fast for me to understand. When I read the English newspaper, I understand only about half of what I read. If I learn more English I will be able to improve my mind because I will have new things to think about, and new people to talk to.

Reflections

When I am lonely I think of Cambodia; but then I think of Pol Pot, and I get so upset. I think, "Why did they kill so many people? They all had the same religion, the same nationality, the same dress; they were all Cambodians!"

I do not cry when I think of what the Pol Pots did to my country and my people, but when I think of those times my head feels very tight, and I feel sick in my chest. At such times, I go to my room, shut the door, and meditate. I concentrate on my breathing, and it helps to relax me. When I breathe in, I concentrate on the cool air that touches the nostril. When I breathe out, I am conscious of the hot air that touches the nostril. I do not think about anything else. When I finish meditating I read newspapers, historical books, or Buddha stories, to forget about Cambodia and my people's troubles.

But when I sleep, I dream of my country. Some nights I dream I am working in my rice fields like I used to, but some nights I dream I am working for Pol Pot, and it is very upsetting. I almost never dream of my life here.

I think Cambodia fell to the Communists because of two major reasons. First, the people in the countryside did not have much education. Most of them went to the temples and became monks, but their temples may not have had highly educated monks who were good teachers. Then, if the people did not go to another temple to study, they would not have learned Dhamma properly, and therefore would not have known what was good and what was bad. When the Khmer Rouge told untruths to such ignorant people, they believed them and became Communists.

Sihanouk's wrong politics was the second reason for Cambodia's fall. I know about Sihanouk's political ideals because when he came to Battambang, soldiers made the people listen to his speeches. Sometimes he spoke for two or three hours.

In 1953, Sihanouk fought for Cambodia's independence and Cambodia became independent in 1954. At that time we all thought Sihanouk was glorious. He kept Cambodia in the middle [politically neutral]. Around 1964–66, however, Sihanouk visited China and his politics changed. He thought that the Communists will triumph over the capitalists, and he formed a friendship with Ho Chi Minh, even though we despised Ho Chi Minh. When Sihanouk left the United Nations in 1966 and started to lean toward socialism, I began to dislike him. Only stupid people in the countryside liked him. The government of Thailand brought progress and peace to their country, but the leader of Cambodia governed the wrong way, and the result he got was Pol Pot.

I had a lot of property in Cambodia. My children would have had good jobs there because we sent them to school and gave them a good education. But we don't think of going back because Cambodia is no longer a peaceful country, and the Khmer Rouge wants to control it again. They have all kinds of weapons they get from China. Even if Pol Pot did not come back, our country is still under Vietnamese Communists, and I don't trust them.

Under Communists, nobody can do what they want. My older sister and her children still live there. She did not escape with us because my nephew wanted to have all our property, but now he has to work as a soldier. His wife works too, in the bank, but their salaries are too small to feed all their children. Since my sister is very old and cannot work, she does not have enough to eat. I wish I had money to spare so I could send some to them every month, but I don't, because I am on welfare. So even though I feel sad about my relatives and I get homesick, I do not think about going back.

Here in America, I have Vietnamese neighbors, but I cannot trust them because I have read the chronicles of Cambodia, and I know that Cambodians and Vietnamese have been enemies through history. Buddha said to treat all people equally, but I cannot become close friends with them. I only say "Hi" to my Vietnamese neighbors, and they say "Hi" to me.

When Cambodian women who live here marry Vietnamese men, I get very angry. I don't know what I would do if my grandchildren married Vietnamese; I don't even want to think about it. I like Chinese people though, they are the same as Cambodians. I would like it if my grandchildren married Chinese people. But I hope my children or grandchildren will not marry American or Spanish people because we have different cultures.

I did not know how different the Cambodian and American cultures were until I came here. When I went to school in the Philippine camp, my teacher was an American Mormon Christian. She told me, "When you come to America, you must not forget your Cambodian culture. Teach your culture to all your children and grandchildren." I could not understand why she said that, because to me it seemed that people will always like the culture of the country they were born in.

I also thought that in America, the government let refugees keep their natural cultures, because in this country there is freedom. Now I know it is not so.

In Cambodian culture, teachers tell the students, "When you go back home, you must never do anything that your parents dislike. You must always obey them." At home, our parents reminded us often to obey our teachers and although we disobeyed them sometimes, we usually did what our parents and teachers told us. However, in America, teachers teach children about their freedom to do what they want, so they don't obey their parents, and many Cambodian refugees have problems with their children.

Some Cambodian youth in this country do not even know about our culture or customs. They grew up in Pol Pot time, and then when they came here, they went to school here; so they know only the American customs. For example, they shout and they jump when they talk to each other, and even if older people tell them not to, they do not listen. Although everybody likes their freedom, it is not good to disturb others by loud and noisy behavior.

I don't dislike everything about American culture, but I dislike people kissing on the road, or on the sidewalk. In Cambodian culture, it is shameful to kiss so all the people can see. I never saw people kiss in public in Thailand, or in the movies we used to get from India. When I wait for the bus, young men and women kiss at the bus stand. I am an old man and I feel ashamed when I see them. If my granddaughters kiss like that I will tell them not to do it, but I do not know if they will listen to me because they grew up here. Also, I can only tell them what is right and wrong. It is up to them to choose what they want to do. Some TV programs have naked people and sex, and then I switch it off. I feel embarrassed to watch them because those stories are for young people.

I want my grandchildren to learn about our history, language, and culture. For instance, when people come to our house, they must greet them respectfully with their palms together, and treat them well. When the people leave, they must again show respect. When we go to another house, they must respect the owner of that house. I am happy to say that my daughter and son-in-law have taught their children these customs.

I would like to teach my grandchildren to read and write our language, but the Cambodian language has many sophisticated words that they don't understand yet because they are too young. Also, the choice is up to their parents. Before I teach Cambodian to my grandchildren, I will ask my daughter and son-in-law if they will allow me to do so. I am their grandfather and I take care of them, but if my daughter and son-in-law do not want them to learn Cambodian, I will not teach them because I do not like to do things that others dislike.

I believe that people must have the freedom to say if they dislike something. For example, if I dislike going to church, nobody should force me to go to church as some people try to do. I think wherever I live, if nobody forces me to do anything, I will have no worries.

Some Cambodians are unhappy here because they came with no education, cannot get jobs, and so cannot have a good life. They do not have enough money to go to Lake Tahoe, Las Vegas, Disneyland, Santa Cruz, Monterey, and other places, like those who came in 1979 with a good education and got good jobs.

As for me, I am neither happy nor unhappy. I am an old man and I am not strong enough to work. The government gives me enough money to get by from month to month, I have a place to live, and I feel contented. I have no desire to go to the cinema or to concerts. I have seen all that in Cambodia. I am happy staying at home, watching TV, reading books. In that respect, I am different from old men in America. They visit places to find ways to happiness. As long as I have the freedom to meditate, to talk about Dhamma, to read, go to the temple, and purify my mind, I will be happy.

All men and women grow old, and I think I am ready to die when the time comes. I do not worry about death because I didn't harm anybody or do anything that others disliked. After I die, I wish to be reborn in a place where I will know Buddhism because the Buddha's word is true.

The Christian religion says, "If you lie, kill, or commit any other sin, you can wash away the sin," but I don't believe that. If people do wrong, they receive bad results. If they do good, they receive good results. For example, if I say bad words to you, you will get angry with me, but if I say good words to you, you will be happy. If somebody touches the fire, they will be burnt, but if they do not touch the fire, they will not burn.

I don't know where I will be reborn, but I will do good in this life because when people are jealous, greedy, steal, lie, or take intoxicants, the results of kamma will not be very good in another life. My only wish is to be reborn anywhere that has Buddhism, so I can listen to Dhamma, study Dhamma, and purify my mind.

CHAPTER FOUR

Bopha: A New American

Bopha means "flower." This narrator chose this pseudonym for herself because her father, who died after the Khmer Rouge evacuation, used to call her Bopha when she was little. Her unblemished, fair complexion and smiling face make it a very apt name for her.

I became acquainted with 35-year-old Bopha when a mutual friend suggested her as a possible narrator. Bopha and I met at several locations away from our homes, and we had twelve interviews, each lasting two to three hours. She was always punctual, smartly dressed, and an articulate speaker.

Bopha is of Vietnamese origin and lived among ethnic Cambodians; but as her narrative indicates, her Vietnamese parentage made her an outsider in the larger Cambodian society. As I probed this subject further, I discovered that Bopha's ethnic experience in Cambodia has had far-reaching consequences for her adjustments to the United States.

Yet as part of the larger Cambodian society, Bopha's family was directly affected by the political and social corruption which pervaded pre–Khmer Rouge Cambodia and which eventually contributed to the downfall of the whole country.

A few months after the Khmer Rouge victory, Bopha was evacuated to Vietnam along with thousands of other Vietnamese Cambodians, and she became a victim of the Khmer Rouge not in Cambodia, but in war-torn Vietnam. However, she has painfully vivid recollections of the initial evacuation of Phnom Penh; and the emotional trauma her family suffered because of the Khmer Rouge atrocities, which caused the deaths of many of her loved ones, was hardly less than the suffering endured by those who were trapped in Cambodia under the regime.

When she recalled the misery caused by the Khmer Rouge, Bopha usually stooped forward, looked down, and spoke in a low, intense voice. It was undoubtedly a difficult subject for her to talk about, but it was important for her that I understood as much as possible her experiences at the time, and Bopha sometimes acted out incidents for me. For instance, when she described how the orphaned babies abandoned during the Khmer Rouge evacuation struggled for breath, she contorted her face and emitted a hoarse, gasping sound I had never heard before. Another time, she sat on the floor with her legs stretched out. A glazed look came over her face as she spread all five fingers across her face and licked them; that was how the child who had fallen out of the crib looked as he ate. Through her actions, which were both pathetic and terrifying, I began to understand better something of the hopelessness and terror the people would have felt from the very beginning of the Khmer Rouge rule.

Her friends' continued confinement in Thai refugee camps adds to the posttraumatic stress she experiences, which is very similar to those of the refugees who actually lived under the regime.

While Bopha displayed deep sorrow, and at times anger, when she talked about the Khmer Rouge experience, she was merry and lighthearted when she recalled funny or happier incidents. For instance, she threw her head back and laughed merrily when she related how she got back at her mother for scolding her. My mother also disciplined me in similar ways during my childhood, and I easily identified with Bopha's resentment. But looking back at my own feelings at the time, I guessed Bopha would have another view of her mother's actions, and as we talked further, she indeed showed much understanding of her mother's behavior.

Because Bopha herself is a parent, I inquired about her own attitudes regarding childrearing and the values and behaviors she wants to impart to her child, and discovered that they are very similar to her mother's. Furthermore, they resonated with the views held by Look Tha and other narrators of this book, which shows the extent to which Bopha's family was integrated with the larger Cambodian society.

After she finished relating her narrative, Bopha invited me to her home. It was an unexpected invitation, and to me was a beautiful culmination to a meaningful experience.

When I arrived at her house, Bopha was out in her front yard, watering rosebushes that were in full bloom. When she saw me she closed the tap, neatly coiled up the garden hose, and put it aside. She took me inside and showed me around her house, gaily decorated with numerous photographs of her four-year-old daughter. Afterward she made a pot of tea, and we sat in the living room. I had intended to make my visit to Bopha a short one, but she extended to me hospitality and friendship without reservation, and I remained there for a good three hours, sipping tea and reminiscing about our meetings and our lives. Even then, I left with reluctance. ❧❧❧

"Eat Your Honesty and Fill Your Stomach!"

I am the oldest daughter of a family of five girls and one boy, of Vietnamese-Cambodian parentage. My father was Vietnamese, but he had some Chinese blood in him too, but my mother, who was his second wife, was Vietnamese. Father's first wife was also Vietnamese. He married her when he went to Vietnam to work, and they had three children. After some years, Father decided to return to Cambodia, but his wife didn't want to leave her aging parents. So he came back by himself, and when he was about 40 years old, he married my mother, who was 19.

My father was an educated man who had passed the examination to become a pharmacist, but because he didn't like that sort of work, and because he got a bigger salary as a civil officer, he worked in a place like the city hall, in Phnom Penh. It was his job to collect the personal tax of 700 riel that Chinese and Vietnamese Cambodians had to pay, issue identity cards to them, and make sure they fulfilled government requirements when they wanted work.

When I was about six years old, we moved from our big brick house in Phnom Penh that my father's mother had given him, to a little wooden house in Kompong Speu. My mom told me that we moved because two Vietnamese men stole a lot of money and escaped to Cambodia, and some of Father's colleagues told him to help the two Vietnamese men for a fee.

Even though he could have made a lot of money helping the Vietnamese, my father refused to do so, saying, "I do not want to get into trouble by doing crooked deals." His colleagues then faked his signature, used his rubber stamp to issue documents, and helped the Vietnamese.

When the police found out about the documents they arrested Father. Although he and my uncle protested his innocence, they kept him in a holding center because his signature and stamp appeared on the documents. Later, the guilty people were discovered and Father was released, but he was so upset about the incident that he resigned from his job, and came to work in Kompong Speu.

Even in Kompong Speu, Father could not escape corruption. The police chief there told him, "Charge an extra 100 riel from each Chinese and Vietnamese person and give me 80 riel; you keep the rest." Again, Father refused, and the police chief threatened to transfer him to a malaria-ridden forest area where newcomers could not survive easily because there was little food. Mother feared the children would die if she took them there and didn't want to go. So Father told her, "I will go to the new place by myself, and come home once a month." Fortunately, the government officer who was the police chief's senior heard my father was doing a good job, and canceled the order to move.

Many government people became rich at that time through corruption, but we became poorer because my father was too good. People gave us gifts of money when he helped them, but he would not allow us to accept those gifts, even though Mom said it was okay.

"If I let them accept that money, I would teach them to be corrupt," Father told her.

That made Mom mad because she found it hard to make ends meet, but Father only said, "God knows I am honest."

When he said that, Mom got more mad and yelled, "Yes, you are so honest! Now eat your honesty and fill your stomach!"

We became quite poor. In Phnom Penh, my father had a big house and a car. In Kompong Speu, we lived in a small house, and my father rode a Vespa motor scooter. Next, he got a motorized cycle, and finally he went down to a bicycle.

Because we did not have enough money, Mom started to do business. She went to Vietnam by the big boat that carried soldiers, to buy goods to sell in Cambodia. We worried when she traveled because the Khmer Rouge bombed the boats. When newspapers reported that a boat had been bombed around the time Mom left or was coming back, we would be terribly depressed and worried until we saw her again.

From Vietnam, Mom brought back things like cloth, perfume, powdered milk, and batteries to sell in Cambodia. Sometimes she smuggled illegal things too, like gold and jewelry, because they fetched a lot of money. She often managed to conceal them by sewing them into the seam of her sarong, but when officials checked her at the border, she got caught sometimes and was charged with illegal activities.

Mom never went to jail, though, because of my father's position in the government. At times, he himself talked to the people who arrested her and obtained her release. But he often said to her, "I really do not like what you are doing. Why don't you stop this business?"

"I do it because I have no choice," was her reply.

My mom also did business as a moneylender, but she was a very kind person, and mostly she got tricked because some people took her money and didn't pay it back.

"Mom, why do you give money to unscrupulous people? You shouldn't do that," I told her often.

But when someone begged, saying, "Oh, please help me. My child is so sick, he is dying," Mom couldn't bear it, and loaned them money.

During the first week of every month I had to collect my mom's money from the market people. When they saw me coming on my bicycle, some of them hid, while some tried to appease me by giving me things to eat. Later I learned that I must not accept food, because then I couldn't ask the people for money. Still others told me they were broke. Then I would sob, saying, "If you don't give me money, my mom will beat me!" People usually felt sorry for me then and gave me the money.

I hated collecting my mom's loans, and I felt angry because she continued to give money to people. Sometimes I refused to go to collect her money from the market people, but she would plead with me so much that I felt sorry for her, and went.

Although I got angry with my mom, I respected her because she was kind, helpful, and reasonable. For example, my father taught her how to give injections, and people came to her for injections. If the customers were well-off, she charged them for her services as well as the medicine, but if they were poor, she charged only the cost of the medicine.

In addition to doing business, Mom also took care of the family. She was reasonable at home too, but when we disobeyed her she beat us with a switch. She beat me too, when I didn't do what she said; like the times when she woke me up at five in the morning to get ready for school which started at seven, and I just sat on the step and dozed.

When she scolded me and beat me I resented it because I like soft, gentle words, and I did things to get back at her. For instance, when she sent me to the store to buy ice because we didn't have a refrigerator, I put the big block of ice in my bicycle basket and rode over big holes in the street until the ice fell and broke into pieces. Then I took just a small piece of ice home to my mother. I did that because I felt my mother was unfair to scold me and switch me, and then use me to do things for her. But I knew that Mom beat us because she had a lot of kids and needed to let go of her anger, and also because she wanted to teach us good behavior.

I went to a coed school, but girls and boys had little to do with one another. We sat in front of the room while the boys sat at the back, and though they liked to talk to us, we usually didn't even say "Hi" to them. I didn't miss the boys' company, though, because I had many close friends among girls. I was popular because I was a good student, and I was also pretty. I still spoke to boys more than other girls, because I was a class leader. Class leaders were usually boys because they had more freedom to walk around the schoolyard, watering plants that teachers grew for agriculture lessons, but the teacher made me a class leader because I always did whatever I promised to do.

My father often told us, "You must study well so you can get a good job when you grow up. That is the only way for you to have a place in society."

I listened to my father and worked hard, and became a good student. I also followed what our proverbs taught us to do, which teachers displayed in the classrooms. The two that I liked best said "Knowledge comes from learning," and "If you try hard, you will always reach your goal."

I tried hard to learn everything that the teachers taught. I wrote good essays and reports in Cambodian even though I am not Cambodian by blood, and usually reached my goal to be the best or the second-best in class. My siblings were only the fifth or sixth in class, so I was the smartest person in the family too. My father was very proud of me and he loved to show my report card to his friends. I was pleased when he did that, but I also felt embarrassed for him because I thought maybe his friends' kids did well in school too.

Although I was a good student, I had a hard time both in school and in public, because I was not Cambodian. In school, the history teacher made Vietnam sound like Cambodia's enemy. He would say, "Vietnam did this or that terrible thing to Cambodia!" When he said that I felt terrible because I imagined everybody looked at me; and I kept my head down so nobody will see my face. Then in the street, when they talked about Vietnamese women, people used derogatory terms like "that female Vietnamese," instead of "that Vietnamese lady."

So when I lived in Cambodia I always tried to look and behave like a Cambodian, as much as possible.

My friends, though, didn't care whether I was Vietnamese, Chinese, or Cambodian. We talked about our cultures, and even about discrimination. We shared food, and if a family had a celebration, we invited each other. We studied together and shared good ideas with each other. Most times I had the best ideas in math and physics because an older boy, who liked me, helped me and my siblings with our schoolwork.

During holidays, my friends and I picked fruit in the forest. Sometimes we took the two statues of a male and a female god from the nearby temple and bathed them in the river, because we believed that the gods liked children. Sometimes people offered food, incense, and cigarettes to those gods and asked for help, but they did not always bring everything the gods liked. Then I got money from them and bought the missing things, because otherwise, the gods would not be happy, and the people wouldn't get what they wanted. After everybody went home, my friends and I shared the food they left behind in the temple.

We also believed in the spirit of a deceased priest, who had lived near our house. He was a vegetarian, and he helped anyone of any race. After he died, people hung his picture in their homes and asked him for help when they had problems. Sometimes when my mom had problems she prayed to him, and he helped her. Once he helped me too, when I lost my new slipper. I was scared to tell Mom because I knew she would beat me, and I prayed to the priest, saying, "If you are a true spirit, please show me my slipper."

That night, I dreamed my slipper had fallen between the piles on which our house was built. In the morning, I found it there. Ever since that experience I have believed in him.

Although we prayed to the gods and the spirits, my parents were Buddhists, and we believed the Buddha's teachings. The Buddha said that if we did good things, we would receive good results, and that if we did bad things, we would receive bad results. If you grew good seed, you got good fruit; it's like that.

The Coming of the Khmer Rouge

In 1972 we left Kompong Speu because our house was burned down when the Khmer Rouge and Lon Nol soldiers started fighting. We salvaged whatever we could, and walked about twenty kilometers to Phnom Penh to live with our father's sister. She lived in a big two-story house that was built on a piece of land that belonged to my father, but when we went to live with her, my aunt did not give us a room in her house. Instead, she pointed to a small house that stood behind her house and said, "You can live over there." Her son, who wanted the whole property, did not like us living even there.

Around this time, Mom fell ill with an ulcer, and we needed a lot of money to buy medicine for her. So after I got my high-school diploma I said to Father, "I will not go to college, but look for a job."

One day, I heard Air Cambodia announce vacancies for the post of airplane stewardess over the radio, and I decided to apply. In Cambodia, when we applied for jobs we had to write our own narratives since there were no application forms. I asked Father, "Can you help me write my narrative so I can apply for the job?"

My father helped me, and I got the job. But when I said that to the boy who liked me, he said, "I don't think you should work as an air stewardess, because air stewardesses must sit on Americans' laps when Americans give them a lot of money."

My cousin-in-law agreed with him and added, "If you did that you will not be a nice girl, but a bad woman."

So I didn't go to work as an airplane stewardess.

Even though my mom was so ill, my cousin kicked us out of their house after a few months, and we went to live with Mom's adopted sister. While we lived there, two men came looking for Father. They gave him a piece of paper, and threatened to shoot him if he didn't sign it. It was an agreement to turn our father's share of his sister's house over to my cousin!

Father had no choice but to sign the agreement. But this upset Mom so much that she flew into a rage and started screaming and throwing everything she could lay her hands on, at Father. She remained angry for a long time and her ulcer got worse. The doctor said she required an operation, but my parents could not agree to get it done because it cost too much money. Finally, Father read his old pharmacy books and gave Mother two injections. Unbelievable as it may sound, she slowly got better.

Mom started working again, and my parents rented a small apartment in Phnom Penh to live with the two younger children. They sent me and four of my siblings to stay with our cousin-in-law who lived in another part of the city, so we could go to better schools.

I entered medical school in 1974. In 1975 Mom had just left for Vietnam on business when the Khmer Rouge came to Phnom Penh.

The Evacuation

When Pol Pot soldiers ordered us to get out of our house, our cousin did not want to go. When the soldiers left, my cousin closed all the doors and windows, and said, "Let's stay in hiding here, and go only if we have to."

My cousin's husband was a wealthy businessman who imported and exported things, and they hid a lot of money and diamonds inside the stove, under the ashes, in the chimney, and various other places. She also sewed a pocket in a pillow and hid about a cup of gems in it, and filled another pillowcase with money. She said we would take those with us if we had to leave.

We stayed in hiding in the house for the next two days. On the third day, the soldiers came looking in the houses, and they ordered the fat Chinese businessman who lived opposite my cousin's house to leave his house. He refused, and the soldiers shot him. Then they kicked his wife, and shouted, "If you don't go immediately with your children we will kill you too."

When we saw that we got out very quickly with some food, clothes, and the pillows with the valuables. I also took four textbooks because I had an examination scheduled three days later, when the soldiers said we would return to our houses.

Outside on the boulevard, thousands of people walked under the hot sun. I saw mothers who had just given birth and who were still in pain, being carried in hammocks tied to poles. Some old people were so tired they could hardly walk. Struggling not to lose each other in the thick crowds, we too trudged along with them. People moved ever so slowly, and though we had walked for hours, we had gone only about a mile from our house when we stopped next to an orphanage to cook some food. I heard a baby crying in the orphanage, and I went over to look.

I remember counting 48 cradles in the orphanage. The Khmer Rouge must have ordered the workers to leave when they first came to the city, because there was nobody except babies in the orphanage, and some of them were already dead. I saw twins in one cradle; one was alive and the other was dead. Some babies tried to cry, but only a horrible sound came from their throats as they gasped for breath.

There were three or four babies who had crawled out of their cribs and fallen on the floor. Other people who had come before had left cans of water and rice on banana leaves for them on the floor, and one child sat there eating. His tummy was bloated, and he looked dazed; but he still kept on eating.

A dead baby lay nearby. I carried him to the side and covered him with a blanket, because I wanted to leave him in a nice place. But as I covered him, he suddenly quivered. I got so frightened, I ran back to my family as fast as I could. But I couldn't forget him. I told my cousin about the baby and asked if we could take him with us, but she scolded me, saying, "Are you crazy? How can we look after a baby when we don't know what will happen to us?"

So I left him there, but oh, God, I felt so bad. I will never forget that baby or that orphanage as long as I live!

We slept by the roadside at night, and walked for days. The Khmer Rouge checked our belongings at various places, and took my books and many other things away. At the checkpoints, we were really worried that they would discover the pillows in which we had hidden our valuables. My cousin told us, "When they stop us, pass those pillows quickly down our line pretending they have been already checked." So we did that, and luckily, the soldiers never found them. But a few days later, the regime abolished money, and the thousands of riel we had brought with us became useless.

The soldiers made us walk until we came to a thick forest, and ordered us to cut wood. It was a dreadful place with snakes, and worms that fell from trees even during daytime. I was so terrified of them that I screamed whenever I saw them. It made the soldiers angry, and they shouted at me, saying, "What is the matter with you? You disrupt the whole group!" whenever I screamed.

I had never worked so hard before, and I became so tired that I often had to rest. But whenever I stopped working, the soldiers scolded me, saying I was too lazy.

"Now hang your pen and your certificate on the tree, and learn to use the ax," they jeered at me.

That hurt me very much. I thought of how I had gone to school for thirteen years and studied so hard, and now I lived in a forest, cutting wood. My education was useless!

At the beginning I argued with the Khmer Rouge about their rules, but my friend from the city told me, "A Pol Pot asked if you talked like that because you had been the wife of a higher officer in the army. I swore that you were not such a wife, but if you talk too much, the soldiers might kill you!"

I stopped arguing with the soldiers.

One day, a Khmer Rouge lady told me that soon I would be married to a handicapped Pol Pot soldier, like an amputee. She said that I had no choice in the matter. At this time the regime still gave us enough food; but I became so depressed when I heard that, that I couldn't eat or sleep. I decided that I would kill myself if they forced me to marry a handicapped soldier.

A Khmer Rouge Victim in Vietnam

In the forest, we lived very close to the Vietnam border. We knew that our mom went to Vietnam just before our country fell, and that she would be still there. Although it too was a Communist country, we heard that the Vietnamese soldiers didn't chase people out of their houses like the Pol Pots did, and it became our goal to go to Vietnam to meet our mom. Some people escaped to Vietnam by pretending to fish and swimming across the river, and my brother, sisters, and I planned to swim across too. But I fell ill with malaria, and we were forced to stay in the jungle.

When the Khmer Rouge allowed the Vietnamese soldiers to take their people back to Vietnam by boat, we joined other people who were going to catch that boat. But I was still sick, and I couldn't walk so far, so someone put me on a bullock cart and told the man to take me there. When we got to the boat, the soldiers placed me in the lower deck with other sick people.

I lay on a stretcher, shivering with fever and unable to see what was happening, but I knew we had reached Vietnam because I heard everyone scrambling to see the crowds waiting to meet those who had escaped from Cambodia.

Suddenly I heard my sister shout excitedly, "Brother, brother, look over there; I see someone whose shape is just like Mom's!" I heard them shouting, "Mom, Mom," and oh, I was so excited. I struggled to get up, but I was so ill that I kept falling back.

When the boat stopped at last, some people carried me out and I saw Mom crying and embracing my brother and sisters. When the people put me down, Mom looked at me, but didn't come over. She stared at me and I heard her say, "Look at that poor child, she is so ill! I almost feel she's like one of mine." "It's sister Bopha, Mom, don't you see?" my brother asked her.

Mom came running and hugged me to her chest, crying hard, exclaiming, "Oh, my poor child! You are so ill and thin!"

When she became a bit calmer, she found a taxi and took me to the hospital, where I stayed for a month.

We lived with our aunt in Vietnam. Mom tried to do some small business to sustain our family, but she had a hard time because she had no capital. She had expected that my sisters and I would bring the jewelry she had kept for us, and that she would use it to do business. But the Pol Pot soldiers did not allow us to go where we wanted, and we could not go back for the jewelry. So we came to Vietnam with nothing, and Mom became really angry. She refused to listen to our reasons and scolded us a great deal.

I felt really bad because I was old enough to work, and still depended on my mom. I would have worked as a cashier or clerk, or anything else, but it was impossible for me to get a job because I didn't speak Vietnamese, and didn't have the necessary influence.

One day Mom went to a neighboring town and brought back two kilograms of chilies, which was a scarce commodity in our area. "Why don't we sell this chili instead of using it ourselves, Mom? I wouldn't mind selling it to our neighbors," I suggested.

Mom couldn't believe I would go from house to house, selling chilies. "You really dare do that?" she said. Then she encouraged me, saying, "It's really okay, because you are not stealing anything from people; you are selling something to them."

Still, I didn't want to do it alone, so I asked my sister, "Will you be my partner? You can carry the wrapping paper while I carry the basket of chilies on my head."

Sister agreed, but when we set out, she was so ashamed to sell things on the street that she walked far away from me. When we sat in the market, she covered her face with the kramar so nobody would recognize her. I was embarrassed, too, but I thought to myself, "These people in Vietnam don't know me, so I will not worry about what they will think of me."

At the end of the day we had made three times the cost of the chilies, and Mom was really proud of us! But selling things at the market was such an embarrassment, that we did it only once in a while after that.

Luck came my way a short time later, when I met one of Mom's friends who offered me a commission if I sold jewelry for her. She became like my adopted mother, and I started a new business for which I needed no capital, and I even made some money. Even so, we were really frustrated living in Vietnam, because there was a lot of crime and robbery there.

In Cambodia, when we wanted to buy fruit, merchants and farmers gave us even a whole bunch to taste before we bought them, so in Vietnam too I tried to taste some fruit in the market. But when the fruit seller saw that, he shouted, "Did you come from the forest? Don't you know you don't eat the fruit before you pay for it?" I felt really embarrassed, and waited until the man gave me the fruit in a bag. When I got home, I discovered he had put rotten fruit in the bottom of the bag, and covered them with a few good ones on top! That had never happened in Cambodia.

In Vietnam, we had to be careful wherever we went. On the bus, people ripped our pockets and stole money and jewelry. I also lost many bicycles, which upset me terribly. But I realized that the Vietnamese stole because their country was very poor.

The good thing about the Vietnamese was that they didn't discriminate against Cambodians.

My father escaped to Vietnam by himself. When the Khmer Rouge evacuated the city people, he went in the direction the soldiers ordered him to go, taking with him my maternal grandmother and two younger sisters. My sisters were five and fourteen years old then.

Father said that like us, they too had walked for several days. Just as they came to a village where some relatives lived, Grandmother collapsed from exhaustion. Since they had to cross a river to get to the village, Father left Grandmother at a resting place and went off with the two girls to find the relatives. After he located them, Father returned to bring my grandmother to the relatives' house, and she was gone. He looked for her everywhere, but he could not find her and had to go back to our cousin's house without Grandmother.

My cousin's family were not only Communists, they were also "Old People" of the village (see Chapter 5), so they had a lot of food. Since Father had worked as a civil officer in the old regime, he thought someone would surely recognize him and turn him and his daughters over to the Khmer Rouge. Thinking that the relatives could protect my sisters and feed them better than he could, Father left them with the relatives, and escaped to Vietnam.

When Father came to Vietnam without the youngest child and our grandmother, Mom became like a crazy woman. Whenever she saw a girl who was about my sister's age, she would run toward her shouting my sister's name. At night she pulled down the mosquito net on the bed and wept, scolding my father and all of us.

"You have animal hearts. If I knew you did not love your grandmother and sister, I would not have raised you so big. You left your grandmother and sisters there and didn't even go back to find them. Why didn't you stay there too? Why did you come to see my face?" she wailed.

We tried our best to explain to her that we could not save our grandmother or our sisters because we were prisoners of the Pol Pot soldiers, but she did not understand or believe that. Even today, she goes to orphanages to look for her daughter.

My father was so brokenhearted from everything that happened, that one year after he came to Vietnam he lost his will to live, and died of depression. We don't know what happened to our grandmother.

I went to Vietnam to get away from laboring under the Khmer Rouge, but I could not endure my mom's scolding. I was angry and depressed because she blamed us for things we could not do, so even though I was terrified of the Pol Pots, I decided to return to Cambodia. I thought that if I sacrificed myself by going back, she would stop scolding my sisters and my father. Secretly, I also hoped to find my sister and the boyfriend who used to help me.

I went back to the riverbank to get the boat to Cambodia, and found a lot of Cambodians waiting to go back because they too couldn't survive in Vietnam. They were too poor, or were too lonely for the relatives they had left behind. We all felt helpless and hopeless at the thought of returning to our country, but we didn't know what else we could do.

I waited all day, but the boat didn't come. When it was getting dark, a Chinese guy who stayed at our house turned up, looking for me. He said, "Your mom told me to bring you back. Please don't refuse to go because if you do not go back, I cannot return to your mom."

I asked if he would go to Cambodia with me, but he wouldn't. Neither would he go back to my mom without me. So I had no choice, but to go back to Mom.

When she saw me Mom didn't say anything, but she didn't scold us anymore. She knew that I would leave and not come back if she scolded us again.

The Vietnamese Liberation

I didn't have any more problems with Mom, but it was so hard to survive in Vietnam that I started to look for a way to escape from there. A person who befriended me told me that he planned to escape with a group of people on a boat, and that I too could join them. I decided to go with them and paid money to the owner of the boat.

On a dark night a couple of weeks later, we all climbed into the boat. The owner told us to be very quiet, because he didn't want to attract the soldiers' attention. He started the engine, and it ran for a minute or two. Then it sputtered and died down. "I have to repair this; just wait quietly," the man told us and began to fiddle with the motor. But before he could get it going, the soldiers started to shoot, and we all scrambled in every direction. I ducked into a house nearby and hid there until the shooting stopped. That was the end of our escape.

I attempted to escape a second time, but I got tricked by a man who took my money and some gold, and never arranged for a boat. After that I didn't try to leave Vietnam until the Vietnamese liberated Cambodia.

When Cambodia became free from Pol Pot, Mom went back to look for her mother and her youngest child. The people of the village in which they had lived told her that first, the Pol Pots killed my cousin's husband because he had been a policeman a long time ago. Next, the soldiers told my cousin's mother-in-law, who had Vietnamese blood, that she would be moved to a new house, and ordered her to evacuate from the village. Since my cousin was widowed, she and her children went with the mother-in-law. The older of my two sisters was away working in the rice field, but my youngest sister went with the relatives because she was too young to live by herself. The villagers never saw them after that.

So Mom came back to Vietnam, really depressed. While she was there, Mom had heard that Cambodians were going to refugee camps in Thailand; and she insisted that I too escape to a refugee camp. So I went to Cambodia by myself, and joined some escapees who were going to the Thai-Cambodia border. We paid a few soldiers some gold to take us part of the way to the border on their truck, and from there, we traveled in bullock carts and bicycles until we reached the border. First I stayed in a border camp, and later I went to Khao-I-Dang camp.

Khao-I-Dang camp was like a prison. We were not allowed to go anywhere. The Cambodian man and his wife who headed our section acted like kings, and gave enough food only to those who pleased them. People became really depressed, and I was too, until the Thai military hired me as a translator because I spoke French. So unlike many other refugees who had hardly anything because Pol Pot took everything we had, I started to have some money. I could buy extra food, and I still remember I bought a bunch of grapes with my first pay; oh, they were so delicious!

Although I felt less like a prisoner because I had a job, I was very lonely in the camp because I had no family of my own. Then one day, I met a friend from Phnom Penh, who had also escaped and was working in the kitchen! She had come to camp with her mother and sisters and brothers. I began to visit them and her mother was very kind, and treated me like her own child! I was so grateful to my friend's mother that I tried to help her whenever I could since, working as a translator, I met important people in the military and could ask them for favors. I remember once I asked one of them to bring water to my friend's mother's hut, so she didn't have to stand in line every morning and evening like everyone else to get water. We helped each other like that, and after a while, my friend's mother invited me to live with them because I had still not found my family; so I moved in with them.

Soon after I moved, I met another friend who said, "Did you know your mom is living in the old people's section of the camp?"

I got so excited when I heard that, and I rushed over to look for Mom. She was there, looking so old and miserable, with her nose and mouth covered with a kramar; the old people's section was next to the bathrooms, which stank so much it was impossible to breathe. Though Mom was very happy to see me, she said, "Oh, daughter, this is worse than living in jail! I think I will go back to Cambodia."

I begged my mom to stay until I obtained permission to bring her to our section, but two days after I met her she went back to Cambodia because she could not bear it anymore.

I felt so bad when Mom left; but soon after I found my sisters, who had also escaped to Khao-I-Dang camp. They were living in the orphans' section, and I brought them to live with my friend's family. My friend helped us all to find work in the kitchen, washing dishes and helping the cook.

Since Cambodia had become Communist, we decided to go to a third country to live. One sister went to France, and she sponsored us to go there; but her application was rejected. I felt very desperate when that happened. But when France went from being capitalist to socialist, I did not want to go there anymore because I was afraid that it would later become Communist. My sister who lived there suggested that we go to Australia, Canada, or America because they were big countries with more space and freedom.

My stepbrother from Vietnam had already come to the United States. I wrote a letter asking him to sponsor us, but it came back because he had moved. In the meantime, my friend's brother came to America, too, and he sponsored them.

We all felt so sad to think that soon, we would part from each other. Then my friend said, "Why don't we say you are our relatives and ask for permission to go with us to the United States?" So I told the Thai refugee office that we were all relatives and asked if we could go with my friend's family to the United States. They said yes, and my sisters and I came to Los Angeles with our friends.

Starting Over in America

Our apartment was quite small, because when my friend's brother rented it, he didn't know that his mom would bring three extra people with her. When he saw us he got quite worried, thinking that the apartment manager might turn us out if the man discovered that twelve people lived in the place. "Don't make noise and attract attention," he told us. Then he said to his younger siblings, "If anyone knocks on the door, run and hide in the closet. Don't let anybody find out that there are so many people living here." It made us feel so bad because we were the extra people, but we were too big to hide in those closets.

Our sponsor's friend invited all of us to dinner on the first night because we didn't have a stove or electricity in the apartment. We all somehow squeezed into our sponsor's car, and he took us to his friend's house, where his friend's wife had cooked us some very nice Cambodian food. After we finished eating, my sisters and I volunteered to walk home so the others could ride back in comfort. Our sponsor wrote down our new address for us, and told us how to get there.

My sisters and I set off and we walked for a long time; but we couldn't find the apartment. I showed our address to a man and said in very broken English, "Sir, I am a Cambodian living at this address, but now I am lost." He told us how to get there, but when we went in the direction he pointed, we got to downtown!

By now it was very late in the night, and we were very frightened. I asked a street cleaner how to get back home, and he said, "Get into a taxi. The driver will take you there." But how could we? We didn't have any money. Finally, we saw an old man who was getting into a van, and we ran and asked him for help. He told us to get into the van, and drove us back to the apartment! Oh, we were so glad to get back, and that man was so good that he didn't even ask for any money.

The next morning, someone knocked on our door. Fearing that the apartment manager had come to check us out, the kids ran and hid in the closet. When we opened the door, though, we found the man who brought us home the night before standing there, with boxes of food, clothes, and blankets given by his church people! We were so surprised and happy, for we hadn't expected such help from anyone, and we opened a tin of Campbell soup he had brought, to eat for lunch. But it tasted so funny, we couldn't eat it. It took us a bit of time to get used to American food.

Our new friend told me he would be my adopted father, and took me downtown and bought me a bookbag to go to school. When he met his friends he introduced me as his adopted daughter or refugee kid. I felt grateful to him for helping us, but I was embarrassed to go around with him in case people mistook me for his wife!

Our sponsor took us to the welfare office, and we applied for welfare. After our applications were approved, my sisters and I received about $400 and some food stamps from the government every month. But I couldn't stand to be on welfare; I wanted a job.

I started to learn English, and went to the refugee resettlement agency nearby to find out how I could get a job. The man who worked there said the minimum wage I could earn was $3.50 an hour, and added, "If you want to work here, I can pay you about $4.50 an hour." I got quite excited and I wanted to work right away. But he said, "First you have to get a driver's license. If you can find a friend to teach you to drive, you wouldn't have to pay for driving lessons."

I asked the people in my English class if anyone would teach me to drive, and a Japanese man who had a beautiful Honda said he could teach me an hour a day for a few weeks. I passed the driving test in my third attempt, and went back to the resettlement agency. "Now I have got my driver's license, and I can work," I told the clerk. He said he would give me a job.

Before I started to work, my half-brother and his wife came to see us. They had heard from somebody that we had come to America. When they realized I came here with a high education they said, "You already have some knowledge, so you should go back to school. It will be better to get more education than trying to earn money right away." But I still wanted to know what it felt like to work in this country, so I got a part-time job as an office clerk, and started going to school.

At school, I learned to read English faster than other Cambodians, because I already knew French; but I was still very slow to understand instructions because I mixed up words like "emergency," "urgency," and "agency."

I also did not know people did things differently in the American culture. For example, I did not realize that in offices there were signs such as those saying DO NOT ENTER, posted on doors; I just walked into people's rooms when I wanted to talk to someone, and they got quite upset with me. I remember the first couple of times I went to the shop or the post office, I walked right up to the counter ahead of everyone else, because in Cambodia, nobody stood in lines to pay for their goods. Over there, people just shoved with their elbows, and usually the men got ahead. One day when I did that here, a woman said to me, "I was here first, madam." At least, I think that's what she said, because at that time I didn't understand much English; I guessed from the way she said it that I should not go ahead of everyone else. From that day, when I saw a line, I just stood behind everyone else.

At the beginning I was also frightened to talk to people because they seemed loud and aggressive. I remember the first time I went to the welfare office with my sister-in-law, I felt very nervous because a Vietnamese man who worked there screamed at people. I really didn't want to talk to him, but my sister-in-law had lived here for a while, and she was not intimidated by him. She said, "Ghosts only scare people who are scared of them," and she shouted at him also. After that he talked to us politely.

I kept on learning by making mistakes! In Cambodia we didn't use serving spoons; when we ate, we just picked up more food with our own spoons. So when I started to work and a colleague had a birthday party, I picked up a second piece of cake with my own fork. My boss saw me do that. She shouted from the other side of the room, "Hey, you are not supposed to do that. Don't you see there's a serving fork?" Everybody turned to look at me, and I felt very embarrassed. I understand now that if you used a serving spoon or fork, you wouldn't spread germs to others; but my boss should have told me that in private and not shout the way she did, in front of everybody.

I worked hard at my job and learned my work quickly, but my boss treated me badly. She never praised me; instead, she threatened me, saying, "You know that so-and-so got fired because she did not do good work, don't you? The same thing will happen to you if you don't do your job properly." I became very unhappy at work, but I didn't know what to do. One day I didn't feel well, and asked my boss for permission to go home early, but she refused to let me go. That afternoon I fainted and fell on the floor, and they had to call an ambulance to take me home. After that I stayed home for a couple of weeks.

I was married by then and my husband, who is usually a kind person, got very upset about what my boss did to me. He said, "Cambodians and Asians are not dumb or stupid; we know the laws here, and we are people too. I am going to sue your boss!"

But that made me unhappy because I thought if we sued my boss, everyone else in my office would get into trouble too. Other people there had helped me a lot, and I didn't want to create problems for them. So I persuaded my husband to drop the idea.

After I recovered, I didn't want to work there any more. I was always tearful, and I didn't want to see my boss at all. I had many emotional problems, and finally I went to a psychologist to get some help.

"Don't avoid your boss," she said to me. "The sooner you go back and confront her, the quicker you would get over your problems."

She taught me how to talk to people here, and also told me about my rights as an employee. Although it wasn't easy, I took her advice and returned to work.

My boss tried to be extra nice to me, but I found it impossible to respect her because of the way she had treated me before. So I quit that job and found another because I could not bear to work with my boss anymore.

I finished school and graduated in computer science, but when I tried to get into an entry-level job in the computer industry, I discovered that people with even higher qualifications than mine had applied for it. So I stopped looking for work in that field, and got a different kind of job.

I need to know more English in my new job, so I have gone back to school again. I want to get good grades, and I study almost every night till my eyes are ready to pop out, but the best grade I ever get is a C. I find my new subjects harder than computer science because I come from a different culture. For example, once the teacher talked about adjustments people have to make when they retire. My ideas about adjustment to retirement are wrong in America, because my culture is different.

I wish I could leave this job and do a mail-order business. My husband prefers to open a grocery store. We can't do what we would like to do for a living, however, because though we have a lot of friends, they are Cambodian people who came here recently, and we don't have the money, or a person who can guide us to do these things, or a place to use for a business.

Love, Marriage, and Childrearing

Before Pol Pot took over our country, a boy who was six years older than I liked me very much. When he had free time, he found me books I needed for my classes, and even taught me mathematics and physics, so I improved a lot in my studies. He never told me he loved me, but I knew it because he did things to show me that he cared for me.

When Pol Pot evacuated us, my friend and I got separated. Later, I heard from another man that the Pol Pots had put my friend to work in a youth group, and that my friend and some other students who disagreed with the policies of the regime had planned to burn a food storage house in their village, as a protest. Somebody informed the Pol Pot leader of their plans, and they killed my friend and all the other students.

He has been dead for almost thirteen years now, but I feel he still follows me. I see him in my dreams, and it disturbs me. I am married to another person now, but I wish I could see him alive and have him as a friend.

Marriage helped me a lot in recovering from the past. It hasn't given me everything, but it has given me something to live for. I met my husband, who is also Cambodian, in the United States. We are almost the same age, but he is wiser than I, and thinks of long-range things regarding family matters. He always thinks about how to become rich. We are not poor, and we have survived here, but my husband thinks we should have more money so we can have an easier life. As in the proverb I mentioned earlier, we work hard; my husband does two jobs to bring happiness to his family. He is a good person who does not gamble, smoke, or womanize; but he has a hot temper!

We have one child who is four years old, and I have such a hard time looking after her because we have no help. In our country people have many children and the kids take care of each other when their parents go out. But over here, I have to take my kid wherever I go during weekends, unless my sister can look after her. But for that, I have to call ahead and make appointments with her! I leave my daughter at a day care center when I go to work, but if I don't pick my kid up on time, the center charges me a lot of extra money. So I always watch the time when I'm at work.

When I come home in the evening, I feel tired, but I still have to make good, interesting food for my family. After we eat I want to do my homework, but my child wants to play. I have to spend time with my daughter at least some of the time, because raising a child is like growing a tree. At the beginning you must water a tree well, so it develops strong roots. Later, it will not need so much water. Children are just like that; they must have good roots. First, you have to spend a lot of time with them, and help them to start from the bottom; then when they can crawl, they learn to walk. Then they run.

In America, it's difficult to raise kids and to discipline them because they have too many rights. Kids should not talk back to their parents, or to older people, but when I scold or yell at my child, she talks back to me. She says, "Why do you have to yell? Then I can yell at you." I want to switch my child to teach her good behavior when she misbehaves like that, but here, you can't switch your child. I think I should have the right to do that.

I have four rules that my child has to follow. First, she may not interrupt when my husband or I talk on the phone. Second, she must ask for permission before she buys something, goes somewhere, or eats anything. Third, she must behave well, and eat all her lunch at school. Fourth, she has to be nice and polite to people, whether they are young or old. This means that she must share her toys with other kids, and not hurt their feelings by saying mean things like "You are not my friend." She has to respect old people. When we have guests, for instance, she should greet them, saying, "Hi, Uncle," or "Hi, Aunty," ask them to sit down, and find out what they like to eat and drink. Even if she is mad at someone, she must not show her anger, but be nice to that person. I will make up new rules for her as she grows older.

My two sisters live together, and last night they came to me because the older sister feels the younger one does not behave properly. If we were in our country, the younger one would have to obey her older sister; she couldn't do whatever she likes. But here, when the older one tells her to do something, she doesn't even bother to answer. She gets in her car and goes out whenever she wants to, without telling her sister. It upsets the older sister because she takes care of the younger sister, and she feels the younger one should respect her like a mother. I think so too.

Reflections

When people sit on fat chairs [gain power], they see only money; they do not see the problems of poor people. When Lon Nol became president he just listened to corrupt people, and didn't go to see what happened in the country. So he didn't know that poor people suffered greatly in Cambodia because there was no public assistance.

In America you have welfare, community lawyers, and government hospitals; but over there, one had to have money for lawyers or doctors, and unless one had relatives to help when one fell ill, one did not even have food. The Communists' main point was that they would help the poor people, and the poor people believed it until it was too late. But how could they know? They were not educated; they were farmers, and the government didn't do anything to give them knowledge or other assistance. So people had no heart and no mind to fight the Communists, who were brainwashed by China, and Cambodia fell because the government was corrupt, and did not help poor people.

Before I came to America, I lived in Cambodia, Vietnam, and Thailand. I think out of these three groups, Cambodians are the most timid and the most honest. The Vietnamese are not very honest; they are smarter, and more selfish and ambitious. They do something for you only if they can get something for themselves. The Thais are in between.

In this country too, many Cambodians only want to live a good life; they are not bothered about getting rich. Most people who came from villages live among other Cambodians, and do things the way other Cambodians do.

My mom told us, "People judge you by your dress, so always dress smartly." But Cambodian people who came from villages walk around in the shops, wearing sarongs. Sarongs should be worn only at home. They are like pajamas, and when I see my people walking around in shops in sarongs, I feel embarrassed because I am also Cambodian. However, I don't criticize them directly, because then they will feel insulted, especially if they are older. Instead, I tell them indirectly, "Oh, you were rushing, and you had no time to change clothes?" hoping they will realize that they should wear something else when they go out.

I also feel bad because some Cambodians have not learned English. Even when they are sick, they won't phone for doctor's appointments because someone might speak in English. I tell them that unlike in our country, children don't stay at home and look after the parents, and if they don't learn English, they can't look after themselves when their children leave. But they say they haven't learned English because they can't remember what they learn. Whatever the reasons may be, I don't judge them too harshly. When Vietnam became Communist, the people did not suffer the way Cambodians did. Cambodians suffered too much to forget.

I changed in many ways after I came here, but while my friend became a Christian, I remained a Buddhist, even though I was also exposed to Christianity when I came here. In Los Angeles, every Sunday morning, people came in a van to take us and other Cambodians to church. When they came, I put away the picture of the Buddha I kept in the living room, and went to church just to please them because they helped us. When I came home, I still prayed to the Buddha. I also pray to my father when I have problems, and I feel he helps me.

I believe all religions make people good; but what part of Christianity do you believe? In Buddhism sin can't be subtracted and become zero. In Christianity, if you do something bad, you tell God, and it's all over. I don't think that's fair.

I still go to church sometimes when my friend invites me, because I like her, and I don't want to hurt her. I also enjoy going there because I meet other people. But when they pass a paper asking if we want to join the church, I write saying that I will join later. I don't say I will not join, because I don't want to hurt them.

If Cambodia hadn't been taken over by the Khmer Rouge, I wouldn't have left my country. It is easier to live in a small country than in a big country like America, because in a small country, it's easier to get used to the culture, society, and food. Even when I lived in Vietnam after Pol Pot came, I missed Cambodia terribly. But when I went back there after the liberation, I knew I couldn't live there because of all the trauma I suffered under the Communists.

I feel so sad when I think about what happened to my family and my boyfriend. Every time I see pictures of refugees in newspapers and magazines, I look closely at them to see if I can spot my little sister. If she is alive, she would not remember us because she was too young when we got separated, so we have to find her.

My sister who was fourteen years old when Father left her with the relatives told me what happened after he left. The Khmer Rouge sent her away to work in the rice fields, but allowed my little sister to remain at home. When the regime began to starve people, the relatives became very mean to my little sister. They forced her to do all the housework, and if their children cried, they accused her of fighting with their children and beat her. She had no food, no school, and no religion; she had only suffering and sadness. Yet, when the Communists had once given a piece of palm sugar to her, she had given a piece of it to another woman and asked her to give it to her older sister. When the older sister came back to the village, my little sister had asked her if she got the piece of sugar, but the older one never got it.

Before I got married, I felt so bad because I missed my boyfriend, my family, all my classmates, my house, my neighbors. I missed everything and everybody I lost to the Khmer Rouge. Right now I feel a little better because

I have my husband and my child, but I won't forgive the Khmer Rouge. In my heart I have the feeling that I want to take revenge on them, but I will not go to the extent of killing them. I don't think I could use a knife or a gun, and I will never kill people, but I want to beat the soldier who killed my sister. I do not feel as upset and angry with my relatives who did mean things to my sister. I think they became mean because they were hungry too. When you have everything, you can be nice to people; you can share. But when you are hungry and don't have anything, you become mean.

I am happy with my family, yet I feel lonely here. I want to have a best friend, someone around my age to whom I should be able to tell everything. I need someone to joke with, and ask for help; but I don't know how to make a best friend here. Some American people look at me as if I was completely different, and I can't find someone from my own country to match my social and educational background because so many were killed. I had many close friends in school in Phnom Penh, and I asked my mom and sister who still live in Cambodia to find out if any of my former friends are alive so I could help them, but they have not been able to find even one.

Right now my sister and I help three Cambodian sisters living in a refugee camp. The Khmer Rouge killed their parents. Although we were not very close friends, the oldest of the three sisters gave me a ride on her scooter when I went to medical school. She is so unhappy in the camp, that she once sent me a letter written with blood, saying she wanted to kill herself. Sometimes she says she wants to become a prostitute so she can earn money. I get very upset when she writes such letters, but other than sending her money, there is nothing I can do to help her.

Though I feel sad about what happened to our country, and we find it hard to live in America, I appreciate living here. In Cambodia we lived under discrimination and prejudice. Without money, we couldn't have a place in society. In America, we have more freedom. Even if you don't know the language, people help you. I am free to work without people abusing my nationality. I like this country, and we have now become American citizens. I will go back to Cambodia to visit, but not to live.

The Desecration
of a Culture

CHAPTER FIVE

The Khmer Rouge Revolution

When the Khmer Rouge defeated the Lon Nol government in 1975, warfare and American bombings of the countryside had driven thousands of people, including some of the narrators, to seek refuge in the cities. As early as 1971, the population of Phnom Penh had swollen from 393,995 in 1962 to about 1.2 million (Ross 1990: 85). Those without relatives were forced to beg on the streets, and even those who received help faced great hardships because many people were jobless, and food and other necessities were scarce because of the destruction of farms and transportation. Schools had been closed down, and people were too afraid to venture out except when it was essential.

In Phnom Penh, little was known about the leaders of the new regime or their policies, and for every negative report, there was a positive one of the Communists helping the peasants. Many urbanites regarded the occasional news they heard of brutality and repression in Communist-controlled areas as government propaganda or rumors by the sophisticates in

Family life before the Khmer Rouge revolution

the capital, and unlike the South Vietnamese elite who fled their country before it was taken over by the Communists, few middle-class Cambodians attempted to flee Cambodia. Like Nya Srey's husband (see Chapter 11), who was a lawyer, they remained to help the new regime rebuild their nation.

On April 17 the Communists entered Phnom Penh as victors. The Cambodian people, whose lives had been utterly disrupted by war, wished only for peace and stability. The new regime's ideals of independence, peace, neutrality, nonalignment, sovereignty, democracy, and prosperity for the Cambodian people (Ngor 1987: 91) appeared to grant the populace their hopes for peace. Particularly because the Khmer Rouge cadres were ethnic Khmer, brothers of the same race, people believed that the Khmer Rouge would uphold the social values and traditions that had evolved from ancient times. Moreover, unlike the two previous regimes, the Khmer Rouge were nationalists fighting for a more just, less corrupt social order. When the Communists won, people believed that the fighting and bloodshed that had ravaged their country for so long would be over, and welcomed the new rulers with joy.

The Khmer Rouge goal was to force a social, cultural, and economic revolution, without any Western technology or aid, that would create a racially pure Khmer society that was self-sufficient and socially and economically egalitarian. However, the revolution turned out to be based not on progressive change, but on eradication of the existing social system, and on revenge.

The first revolutionary act to achieve social equality started with the completely unexpected forced evacuation of city dwellers to the countryside, where all would become peasants. The regime called them the "New People" (as opposed to long-time peasants, who were called the "Old People") but in fact, according to Ngor, the regime thought of the evacuees as "War Slaves" (1987: 202).

In the countryside, the Khmer Rouge starved people systematically, and forced them to do hard manual labor for up to sixteen hours a day. They were denied food, sleep, and medical treatment, and social needs such as currency, education, and religion were stripped from the victims' lives. The Sangha were either killed or unfrocked and put to work, and Buddhist temples were turned into brutal prisons where prisoners were starved, verbally and physically abused, left to die, or were killed. Educational establishments became centers to torture the educated, and hospitals became morgues where the infirm were left to die, or discarded before they died. But the survivors were not allowed to perform funeral rites. Instead, corpses were carted away to be thrown into massive pits, partially buried, or left in the fields to be devoured by wild animals. Relating an incident when the bodies of two women who suffocated to death inside a truck packed with people were abandoned on the wayside by the soldiers, one evacuee wrote:

> When they saw what was happening, the families of the two dead women protested, weeping. Traditionally, the dead must either be buried or cremated. The idea of leaving them there by the roadside was unthinkable, sacrilegious. . . . "Now we are no longer human beings." (Yathay 1987: 73)

Under the new regime, individuals were not worthy of consideration. They were erased, except as units in a group. The only thing that mattered was Angka, the high revolutionary organization governing the country that would make Cambodia an egalitarian, agrarian, self-sufficient country using only the labor of the people. The duty of the people was to serve Angka without question. Ngor quotes a soldier who instructed the populace in their new order of life:

> "If Angka says to break rocks, break rocks. If Angka says to dig canals, you must dig canals. If Angka says to farm, you must farm. . . . We don't need the technology of the capitalists. We don't need to send our young people to school. Our school is the farm. The land is our paper. The plow is our pen. We will 'write' by plowing. We don't need to give exams or award certificates. Knowing how to farm and knowing how to dig canals—those are our certificates," he said. And, "We don't need doctors anymore. They are not necessary. If someone needs to have their intestines removed, I will do it." He [the soldier] made a cutting motion with an imaginary knife across his stomach. "It is easy. There is no need to learn how to do it by going to school." (Ngor 1987: 133, 139)

In some cases, the Khmer Rouge cadres were mere children of twelve or thirteen years, but they had full power to control the lives of the "New People," who were separated into age- and sex-graded labor camps. Vocabulary denoting former social and family relationships was abolished, and parents, teachers, elders, monks, children, all became "comrades": "Everybody is equal now! Everybody is the same! No more *sompheahing*! [gesture of greeting or submission]. No more masters and no more servants! The wheel of history is turning! You must follow Angka's rules!" (Ngor 1987: 83) The wheel of history indeed turned. Every man, woman, and child was caught in the spokes; all were broken and many were crushed, when the regime publicly declared "BLOOD AVENGES BLOOD!" As Ngor explains:

In our language, "blood" has its ordinary meaning, the red liquid in the body, and another meaning of kinship or family. Blood avenges blood. You kill us, we kill you. We "new" people had been on the other side of the Khmer Rouge in the civil war. . . . Symbolically, the Khmer Rouge had just announced that they were going to take revenge. (Ngor 1987: 140–41)

At the beginning, the Khmer Rouge killed those they perceived as enemies of the revolution: officials of the former government who, as allies of American imperialists, had been their enemies in the civil war; the educated and wealthy urbanites who were "New People" tainted with Western ideas; Buddhist monks considered parasites living off other people's labor; the Vietnamese, who were historical enemies of the Khmer people. As time went on, however, killings became indiscriminate, and nobody, not even the poorest peasants the regime had set out to liberate, escaped abuse and death.

Though North Vietnam initially helped the Khmer Rouge gain power, the regime's distrust of the Vietnamese led to repeated border clashes with Vietnamese forces. In January 1979 Vietnamese invaders ousted the Khmer Rouge, installed a puppet regime with Heng Samrin as president, and renamed the country "People's Republic of Kampuchea." Hun Sen was appointed prime minister in 1985.

The narratives in this book describe graphically, not only how (until they were ousted) the Khmer Rouge regime violated the Buddhist precepts and code of conduct that had been the essence of Cambodian society, but also how the victims themselves were forced to violate those norms in order to survive. But the narratives also show that though the Khmer Rouge tried so hard to eradicate the former Khmer society and culture, they only succeeded in doing so outwardly. Inwardly, many victims continued to look to their past for survival.

CHAPTER SIX

Pu Ma: A Welfare Mother

As I turned my car into the street leading to Pu Ma's apartment on a sunny September morning, clouds of brown dust from road and building construction sites swirled into my face, choking me and making my eyes water. There were no trees to shade me from the glaring sun; only rows of substandard apartment buildings that stood on either side of the street. When I parked the car near the entrance to Pu Ma's home, several children who were playing on the gritty roadside, and who knew me, came over to greet me. I stopped for a moment to talk with them, and to admire a toy car one little boy timidly held out to me; then I walked up the flight of concrete steps leading to the two-bedroom apartment Pu Ma shares with her children, another family of four adult refugees, and a sole survivor of a family that perished in the holocaust. (See Chapter 13 for Pu Ma's daughter's narrative.)

When I first met her at another refugee's house, I thought Pu Ma had adjusted well to her new life in America. A vibrant woman of 39, she

Khmer Rouge soldiers wielding their authority

donned skirts or jeans to go to the store, while many refugees of her age and background continued to wear sarongs. She attended English-as-a-second-language classes and parent-teacher conferences at her children's schools. Soon, she became the *pu ma*, or friend, who introduced me to other refugees in the community.

I found Pu Ma's apartment even busier than usual, since it was a school holiday. Two sons of the family who shared Pu Ma's apartment sat at an old sewing machine, altering jeans they had bought at the flea market. Pu Ma's six-year-old daughter sat on the floor, absorbed in mixing an orange drink with more orange than water. The older woman, who was the head of the other family occupying the house, was pulling out her betel leaf and condiments. As was her custom, she offered me some, but I declined, for while I am used to the strong-tasting betel leaf from my childhood in Sri Lanka, I have not developed a fondness for it. On rare occasions I accept her offer, to please her. Pu Ma, her daughter Koun Srey, and two other women sat on woven mats on the floor. They were looking at photographs taken at the last wat ceremony and I joined them.

When we had finished, Koun Srey brought out another batch of older photographs that I had never seen before. Among them were two of Pu Ma's wedding pictures. Pu Ma had been a beautiful bride—radiant, yet innocent. Her eyes were filled with love as she stood next to her tall, handsome husband. When I told Pu Ma how beautiful she looked, she said, "You know, my mother, my stepfather, my aunts, my sisters, didn't like my husband because he was very poor. But I loved him because he was very good."

Slowly, Pu Ma took the photographs from my hand and gazed with immense tenderness at the picture of her husband, who was murdered by the Khmer Rouge. With tears welling up in her eyes, she caressed his face slowly. She uttered no sound, but the indescribable sadness that spread over her face conveyed all the pain she felt. For the first time, I realized I may never understand the pain and suffering the Cambodians endure because of the holocaust; and I was humbled by the courage and humanity with which they bear it.

I spent over a hundred hours collecting this narrative, because when memories became too painful for Pu Ma, I either terminated or prolonged the interviews, to give her as much time as she needed to recover. Because of her limited English skills, a large portion of her story was related in Khmer. When my understanding of Khmer was insufficient to fully comprehend her story, I tape-recorded those portions and took them to a third party for translation.

Even though talking about the Khmer Rouge atrocities was immensely sorrowful and painful for both of us, I asked many questions to find out how Pu Ma copes with the holocaust experience. In doing so, I also discovered the extent to which Cambodian folk beliefs about death and ghosts pervade people's everyday lives, and how they contribute to making the holocaust experience even more traumatic, if that is possible.

Though Pu Ma is now here in the United States, she continues to turn to her traditions and beliefs to make sense of her present life, and yearns to return to Cambodia. Her sentiments are shared by many middle-aged and older refugees who are uneducated, and unemployed, and therefore even more removed from mainstream American culture. ❖❖❖

A Childhood in Poverty

I remember when I was little, my mother, who lived in Battambang, was very, very poor. She had married a farmer when she was fourteen years of age, but when she was pregnant with her third child, her husband became sick with diarrhea and died. After his death, Mother went back to live with her parents. There, a soldier fell in love with her and asked her parents for permission to marry her. Her parents told him, "We do not think you should marry our daughter because she already has two children, and a third one in her stomach." The soldier went away, but after her son was born, returned again and again, asking to marry her.

In the meantime, my mother had seen her dead husband in a dream, and he told her, "If you get married with another man, I will take away one of your children."

Mother became frightened, and told her parents that she did not want to marry again. Her parents tried their best to keep the soldier from seeing their daughter. At night she slept in a hammock tied way up near the roof so those who came to the house would not see her.

When he couldn't get his way, the soldier began to threaten her parents, saying, "I will kill you all if you will not give your daughter to me." So even though she did not want to, Mother was forced to marry the soldier. That soldier was my father.

After their wedding, one of Mother's children died. The child was not sick, and she believed he was taken away by her first husband's spirit.

The people in my country believe that every November, the ghosts of their dead relatives come to visit children. To stop ghosts from entering our house, Mother drew an angry-looking face with lime paste on a cooking pot and left it in the front yard. It looked like a carved pumpkin American people leave outside at Halloween time.

My mother was a good person and I liked her very much. I didn't like my father, though, because he was a bad man. He wouldn't give money to Mother, and fought with her every day. I don't know why he fought, but she said that he had another woman.

Mother worked hard making sweetmeats to earn money, and my older sister and I sold them at the nearby temple. Sometimes a neighbor gave us a bit of food, and my mother also visited Grandmother, who lived across the river, to ask for help. Once I remember the boatman agreed to take Mother across for two cans of rice because she didn't have money to pay him, and when the boat was in mid-river she saw a dead fish in the water. She dove in, caught it, and brought it home to cook for the children.

My mother had such an unhappy life because she didn't have merit. Whenever she could, she tried to do good things so she would have a better life in the future. Sometimes she cleaned the temple, and if she had enough food she would take some to the monks. I used to go with her, and I heard her pray, "When I am born again, please let me not be married to this man."

Although she was so poor, Mother insisted that my stepsister and brother and I go to school. I said, "Mother, I like going to school, but I don't want to go because you are so poor." She said that to the teacher, and the teacher said, "Your older daughter does not come to school regularly, but Pu Ma is a hard-working student, and I will help her."

I went to school until I was about nine years old, when our king, Norodom Sihanouk, visited our school. My teacher chose me to perform the "butterfly dance" for him, and told me to buy some white fabric to make the costume. I knew Mother didn't have money to buy the cloth, and I didn't want her to borrow money from other people, and I quit going to school.

When King Sihanouk came, soldiers had to guard him when he appeared in public to speak to people. But instead of staying at his guard post, my father, who was a bad soldier, loitered around, drinking wine. After Sihanouk left, Father's boss put him in jail, where he was forced to walk around the prison yard twenty times, with big rocks tied to his back. We saw that when we visited him in jail, and Mother cried.

One morning Father was released and he came home. In the afternoon he put on a pair of new pants, a shirt with long sleeves, and his soldier's red hat. He took his kramar and called out to Mother, "Pu Ma's mother, I am leaving. I want to say goodbye."

"Where are you going?" she asked.

"I don't know, but I have a problem with you, Pu Ma's mother," he replied, and left the house.

He always called her "Pu Ma's mother"; he never used her name.

About an hour later another soldier came running and said to Mother, "Your husband is dead." "But he only just left the house!" she said in disbelief. But she ran with him to see. I went too. We saw Father hanging from a rope round his neck in the cell where he was kept.

After Father killed himself we lived with my mother's brother, who was a teacher. He looked after us well, and told Mother to save the money she earned by selling sweetmeats. In time she became rich. She built a house, and bought me a necklace, a bracelet, and a wristwatch.

When I was about twelve years old, Mother married again. My stepfather had been a poor farmer, and because he had been unable to find work in the countryside, he now worked as a cyclo [pedicab driver] in town. After they married he helped Mother with her business, and I started working in a mattress factory when I was about fourteen years old. A year and a half later, I got married.

Love and Marriage

My husband worked in the factory as a mechanic. Like my stepfather, he too had come to the town looking for work, because when his father had an accident and was crippled, they lost their rice fields. My husband's mother left them, and my husband and his two brothers looked after their father.

Before we got married, I had been friends with my husband for some time. One day he said, "Pu Ma, I come from a very poor family, but I love you and I want to marry you."

I loved him too, but I told him, "Until you speak to my mother and get her permission, I cannot say anything."

When Mother heard my husband's family was destitute, she told me, "I don't want you to marry such a poor man. You should marry a soldier from the city; you will have an easier life then."

I said, "Mother, I love this man and don't want to marry a soldier. I want to marry him." But Mother would not agree, and my husband asked his boss to speak with her. His boss told my mother, "I know this man, and he is a good person. If you will not let your daughter marry him, I will help her to do so." So with his approval, I married my husband, even though it displeased my mother.

In Cambodia, the man usually came to live with the wife's family, but after we got married, I went to live with my husband because nobody in my family liked my husband—he was too poor.

Before I left I said, "Mother, if my marriage turns out to be good and I am happy, I will come back to see you. But if I have problems with my husband I won't return, because it was a mistake that I made." Then because I had displeased her, I gave back the jewelry and the watch she had bought for me, and left with my husband.

I hadn't realized how poor my husband was until I saw my father-in-law's hut in the countryside. They had two chairs and a table, but no beds, or even pillows. That night, as I lay on the mat next to my husband, I could see the stars and the moon through cracks and holes in the walls and roof. I began to feel very unhappy because my husband was so poor. After he fell asleep, I stayed awake for a long time, crying bitterly to myself, "Oh, why am I going to be so poor? Maybe I have no merit!"

Although they were so poor, my husband's father and brothers were very good people, and I loved them dearly. My father-in-law always spoke lovingly to me, and constantly reminded my husband to take good care of me. Because my father-in-law wanted to make us happy, he had borrowed money to give us a good wedding. With the money we received as wedding gifts, we first helped him to repay his loans, and from the remainder, we bought furniture for the house. My brothers-in-law helped me with housework, and when they worked for rich farmers and got rice as payment, they brought it home. We lived together peacefully until my husband and I moved to a factory house we won from a lotto drawing.

A few months after we moved to our new house, my mother gave birth to another boy. After he was born, Stepfather left her and went to Phnom Penh to work as a soldier. Soon after he left, mother became sickly and we brought her to live with us. We also continued to visit my father-in-law often.

My husband worked hard to get rich. When he didn't have to work in the factory, he earned money by working as a pedicab driver, or by selling the fish he caught in the river. We saved all my earnings for a whole year and bought some gold, a motorcycle, and furniture for our house. About this time, my mother returned to her house with my brother.

I got pregnant soon after we moved to the new house, and my father-in-law was overjoyed. "Oh, daughter, I have waited so long to have a grandchild!" he told me, over and over.

But after five months, I suddenly started to bleed when I was at work, and the doctor in the factory rushed me to a hospital by ambulance. My husband came with me too. I don't remember what happened when we got there, but when I opened my eyes I saw my husband crying. A doctor told me that my baby had died.

My father-in-law was heartbroken about my miscarriage. A few months after that, we were at work when my husband's brother came and said, "Sister, come quickly, Father has died!" We left right away, and found that he had died inside his house, all by himself.

I loved my father-in-law very much, and I was so sad that he never saw my son or daughter, who were born before Pol Pot took over our country.

Khmer Rouge Prisoners

When my son was four years old and my daughter was two, I got pregnant again, and we decided to build a house for our family. My mom gave us some money too, and with her money and our savings, we bought a piece of land. But before we began building, the Pol Pots took over our factory. They said, "Good people can stay and work here. Everyone else must go to the farms." We were allowed to remain. My second son was born soon afterward.

About a month after the Pol Pots came, my husband went to visit my mother. When he came back he said, "Pu Ma, I didn't see your mother or the people who lived in that village. I only saw Pol Pots there." None of my friends in the factory knew what had happened to the villagers. I got permission from the soldiers to visit Mother, and took along some rice and fish for her. But I could not find my mother. Her house, as well as the others around it, were deserted. "The people have gone back to live in their hometowns. If you want to find them, you have to go there," the soldiers in my mother's town told me.

I knew my mother would have gone to her first husband's farm, because she would get food there. But when I went there, I found her seated on the floor, eating rice husks! "I have nothing else to eat," she said, "the farm now belongs to the Khmer Rouge."

Although I had not asked for permission from the soldiers in the factory to bring Mother there, I decided to bring her and my little brother to live with me, because we had a lot of food in the factory. Mercifully, when the soldiers saw Mother and Brother they didn't say anything.

A few days later, my stepfather—having heard that Mother was with me—came in search of her, and asked to live with us. I didn't want to help him; I was angry with him because he left Mother. But my husband said, "Let him stay. It's difficult for him to go anywhere else in these times." So he ended up living with us.

We worked in the factory until 1977, when the soldiers brought a new group of people to work there. "Now it is your turn to go and work in the rice fields," they told us. "Take your belongings and get into those trucks with your families."

The soldiers drove us far into a mountainous area. There, for the first time, I saw others who had been evacuated much earlier. "Oh God," I thought, "they look so pale and haggard; they are dying!"

Soon after we came to live in the mountains, the Khmer Rouge ordered my husband and my stepfather to go to a men's camp in a different village. They took away my seven-year-old son and my nine-year-old brother to a Pol Pot school. I lived with my mother, my infant son, and my daughter. Mother took care of them while I worked in the rice fields all day.

I hadn't seen my husband for a year when another man who had worked in the factory, and now worked in his team, came to our village on some errand. "Pu Ma," he called me softly. "Your husband has a big wound on his knee, and he is very sick. He wants to see you." I was a good worker and my leader liked me. He gave me permission to visit my husband for half a day.

I hardly recognized my husband. He looked like a matchstick except for his leg, which was swollen with the festered wound. "Is that really you, Pu Ma?" he said softly, looking at me with sunken eyes. He held out a hand. "Please take me with you. Otherwise I will die soon," he moaned.

I went to his leader. "My husband is so sick he can't work. Please let me take him to my village and look after him; when he's better he will come back," I pleaded. His leader was an old man, and he must have felt sorry for me, because he allowed my husband to go with me.

On the way back, I half-carried my husband, who dragged himself slowly and painfully, leaning on a stick. Even though he got very little food, once he came to live with me, my husband got better little by little. When he was able to hobble around a bit, instead of sending him back, my village leader assigned him to carry vegetables from the farm to the kitchen. He was very happy doing that, because he was able to steal some food for us too, and at that time, we ate well!

About three months after my husband came, we heard that my sister who lived in another village had just had a baby, and that she was starving. This upset my mother a great deal, particularly because we had enough food since my husband stole from the kitchen.

"Pu Ma, you must help your sister. You cannot let her die. Please take her some food," Mother begged me. I told her, "Mother, Sister lives far away, and you know there are Pol Pots everywhere. I am too frightened to go to see her." But she was determined to help Sister, and declared, "If you will not go, I will take her food!" But I couldn't let Mother go on such a long journey. She was too old and too weak. "Okay, you take care of the children. I will go," I said to her, unhappily. When I told my husband I was going to see Sister he said, "You must not go on such a long journey by yourself. I will come with you." Although I wanted him to go with me, he still limped badly, and I told him to stay. But he was determined to go with me.

Our group leader gave us a note authorizing us to travel to my sister's village. We took some rice and yams that we had hidden, and walked all day. We reached her place late in the evening. Too tired to say much, we gave my sister the food we had brought, and went to sleep. Early next morning we left because we wanted to get back to our children as quickly as possible. We had walked only a few kilometers when we saw a group of Pol Pot soldiers.

"Stop there. Where are you going?" they demanded, running over to us. Terrified, we handed one of them our permit. He read it and said, "This gives you permission only to walk from your village to your sister's village. It does not permit you to return to your village."

He accused us of running away to join the Vietnamese, and ordered the other soldiers to tie our hands behind our backs. Then they walked us to a jail. It was in a temple.

One soldier took my husband away, and another took me to a small room and shoved me onto a bed. He poked the barrel of his gun hard into my chest. [Pu Ma still has the indentation made by the soldier's gun.]

"Why were you running away to join the Vietnamese?" he demanded.

"We were not running away to the Vietnamese," I said, trembling. "Yesterday my husband and I came to visit my sister because she's sick. This morning we were going back to our village, where I have a baby and two older children."

My breasts were swollen because my son had not drunk milk for two days, but the soldier did not believe me. He started to hurt me more, and to prove to him that I was telling the truth, I showed him the milk in my breasts. The soldier untied my hands, but he didn't let me go. Instead, he took me to another room, where about 80 other women prisoners and their children lived. Every day, I worked with them in the rice fields behind the temple, and we got two meals of watery rice to eat.

The Pol Pots kept my husband and about 700 other men in chains in a filthy room, and starved them day after day. The men looked like skeletons, but mosquitoes still bit them all night through. Unable to move, they defecated and urinated where they lay, and the room stank dreadfully. Although we couldn't visit them, a soldier who liked me because I sewed his torn sweater allowed me to see my husband every now and then for ten or fifteen minutes. So every day, I saved a bit of my rice gruel in a can to take to my husband, if the good soldier allowed me to see him.

When the other men saw me, they pleaded for food and water too. "Please lady, will you help me? I want some water to drink," they cried. I felt sick at heart when I saw them and heard their whimpers, but all I could say was "No, I can't help you, because I am a prisoner too!"

The first time I went to see him, my husband said, "Pu Ma, you must not stay here. You must run away. Go back to the children and to your mother." It made me cry because I missed my children and my mother so much. That night I ran away. I ran for about four blocks, and then stopped. I knew that if I escaped, my husband would be killed. I went back to the temple.

The next time I went to see him, my husband wept, "Pu Ma, I want to see my children." I said, "Okay, but you eat first," and gave him the food. He smiled. "Maybe I will not die. Maybe I will see my children one day," he said. But after that my husband grew depressed and refused to eat. "I don't need to eat, Pu Ma. You eat alone; because you are a woman they might allow you to go back to the children. Don't worry about me," my husband said. His legs were scorched by red-hot embers that one of the soldiers had thrown into the room. My husband did not expect to live. He was very thin and very white because there was no blood in his veins.

One month and five days after Pol Pots took us to jail, I saw the soldiers put all the men into a truck. "Where are you taking my husband?" I asked them. "We are taking your husband to work in another place," one of them said.

But later that night, the soldier who was my friend told me, "Pu Ma, your husband is dead. They took the men to a big mountain, killed them with axes, and pushed them all into a big hole."

So I know my husband is dead.

Two nights after they killed the men, the Pol Pots ordered all the women and children to walk to the farms behind the temple. When we were walking, the good soldier said to me, "Pu Ma, Pol Pot is going to kill all of you. Run; you may get killed, or you may escape."

When the soldiers started to kill, I ran away into the jungle, and hid in some bushes. I lay there until it became quiet, and then started running as fast as I could. I ran and walked all night, and hid when the sun came up the next day. Every day I thought, "Maybe tonight I will see my mother and children." But I ran for a week before I finally reached them, surviving on leaves and fruits I picked off the trees.

Three days after I reached the village where my mother was staying, my stepfather lost a cow belonging to Angka, and the soldiers ordered him to go and find it. He hadn't come back after two days, and the group leader in our camp asked my mother, "Perhaps your husband ran away to live with the Vietnamese?" Mother got very scared. "No, he did not go to live with the Vietnamese. He went to look for the cow," she replied.

That night a *chlop* [a young Khmer Rouge spy] came and took my mother away. I didn't see her for a week; I didn't know if she had been killed. On the seventh day, I saw her working in the fields. She was very, very thin. I saved some rice gruel and gave it to her when nobody was looking, and she said that the Pol Pots hadn't given her anything to eat for a week. My mother worked for three more days. On the fourth day, when I took her a bit of food, she took out the gold she kept hidden in her bosom and gave it to me and said, "Pu Ma, I will not live long. Keep this gold, and take care of your brother." I never saw her again. That night my stepfather returned with the cow. When he heard my mother had been taken away, he ran away from the village.

After my mother disappeared, the soldiers sent back my son, my brother, and the rest of the children from the youth camp, but they did not say why. Soon after that, a young chlop who was a neighbor's son came to my hut. "Pu Ma, tonight at twelve o'clock they want to kill your family," he whispered. That night, I took the rice I had stolen and hidden whenever I could, a pan, and a bottle of water, and went again into the jungle, this time with my brother and children.

It was cold and raining and so dark that we could not see where we were going. I forbade my children to cry or make any sound, and sat under a tree, waiting for the rain to stop. As we waited, I saw a red glimmer from the Pol Pots' cigarettes, moving far away. After a while, we heard children crying and women wailing very loudly. The Pol Pots were killing them. Too frightened to move, we just sat where we were, until the soldiers finished killing and it became quiet again. When they left, I took my children and ran again.

In Search of Refuge

I didn't know the Vietnamese had taken over our country until I met two Vietnamese soldiers in the jungle, some days after we had escaped. "What are you doing here?" one of them asked in simple Khmer. I explained that we had run away from the killing fields. He said, "You don't have to worry anymore. We have defeated the Khmer Rouge, and you are free to go back to your own house." At first, I thought he was lying, but he insisted that the Vietnamese had liberated us.

I decided that instead of going to the factory, I would go to my father-in-law's house, because I knew I would find my brothers-in-law there, if they had survived. When we got back, we found that not only my husband's brothers but also his mother too had survived. In the following days, my aunt, sisters, and older brother too came looking for us, but some of my nieces and nephews had died.

About a week after we got back, my little son, who had always been too small because he never had had enough to eat, fell ill. My aunt searched high and low and found a doctor who gave medicine for my son, but he was too weak to recover, and he died. When he died, I think I went crazy. I could not stop crying. I wept when I ate, because I remembered my husband and my mother who died of starvation. I cried whenever I saw the coconut tree my husband had planted when we lived with my father-in-law. Everything around me reminded me of my mother and husband, and finally, it became so unbearable, I went to live with my aunt.

My aunt and I made sweetmeats to sell. The Pol Pots had burned all the money, and the Vietnamese had still not given us new currency, so everybody paid us with rice or gold. But when the soldiers discovered that we didn't have husbands, they began to bother us. One night they tried to rob us, and the next day my aunt and I decided to escape to a refugee camp with our children.

We walked for about eight or nine days with many other families who were also going to the camp, sleeping in barns or by the roadside at night.

Once, soldiers shot at us because we were running away from our country, but we managed to escape without getting hurt. Finally we hired an ox cart to take us to a camp in the Cambodia-Thailand border.

At the time I left, I thought Cambodia would soon be free and I expected to return to my home then. But the Vietnamese didn't leave, and one day when I was gathering firewood in the mountains near our camp, I heard gunshots coming from the jungle. Suddenly, Pol Pots came out of the jungle, shooting at the Vietnamese! I ran for my life. When I got back to camp, I told my aunt that I did not want to live in Cambodia any more, and the next time Americans came to the border camp and asked if anyone wanted to go to Khao-I-Dang camp, my aunt and I took our children and left our country.

A fence surrounded the Khao-I-Dang camp and police and soldiers carrying guns stood around it; but it was not a safe place. At night thieves and bandits terrorized the refugees, and some people slept in the hospital because they were frightened to sleep in the shelters. One night when I was sick, two men came and demanded money and gold. Although I still had some gold, I said, "I am very poor, and very sick, I have no money. Please don't hurt me." I thought they would kill me; instead, they went away.

Soon after, though, somebody stole my gold. So I started to sell cabbages, tomatoes, and other vegetables I grew in the compound outside my shelter. My children went to school in the morning, and in the afternoon, they helped me in the garden. After a while, I too went to school to learn to sew baby clothes, which were given to mothers with newborn babies.

I got married again in camp to a man who told me that he was a widower. He lived with me until I got pregnant, and then he went back to Cambodia. Another person told me that his wife still lived there! If I had known his wife was still alive, I would never have married him. I haven't seen him since, so he doesn't know I gave birth to a daughter.

During my fourth year in the camp, my sister, who had gone to the U.S., wrote that my aunt and I should go there. She said the Americans will bring us back to Cambodia when our country is free again.

We applied to go to America, and the American called me for an interview.

"When you lived under Pol Pot what did you do?" an American official asked me, through an interpreter.

"I lived in the mountains and planted rice and vegetables," I replied.

"What kind of work did you do before Pol Pot came?"

"I made sacks and mattresses in a factory with my husband."

"Where is your husband?"

"My husband died."

"Did you see him die?"

"I did not see him die, but I saw the Pol Pots tie his hands and legs and take him in a truck with the other men. Later a Pol Pot soldier told me he was killed. So I know my husband died."

But the American accused me of lying. He asked me again and again, and I began to cry; I missed my husband very much. Then the American believed me. He said, "Okay, you can go to America."

A few days later I was called for another interview. The American said, "Your brother too has applied to go to America, but while he says his father was a farmer, you say your father was a soldier. Either you or your brother must be crazy!" "No, I am not crazy," I said. "He's my half brother. His father was a farmer, and my father was a soldier." The official told me to go back.

A few months later my family was taken to a transit camp in the Philippines. There, a teacher taught us how to live in America—how to go to the supermarket, to the hospital, and so on—and in 1985, we came to America. My brother had to go for three more interviews before he was allowed to leave.

A Welfare Mother in the United States

When I arrived in San Francisco I was very tired. I hadn't eaten for two days because I didn't know how to eat the American food the people gave us on the airplane, but even worse, my sister didn't come to meet us at the airport. I was very frightened. I didn't know how to find my sister. Although I knew her telephone number, I didn't know how to use the telephone. A Cambodian family who had come to meet their relatives helped us. They telephoned my sister, and found out her address. Then they gave us some money, and put me and my children on the bus going to my sister's town.

My sister and brother-in-law met us at the bus stop, and took us to their apartment. A month after I arrived, I started going to English class with my sister. She went to school in the morning while I took care of the children, and I went in the afternoon when she returned. In this way, we helped each other to cope with our new life, but living with a relative kept me from getting food stamps. Since I didn't know English, I couldn't get a job to earn money, and I needed food stamps. So I was forced to move.

A Cambodian man in my English class said I could live with his mother, sister, and two brothers in their apartment. When his mother agreed, my children and I moved to their apartment. After we moved I got the food stamps, but we had new problems. The apartment had only two bedrooms, and my son and brother slept in the living room. But they got little sleep because my friend went to work in the evening, and came back at three in the morning, and watched television. In the morning my son and my brother were so tired they didn't want to go to school, and they had problems remembering their lessons. And my friend's mother was often moody and depressed, and sometimes she wouldn't speak with my children, which made them feel uncomfortable. She got angry when they took showers, but she wouldn't say why. My children grew so unhappy that after a year, when my aunt's family came here, we went to live with them in their apartment.

Although we have no problems with my aunt, I wish I could find a better place to live. I am frightened to live here because there are bad people around here, and I worry that they will hurt my children. But I know very little English, and I can't get a good job that will pay me enough money so I can find a better house. Right now, I get about $890 from welfare every month. I spend it on food, clothes, rent, gas and electricity, telephone, and whatever else we need. I also pay back the International Rescue Committee for our airplane tickets to come here, so I don't have any savings at the end of the month. I am not happy to be on welfare. I want to work because I can then earn a lot more money, and move to another area.

I am frightened to live here because sometimes teenagers throw broken pieces of glass at our doors and windows. One night when I walked out after my English class, a man blocked my path. I didn't know him. He asked me, "Do you love me?" I said, "No." He said, "I love you, and I want to marry you. I will let you go only if you tell me you love me." I told him I loved him because that was the only way I could go past him. He said, "I will see you in the park next week." I didn't say anything.

I try hard to learn English, but I find it very difficult because I don't understand things like past tense, present tense, and future tense. When I make sentences my teacher says I mix up the word order in the sentences. I have a Cambodian-English dictionary, and I write down in Cambodian the meanings of all the English words the teacher says, and try to memorize them. But some English words are very difficult to remember. I don't know why I find it so hard to learn English; maybe it's because I have a problem in my head!

Reflections

America is a good country. We have Medicare, so when my children fall ill I don't have to worry about finding money to pay the doctor. I don't have to pay for them to go to school. People are polite and say "excuse me" if they want to go ahead of us, and "sorry" if they bump into us, just like we did in Cambodia, but over there, people were more respectful to older people.

My mother told me, "You must never forget to show respect to the monks and the old people." We always worshipped the monks even when we saw them on the street, and bowed to older people and greeted them with our palms together whenever we met them. When I first came to America I bowed to the old people I met on the street, but when I went to English class my teacher said, "You don't have to bow to old people here." But I tell my children that they must show respect to old people, both Cambodian and American.

Although I'm glad that my children can go to school, I worry about their growing up here because they too might have boyfriends and girlfriends like other children, and then they will not study. Here, men and women kiss on the street, in schools, and in hospitals. I don't like to see that because I feel embarrassed. In my country, people kissed only after they were married; but they never kissed in public.

I know that my son and my brother don't have girlfriends yet, because after school, they come back home straight away. I tell them, "If you have girlfriends you must tell me, so I can get permission from the girls' parents."

I worry a lot about my daughter. If she ever has a boyfriend, she will not be able to find a good husband. I tell my daughter, "I will be very happy if you have a good marriage. But if your marriage turns out to be bad, I will take care of you and your children, if you consulted me before the marriage in the proper way. So if you ever have a boyfriend, he must come and talk to me before he proposes to you." She tells me she doesn't have a boyfriend, but she's still young; maybe when she goes to college she will have one.

If I lived in Cambodia I wouldn't worry about my children. My children tell me that their classmates here cut classes and drive around with boyfriends and girlfriends. Over there, they would walk to school and back. They don't have cars to go to various places with bad friends. My children are good because they don't have bad friends who take them out all the time. When they visit other people they go with me.

People ask me if their son can marry my daughter, but my daughter wants to go to college so she can be a nurse. She worked in the assembly line in the summer, but she didn't like it. My son and my brother want to become mechanics. My son says he is not a smart student. He can speak in English, but he can't read and write well. He learned to read and write Khmer, and writes to his relatives in Cambodia; they don't know English because in my country they study only Cambodian and French.

Here, when children are eighteen or nineteen parents don't take care of them, but in Cambodia, even after children are married, mothers take care of them when they have problems. So I hope my daughter will marry a Cambodian, because I want to help her if she has problems with her husband, and I will not be able to help if she marries an American or a Vietnamese.

I hope my daughter will not marry a Vietnamese because we always had problems with the Vietnamese. There were many Vietnamese men in my English class who told me they wished to marry me, but I said, "No, we cannot marry because our countries always fought with each other."

Cambodians are different from Vietnamese. My friend's daughter married a Vietnamese, but the marriage lasted only six months. In my country the man gives the money to his wife so she can look after the family, but my friend told me that her daughter's husband gave the money to his mother. So my friend's daughter separated from her husband.

I miss my country and my husband's family. They are very poor, and in the rainy season their house leaks badly and they don't have rice to eat. I would like to help my husband's mother and his brothers, but I don't have money to send them regularly. One time I collected some money over many months and bought a small radio and two watches and sent them to my family. But it didn't help very much because my family lives in Battambang, and my brother-in-law had to go to Phnom Penh to collect the things I sent. He sold them for 7,000 riel, but his bus fare alone was 2,000 riel.

I have a lot of food here, but sometimes I feel bad about eating because I think about my mother and my husband who died with no food in their stomachs. My mother and my husband were always very polite people who never fought with anybody. I don't know why Pol Pot killed them. I want to know why. I think if they could have come with me to this country, I would have been happy here. I think about my husband and my mother, and dream about them a lot.

Even though my mother is dead, I believe that she still takes care of me. When I have problems I pray to her at night. I say, "My mother, I miss you. I live in America, and I have many problems. Please help me."

Sometimes I dream that I am living with my husband again, but I only dream of living with him in Cambodia, never in this country. In my last dream, my husband took my son to the store to buy him a bicycle. About two months ago I dreamed of him a lot, I don't know why. "Could it be that he is not yet reborn?" I asked my aunt. "I don't know," she replied. We gave food to the monks last month, and gave my husband and my mother merit to help them to have good births.

I also dream about Pol Pot. Then the hole in my chest begins to hurt, and I have problems in my head. Then I tell my aunt and my children, "I am unhappy because last night I dreamt of Pol Pot. So don't bother me." The doctor x-rayed the hole in my chest and said there is no injury. When I tell him that my head aches and that I feel dizzy, he asks me, "What do you think about?" I tell him I think about my husband and my mother. He says, "Don't think about them; then you won't have problems." But I cannot forget them.

Right now I feel very depressed because I am pregnant, and although the man promised to marry me, he left me after I got pregnant, saying, "My mother does not like you; you are too poor. She has chosen a rich girl for me to marry."

If Pol Pots didn't kill my husband, I wouldn't have these problems. Before he was killed, my husband took good care of me, my mother, and our children. He quit smoking because I didn't like it. He worked hard and didn't go around with bad people. He shared the things we had with both our families. If I suggested going to a restaurant, he said, "Why do you want to go to the restaurant? You can buy some nice food and cook at home so all of us can enjoy it together." He was a good father and a good husband, but my two other husbands were bad people. Sometimes my third husband calls me and says he wants to move back. But I will not let him come back unless he marries me.

The Cambodian newspaper says my country will become independent soon. I want to go back then, but if Pol Pot comes back to power, I don't want to go back. Maybe if America helped my country, Pol Pot wouldn't be able to come back. I know my country is very poor, but I lived in it for a long time, and I miss it.

People tell me America is the Freedom Country, but in my heart, there is no freedom. So I would like to return to my country again.

CHAPTER SEVEN

Bun Thab: A Khmer Rouge Escapee

Bun Thab (a fictitious name this narrator chose for himself) is of medium build, and has the reserved, quiet countenance of a man who keeps to himself. At his wife's suggestion, I asked him if he would tell me his story, but I did not expect him to be a good narrator because of his reserved appearance. How wrong I was!

Bun Thab turned out to be an articulate storyteller, one who brought his narrative to life with wonderful facial and bodily expressions. I remember vividly the afternoon when he sauntered up and down his living room as he had done in the marketplace in Sisophon, gaily swinging his left hand, while his right hand held an imaginary basket of clucking chickens on his shoulder. At that moment, I could almost see the rest of the scene: vendors sitting beside sacks and baskets of chilies, onions, corn, pineapples, eggplants, cucumbers, mangoes, papayas, and a host of other fruits and vegetables, and throngs of people milling around the noisy stalls and bargaining to get the best deals.

In Cambodia, Bun Thab was a poor peasant—the largest group in the classes of peasantry. Even though his burdens became heavier after his father left the family and hastened his mother's death, Bun Thab's narrative is a testimony to the richness of life, rather than to its poverty, until he became a victim of the Khmer Rouge. But even in the face of death, Bun Thab got the better of the Khmer Rouge with his wit and determination; his extraordinary escape from the regime in 1977 makes his narrative unique in this collection.

Bun Thab's perseverance did not end after his escape to America. He refused to give up his efforts to win the hand of the woman he loved despite continued rejection by her family, and ultimately he succeeded. Now he and his wife and their five-year-old daughter share their two-bedroom apartment with another young couple and their two-year-old son: a lively little boy who, in Bun Thab's words, is "always too busy!" It is a far cry from the open air of the rice fields, and when things become too hectic in the kitchen-dinette adjoining the living area, Bun Thab retreats to the quiet of their bedroom for a while.

Bun Thab's daughter takes after his quiet manner, and during our interviews, she often sat contentedly on his lap, listening to Bun Thab as he told his story. While he is quite adaptable, Bun Thab's expectations and ambitions for his daughter echo those of the mothers whose stories appear in this book. Not only is Bun Thab a gentle father, he is also a considerate husband and a handyman. Once when I went to his house, he was fixing their broken stove, and I often see him help his wife with cooking and other household chores.

One of Bun Thab's greatest joys is eating good food, and some of the tastiest Cambodian food I have eaten has been at his house. A particularly nice dish was the quick-fried beef I was invited to have one evening when Bun Thab's mother-in-law was visiting. The beef had been marinated in a delicious sauce for several hours, and Bun Thab's wife set up a wok on the living-room floor, and heated some oil. We all sat around the wok on beautifully woven mats, chatting and, using chopsticks, frying our own portions of beef till it was done to our liking. We then placed the meat with a variety of salad greens and pickles on sheets of rice paper that were first moistened with water, and rolled them up to eat. A couple of weeks later, I prepared my first Cambodian meal of quick-fried beef for my family, and it was a great success. ✦✦✦

Farmer Boy

My father was a rice farmer, and because we were very poor, my mother raised silkworms and wove silk cloth at home. When I was little I liked to play with Mom's silkworms, especially when they grew to be caterpillars. I loved to drape the caterpillars on my head and around my ears; they felt so soft and cool. But if Mom saw me playing with them, she scolded me, saying, "Haven't I told you not to play with those caterpillars because ants and flies will attack them and make them sick? I don't want them dying from disease like those other people's did. Put them back this minute!"

Mom took care of those caterpillars as if they were babies! They lived in tightly woven baskets that were hung from the roof inside the house, to protect them from dampness and from the ants and flies that gave them diseases. From time to time we cleaned the baskets and lined them with fresh mulberry leaves, and sometimes in the quiet of the night, we could hear the caterpillars munching the leaves.

When our caterpillars became cocoons, we identified males and females by shaking the cocoons and carefully listening to the sound they made inside. We placed some on large clay trays so they could become moths and breed. We covered the trays with porous cloth and they laid their eggs, which were really tiny, on that cloth. We put the rest of the cocoons in boiling water to get the silk. After we took the silk, we boiled the worms together with papaya skin to separate them. They were a real delicacy in Cambodia, and when I was older, I sold them in the market. Since we had no refrigerators I had to sell them before they rotted, within about three days.

My parents, who were ethnic Cambodians, worked very hard, and even as children we had to help them. My older sister helped Mom to weave silk sarongs to sell in the market, and my two younger sisters gathered mulberry leaves to feed the silkworms. I was the second of the four children and the only boy, and I helped Dad in the rice fields. At harvest time, Mom and my sisters worked in the fields too.

About 700 people lived in our village, including many of my mom's relatives. We built our houses on stilts, to prevent floodwater from the river coming inside the houses during the rainy season. Our houses had big gardens around them, and weren't built close to one another like American houses. Most people grew a variety of fruit trees in their gardens, and I remember having coconuts, mangoes, pineapple, papaya, and a lot of bamboo growing in ours. While people preferred to have clay tile roofs, really poor people had to cover their roofs with cheaper material like hay or aluminum. Aluminum roofs lasted longer, but they made the houses terribly hot during the dry season. We used wood for walls and floors because it made our homes cool and comfortable.

Our home had a clay tile roof, two bedrooms, and a large living room in which we built a little altar, so we could pray to the Buddha and to our relatives who had died. Our beds, which were very big, were made with nice and shiny red-colored wood. At night they looked like cocoons because we drew nets around them to keep mosquitoes out. Since we didn't have enough beds for the family, I slept with my grandmother. We kept our clothes in big trunks, and didn't have sofas and chairs because everybody sat on handwoven mats. We even ate sitting on mats.

Our kitchen was just outside the house. Some people in the village made clay stoves for a living, and we used kerosene oil or wood for fuel. Our toilet was at the bottom of the garden. I don't think anybody in my village had flush toilets. Maybe they had them in Phnom Penh.

We had no electricity or running water in our village. In the night, we lit kerosene lamps and candles made with beeswax. During the rainy season, we collected water that poured down from gutters into a big vessel and used it for our needs, and in the dry season, I carried twelve or fifteen buckets of water every day from the water tank in the village, and filled a huge clay pot my mom kept in the kitchen.

I loved to go to the water tank because it was a favorite meeting place of the people. Some even bathed there. The tank was made with cement and filled with clean, clear water, and people grew bamboos and palms nearby and built a fence around the area to prevent animals from drinking there. Because the tank was always full, all we did was to scoop the water into two buckets. We hung the buckets on the ends of a pole we carried on our shoulders, and took them home.

Most of the villagers had work animals and pets. We owned six oxen that worked in the rice fields, and at night, we tied them up underneath the house. We also had a few chickens and ducks, and a cat.

The people in my village were good. They never stole from their neighbors. But there were people in other villages whose livelihood was stealing; so to protect our animals from thieves we had three really good watchdogs. Whenever strangers approached our house they barked so fiercely that we never lost anything.

When I was about eight years old, Dad started to earn extra money by selling rubies. He bought the rubies cheaply from miners in the country-side, and sold them for a higher price in the city of Pilan, about 180 kilome-ters from our village. When Dad went to Pilan, he stayed there for a month or so, and we hired people to work in the rice fields. We paid them with rice and some money.

Dad traveled back and forth between the village and Pilan for a few years selling rubies, but one year he failed to return home. We heard that he had found another wife. Mom fell ill with a broken heart when she heard that, and the kids in the village taunted me, saying, "You're the boy with no father." They said it in a really mean way, and their parents didn't like Dad anymore because he took a second wife. My mom never recovered from the shock or from the sickness. She started to cough blood and after about six months she died.

I was about twelve or thirteen years old when Mom died. Before she died I had gone to school for about four years. I also used to go to the tem-ple often with her. I remember when everybody in my village worked to-gether and built a temple because the other one was too far. We always went to the new temple, but some people continued to go to the old one. Some went to both. I loved to go to the temple because we met a lot of villagers there. At New Year's we played many games on the temple grounds.

If my parents had stayed together, I think they would have wanted me to become a monk for a while like other boys in the village. I became a monk once in my life, but just for two days. In Cambodia we believe that when someone dies we can give him a good life in his next birth if a male person from that family becomes a monk for two or three days. So when Dad's mother died, I became a monk for her. An old monk shaved my head and dressed me like one of them. I lived in the temple for two days.

Dad came to his mother's funeral, but he didn't even recognize me. He asked my sister, "Whose child is that? Why has he become a monk for my mother?" That made my sister very sad and she cried for a long time. After that he came once in a while to see us, carrying food and other gifts. But when Mom died, even though we let him know, he never came to see her.

When Mom died, I became the "big man" in my house because Dad wasn't there. I was young and physically not very big, but I was strong, and because I had helped Dad in the rice fields since I was six or seven, I knew how to grow rice.

I got up even before the sun rose, when the rooster crowed three times, and gathered all my equipment, hitched the oxen to my cart, and left for the fields, which were about two kilometers away from my house. All the farmers in the village left for the fields on their oxcarts around the same time, and as we set off, there was a lot of shouting and cajoling by the farmers because the oxen were restless and tried to butt one another when they met.

We plowed the fields with oxen because we didn't have farm machinery, and then walked up and down the field, scattering handfuls of rice seeds we carried in big buckets. Next, we hitched the oxen again to our plows, and turned over the earth to cover the seeds. Thereafter, we kept the fields really muddy and wet until the seeds germinated and rice plants grew to be about six inches tall, when they looked delicate, but were quite strong and could be transplanted. Then it was time for the rains, and the fields got completely flooded with water. With all that water, the rice just grew.

With the water came loads of fish from the rivers. So we left fish traps along the dikes that separated the fields, and in the morning, we collected the fish that were caught in them. Since I couldn't work in the rice field in the rainy season, sometimes I sold lotto tickets and earned some money. After the rains stopped and the rice had ripened in the sun, we harvested our crops. We kept part of it for ourselves and sold the rest. We fed some of the straw to our oxen and used some for bedding.

We carried no clocks or watches when we went to the rice fields. Those who had watches kept them at home because the fields were muddy, and they didn't want the watches to get dirty. We knew how to tell the time by looking at the sun. When it was nearly at the top we stopped for lunch, and untied the oxen and sent them off to graze. Some farmers caught a few fish at the nearby lake and cooked them there, but my sisters usually brought some rice, fish, and soup for me in a tiffin carrier.

After we ate, we rested for about two hours under the trees or inside our carts, and then gathered our oxen and went back to work. Growing rice was hard work, and made us sweaty and tired. So about five or six in the evening we bathed in the lake, scrubbed down the animals, and headed back home.

I liked farming and I was always busy. But my heart was filled with sadness because Mom died so early, and life had become even harder with nobody to support us. Dad's two brothers and three sisters who were richer than we were didn't care for us, and even Mom's two brothers didn't help us much. So we lived with our grandmother, but she was about eighty years old and she was sickly too.

As farmers, we worked hard for six months, growing rice. Most people took life more easily the next six months, but because we were so poor, I had to do other things to earn money. Some days I went to the jungle and collected firewood with other villagers, and at other times I bought chickens, ducks, and pigs cheap from people living at the edge of our village, and sold them for higher prices at the marketplace in Sisophon.

Most villagers went to Sisophon to sell various things, but we didn't wait for one another. If we had something to sell, we just went. Some rich people earned a living by hiring out trucks and taxis to farmers taking their goods to the market, but I usually hired a *momoto* to go to Sisophon. A *momoto* is a two-wheeled motorcycle with a passenger compartment at the back, carrying up to seven or eight people. I liked it because it had no roof, and in the hot season, the breeze blew through my hair.

The marketplace was always crowded, noisy, and busy. It was a bit like the flea market here. Some people walked around, carrying their baskets of wares on their shoulders, and others sat on benches and boxes under awnings. But everybody yelled to attract people's attention, "Come over here, I'll give you the best bargains! Mangoes, papayas, pineapples, chili, onions," and so on and on. The customers walked from one display to the next, eyeing and handling everything, and bargaining to get the best deals.

I gave all the money I earned by selling things to my older sister, and until she married a Lon Nol soldier, she bought clothes and everything else we needed, and looked after us like a mother. But after she got married, even though she lived with us, she did not do much for us because she liked her husband more than her brother and sisters.

The Khmer Rouge Youth Brigade

In 1973 or so, the Khmer Rouge started fighting with the Lon Nol soldiers around my village, and when their fighting burned our house and two other houses in the village, we lost everything. So even though our relatives didn't like us, we were forced to move into a small thatched-roof house that belonged to my uncle from my mom's side.

One day in 1975, when I got back from the farm, the house was quiet. There was no food for me as there usually was, and my sisters were not around. I was just leaving the house to look for them when I heard my grandmother screaming from the room. She said, "Some soldiers came and chased the family out of the house, but I hid in the room and waited for you, because I wanted to go with you."

I knew that she liked me even more than she liked her own children, and that was why she waited. "We'll go soon, Grandma, but I'm hungry, and I must eat. I'll cook some rice," I told her, but she wouldn't let me. She insisted that we should go before the soldiers came back, or they would kill us. But she was too old and sickly to walk. I ran over to my Chinese neighbors' yard and found a handcart they had left behind. I put Grandma in the cart and left the house. About four or five miles down the road, I met my sisters.

On the third day of evacuation, the soldiers told us that we could return to our houses. We didn't know why they changed their minds. But a week later they ordered us to evacuate our village again, and over the next two days, walked us about 20 kilometers into the countryside. This time my whole family left together. I put Grandmother in the handcart again. My uncle had a cart too, but he preferred to load that with food.

When we got to the countryside the Communists took us to a big building. There they told us, "We are all equal now, and Angka will look after all your needs. So give everything you have brought to Angka: clothes, money, jewelry, food, anything."

We had to give up our personal belongings, whether we liked it or not. The next day, the soldiers ordered us to build huts for our families, and when that was done, they assigned us to work.

I was separated from my family and sent away to build dams with other young men. The dam was about twenty feet high, and we had to work fourteen or sixteen hours a day. We labored day after day, but at least we got enough rice to eat until the Pol Pot soldiers brought a lot of "New People" to our village in late 1976, and they ran out of food. After that they gave us only two meals of watered-down rice a day, but our work load did not go down. People got so weak, they started to fall ill with all kinds of diseases.

I became sick with night blindness. With this disease, I couldn't see anything, except something like a bright flame from a fire, after sunset. I was really frightened when I went blind, but the soldiers didn't believe me when I told them I couldn't see, because people pretended they got night blindness to stay away from work in the evening. Because they suspected us, the soldiers took us to the jungle in the night and left us there, and they watched to see if anyone found their way back home. Those who were caught were called traitors and killed.

The Communists didn't give me any medicine for the disease. Some people got cured when a person threw a lotus leaf filled with water against their foreheads, but it didn't work for me. Instead, I discovered that I could see if I ate cow's liver, and I started stealing the livers from dead cows. If the soldiers had caught me stealing they would have killed me, just like other people I saw being killed with blows to the backs of their necks with bamboo poles. If a person didn't die instantly, he was just left in the jungle.

I learned that to survive the regime, I had to be a good worker. I didn't talk to people, I didn't defy the soldiers, I just acted dumb, and after we finished building the dam, I was made a junior group leader. My new boss was an old man who had been a monk. He had studied books about herbs and knew which trees and plants should be used to make medicines, so he was now looking after sick people.

We frequently went into the jungle to collect the plants he needed for the medicine. Among the ten people in our group, we had one bicycle to ride to the jungle, which I rode as the junior leader. I also had to write down people's life stories each month, and if what they said this month was different from what they had said the previous month, I had to report them to the leader. That was enough to get them killed.

I had been with the old monk for about a year when a new group of Communist soldiers came to our village. They were a lot meaner than the old leaders, and killed many of the old leaders because they had asked for more freedom. They also killed a lot of "New People" that the soldiers had brought to our village in 1976. One of them was my cousin, who had lived in the city and couldn't do hard labor because he got tired very quickly. A chlop followed him around for a few days, and one morning the chlop said, "You have been called to attend a special meeting. Come with me." That was all. My cousin just disappeared, and we knew he was killed because two or three days later the soldiers brought his clothes back and gave them to his own wife to mend. When she realized what had happened, she became so upset and depressed, but she had to pretend that nothing was wrong; if she had cried or asked any questions, she would have been killed too.

None of us knew when we would be killed. Many people I knew had disappeared, and I was so frightened about what might happen, I asked the old monk, who was a fortune-teller, to read my palm. He said, "You should not fear because you will not die just yet." But how could I be sure he was right? People just disappeared every day. I never stopped praying to the Buddha, in my mind.

One evening, we had just sat down to eat when two soldiers came and chose three people to go to a meeting in the soldiers' house. First they called a man who had been a monk but had been forced to unfrock and marry. Next they called my friend, and then they called me. We knew that the night before they had killed two people in my group.

Running for Life

The two soldiers escorted us back to the soldiers' house, where four or five others had cooked us a very good dinner. They invited us to eat as much as we wanted, but we didn't know why they gave us such good food. After we ate, they gave me an ax, and gave my friend a long knife. Then the leader announced, "Tonight we have three enemies here." We knew that they meant us. Two soldiers grabbed my friends, pulled their arms behind their backs and started to tie them up tightly. I was terrified because I knew what was coming. I needed to urinate. A soldier took me outside. It was dark and raining a little, but suddenly the rain came pelting down. I ran into the darkness.

The soldier saw me run away, and started yelling and shouting, and I heard many people coming after me. I ran as hard as I could, and stumbled into a banana grove. I pressed myself hard against the trunk of a banana tree. I heard the soldiers searching for me, but it was raining hard, and they didn't see me. After a while, they gave up and went back.

When I was sure that all of them had gone, I started running again, and in the distance, I saw two other people running away also. Their arms were tied behind their backs; when I got closer I recognized my friends. I called out to them, and they stopped. Using the ax the Khmer Rouge gave me, I cut the ropes that bound them, and we decided to escape from Cambodia together.

Before we left the village the former monk wanted to see his wife one more time. So, very carefully, we slithered up to his house, and called her. But when she saw her husband she thought was dead, she got such a fright she began to scream. Fortunately, it was raining too hard for the soldiers to hear, so no one came to see. We told her of our plan to escape. She gave us a homemade lighter and a little bit of food, but refused to come with us. She thought she would be safer in the village. We said goodbye to her, stole some yams from the farm, and set out for Thailand.

Until that night none of us had thought about leaving our country. We were farmers and we had always lived in the village. I had heard about Vietnam and Thailand, but I didn't know where they were because I didn't have much education. The monk knew from old stories that Thailand was to the north of our country, so we began going in that direction.

We tried to avoid meeting any Pol Pots by escaping through the jungle, and we always kept very close to one another so we would not get separated. We kept going day and night, and after we ran out of food, we lived on fruits and leaves from the forest trees. We had been on the run for about a week when we spotted some people working on a farm far away. We had to go across it to get to Thailand, but we didn't have a permit that allowed us to travel, to show the Khmer Rouge leader of that village. "Let's pretend we are chlops looking for crabs," my friend suggested. "We must stop running and keep our heads down, so no one can see our faces." And we ambled slowly along, looking at the ground, until at last we crossed that village. Then we started running again.

About four days after we had walked through that village, we came to some high mountains at the Thailand-Cambodia border. We had climbed a fair distance when the monk whispered, "I can see Pol Pot soldiers patrolling the area with guns!"

We began running away as softly as we could, but they saw us and came after us shouting, "We see some enemies escaping! Come on, catch them!" But they didn't shoot us; maybe they wanted to capture us alive.

We kept running wildly, and at last we escaped, but we didn't know where we were anymore. Everywhere we looked we saw only trees, and they all looked the same. We had no choice but to keep going, taking turns to climb trees every now and then to see if we could see the mountains of Thailand.

One afternoon, the old monk had just reached the top of a tree to look for the mountains when I heard a faint sound of dry leaves crackling. "Khmer Rouge, lie down!" I whispered fiercely to my friend. We dropped down and waited, hardly daring to breathe. A shot rang out. Our friend fell from the tree, screaming with pain. While we watched, the Communist walked up and he chopped our friend to pieces with his ax. We fled, and he shot at us too, but I don't know where the bullets went. We kept on running and we came to a river. We jumped in, and hid under water. I know the Communist kept running after us because once, as I looked up from under the water, he jumped right over my head. I still have nightmares of that Khmer Rouge jumping over my head, and I wake up, shivering with fear.

After some time we came out of the water. Our friend had been killed, we had no more food, and we had lost the ax and the knife we carried. The only thing that remained was the lighter our friend's wife had given us. But we had to go on. We decided, "If we die, we will die together," and started walking again, holding hands.

We walked for two days with nothing to eat. Our feet were cut from the bamboo splinters that covered the ground, and they were swollen and smelly, and really painful. But we kept on going, and suddenly, we saw a huge turtle. At last, we had found real food! We couldn't believe our luck, for we even had a lighter to make a fire.

But neither my friend nor I could bring ourselves to kill the turtle. Instead, we prayed and promised the turtle, "If you bring us good luck and take us to Thailand, we will not kill you. We will let you go." We started walking again, carrying the turtle.

The following day we heard a new sound. It was the whirring of an engine, and we thought it came from Communist planes that were searching for us. We threw ourselves into the bushes, and looked at the sky. The sound continued, but we couldn't see any planes. Very slowly, my friend and I crawled in the direction of the sound.

After a while we began to hear people's voices. We stopped and listened hard, thinking we had come to another Pol Pot camp, but we couldn't understand what the people were saying. After a while we realized that we couldn't understand them because they were speaking Thai! We had reached Thailand! We thanked the turtle and set him free.

I crawled up to an old man who was digging by himself, and spoke to him very softly. But when he saw me, he got such a fright that he jumped and screamed, and people came running from everywhere. When the old man realized we had escaped from the Khmer Rouge, he took us to his house, and his family gave us rice. We hadn't eaten for three days, and we ate until our stomachs bulged. But although our stomachs were full, our hearts were heavy; we couldn't forget our friend who got killed.

After we ate, the people took us to the Thai soldiers. When they saw our black clothes the soldiers thought we were Khmer Rouge who had attacked them five days before, and they threw us on the ground and began to kick us. I don't know what would have happened if another Cambodian, who had also escaped, had not come to see what was going on. To our luck he was a man who knew me, and he convinced the Thai soldiers that we were not Communists. The soldiers released us and took us to work on a peanut farm. We worked hard, and though we got food from the farmer, we didn't get wages. But we didn't mind; we had worked much harder with no food or rest, under the Communists.

Freedom Fighter

When we had worked on the farm for about three months, we heard that about fifteen more Cambodians had escaped, and that they were going to join the resistance fighters to fight against the Khmer Rouge. We too volunteered to go with them, and one night, Thai soldiers put us all in a big covered truck and drove us to the jungle where the resistance fighters lived. But as we went round a bend, the truck turned over. I escaped with a bump on my head, but one man died, and my friend and many other people got badly hurt. The soldiers took us to a hospital, and after two days a few of us who were not seriously injured were released. My friend was not released, and we got separated. I never met him again.

We got to the jungle and joined the resistance fighters, who numbered about a hundred men. My first job was to go to the border with twelve people to fight with the Communists, and in that battle seven people got killed. When we returned, our leader rewarded us with a lot of clothes and other gifts. My next mission was to go with five others to take photographs of Communists cutting a trench in the Prea Vihear area. The route was covered with mines, and though we took the pictures, three people from the group got their legs blown up. After that, I didn't want to be a freedom fighter anymore.

When the truck came again to take us on another mission, I escaped with five other people, and we ran away to a Thai village. There, the villagers helped us to escape to the province of Suren. In Suren, I again worked on a farm, but I had an easier time there because the people on the farm spoke Khmer and they liked me. Even more important, the farmer paid me fifteen baht a week. I collected all my wages, and when I had enough, I paid a guard and got into a refugee camp.

I was still in the refugee camp when I heard that the Vietnamese had defeated the Khmer Rouge. I was very happy to hear the news, but I didn't know if Cambodia could have peace under the Vietnamese. I didn't know whether to return to Cambodia or stay in the camp. At that time I didn't have any ideas about going to a third country.

Unable to decide what I should do, I lived in the camp until it was closed in 1979. When I heard that many of my people were going to a country called America, I too decided to go there, and went for the interview with American people. They asked if I had any relatives in America. I had no relatives, but I knew a friend had gone there because I saw his picture and address posted in the camp library. I gave his name to the American, but he said I needed a sponsor to go to America.

In 1980 I was taken to a camp in the Philippines. There were about 100 refugees in my building, and most of them had sponsors in America. But I did not have one, and because I was single, it was very hard to find a sponsor for me. Even so, living in that camp, I learned English and about living in America; how to turn on lights, how to use flush toilets, how to talk to people, and so on, and finally, the camp people found me a sponsor. It was an American living in Oregon.

Coming to America

I left the refugee camp in November 1981, along with many other refugees who were also coming to America. We were very happy, and looked forward to living close to one another in the new country. After a long flight, the plane reached San Francisco airport in the evening, and we were taken to a refugee camp for the night. The next morning, the officials took us back to the airport, and they put me on a plane to Oregon. I was the only Cambodian going to Oregon. All my other friends were going to different places. When the plane reached Oregon, I was crying. I was in a new country, and I had no family and no friends.

I walked on snow for the first time in my life and went inside the building. My sponsor was waiting for me, and I recognized him from the picture I carried with me. He recognized me, too. He rushed over and hugged me, and then took me to his house in a small car. He gave me hamburgers, but they tasted so funny, I couldn't eat them. I had eaten only Cambodian food all my life, and I couldn't eat the new food. So here I was in America, the "freedom country," where I thought I would live well with a lot of food to eat, and I was still hungry. I was miserable too, because I was so cold. My sponsor and his wife were very good and looked after me well. I helped around the house, and collected wood for their stove. Although I was happy to help, all I could do was what they showed me to do, because I didn't know English.

My sponsor enrolled me in school to learn English, and there I met another Cambodian man. We soon became friends, and he invited me to live with him and his wife. I wanted very much to do so, but I felt bad to leave my sponsor because he had been so kind. In the end, because of the problems I had with food and language, I asked him if I could go to live with my friend. My sponsor was very sad. But he understood my problem and gave me $160 he had received from the refugee office, and I moved in with my friend. But even after I left his house, my sponsor continued to help me.

I went to school for four months, after which the teacher said I knew enough English and that I should find a job. Until then, I had been living on welfare. I got a job working in the electronics industry for three dollars an hour, but I went back to school in the evening because I wanted to learn more English.

Love and Marriage

I am glad I went back to school because a Cambodian girl who had just come to America joined my English class. I liked her when I saw her, and after I came to know her well, I wanted to marry her. But when I asked her if she would be my wife, all she said was, "It's up to my mother."

I went to her house to meet her family. They had been rich people living in Phnom Penh, and they didn't like me because I was a farm boy, and now I earned only three dollars an hour. Her mother explained she wanted her daughter to have a good future, and that she had already chosen another man, who had a better job than I did, for her daughter.

I could not give up the girl. I loved her very much, and she seemed to like me too. One evening I spoke to her on the telephone and asked if I could send another proposal, this time through an older Cambodian man, and she said yes. By now, I owned a car. I bought a lot of food and other gifts for the girl's family and drove my friend to the girl's house, dropped him there, and went back to his house and waited. He came back after a while and said, "I am sorry, but the people still don't like you because you are not making enough money. They also say that the horoscopes don't match." I spoke to the girl again, and I was convinced she liked me. I continued to see her, and about three months later I sent another proposal through my friend. This time her mother agreed. I guess she thought she couldn't stop her daughter from marrying me. So we got married in 1982. I invited my sponsor to my wedding but he couldn't come because he was away at the time. After the wedding I moved in with my wife's family. Her mom helped us with food, and I paid her rent.

I found my wife a job in the company I worked in, but a year later my company moved to Seattle. Because Seattle is a cold place we didn't want to move, and we lived on unemployment money for about six months until my wife had a baby. Then we moved to Los Angeles, to live with my sister-in-law in a small town, but the only work we found there was in a bakery, which paid just enough to buy food. So when a friend moved to northern California and said he will help us to move here, we came to northern California, and rented a room in a house shared by many Cambodian people. A few months later we found jobs, and after we saved some money we moved into the apartment next door when the people who lived there moved away.

Both my wife and I like to work, and for me, even three dollars an hour was better than getting welfare money. Now I work in an electronics company, and because I work hard people in my company like me, and I feel happy when I go to work. Once in a while we invite American friends to our house, and cook egg rolls or noodles for them, but we work hard and don't have too much time to spend with friends.

My wife was born to a rich family in Phnom Penh, while I was born to a very poor family in the village, but we have a good marriage because I respect her and she respects me. We do not say things that can hurt each other. Usually if I get angry with somebody I keep my feelings to myself. I don't say anything unless I have thought about it. I was like that even when I was a child too. I remain quiet because I do not like to make people feel bad.

Both of us earn, and I give my paycheck to her, but we usually make decisions together about the things we want to buy. If I want a new car I don't just go out and buy one as if I was single, and she will also not buy anything without asking me. Moreover, we buy things only if we both agree we can afford them.

We also make decisions about our child together, and we try to live so that the other person will not have to worry. For example, when she goes somewhere and is going to be late returning, she calls to let me know, and I do the same thing because otherwise she will worry that I have been in an accident or something like that. So we have a good marriage because we respect each other.

Reflections

When I was a freedom fighter I went back to Cambodia to look for my sisters, but before I got to my village I was attacked by the Vietnamese, and I had to escape back to the jungle. While I lived in refugee camp and after I came here, I wrote over a hundred letters trying to find out what had happened to my sisters, and finally, in 1988, I heard from them! It is hard for me to describe to you how I felt when I found them. I was choked with happiness that they were alive. But I was also choked with sadness because they still live in the same village, and though they have more freedom than they did under the Khmer Rouge, they are very poor and have no food. They are also very sad because my sister's husband had been killed by the

Communists. My father had died too. They had thought I died also, and many people had become monks to make my next life a good one.

We liked Cambodia with Sihanouk as the ruler, and I don't know why the Communists took over my country. I was young when all that happened so I don't know what was going on then. I only know that Communists lied to people and destroyed our country. They took everything away from us—our monks, our temple, our culture.

I hate the Pol Pot soldiers. If I meet those soldiers I will kill them. Although I believe in kamma, I don't think I would commit a sin if I killed Pol Pots; they did such bad things to people. Some say that Pol Pot soldiers killed only because the leaders told them to do so, but I don't know if that is so. I hate them all.

I learned from my experience of living with the Communists that I am a survivor and that I can overcome many difficulties. In that respect I am different from the Americans. If they have no lights for a day, they worry because they can't cook. But I know I can survive without food for many days. But I don't want to think of Pol Pot; it's too painful. Usually when I talk like this I can't sleep. If I sleep I have nightmares. So I don't talk much about that time. But even if I have not talked about Pol Pot, I dream mostly about my country and I don't know why. I think I should dream about America because I live here now.

I think America is a good country to live in. I have the freedom to work, keep my own money, buy whatever I want, and say whatever I want. If you have money you can have anything you want. I also feel safe over here because there are laws to protect people; in Cambodia there was no law. But sometimes I am bothered because Americans don't really know much about Cambodians. If they meet one Cambodian who can't speak English, they think all Cambodians are like that, and that's not true.

The other thing I don't like about America is that girls and boys date. They have too much freedom, and if they don't like one partner, they find another. I don't think that's good, but Cambodian kids who came here when they were very young fool around, have boyfriends, and don't listen to parents. I have a daughter, and I will tell her to behave well and not to go around with many guys. But she was born here, and she may think differently and want to date like Americans. My father left my mother, but in our culture people generally live with their wives or husbands till they die. We don't walk away from our spouses. I want my daughter to be like that.

In Cambodia people do not date. Men and women get married before they go out together. Sometimes when people marry they don't even know each other, but they learn about each other after the marriage, and they have good marriages. When my daughter is old enough to marry, I think it's all right for her to marry an American, but I would prefer her not to marry a Vietnamese, because Cambodians and Vietnamese have had a lot of trouble throughout history. But I like my own people and I hope she will marry a Cambodian.

In our culture we believe that parents should be like teachers, and teach their children how to do things. In Cambodia, parents controlled everything and children listened to their parents, and asked for permission before they did anything. When I was a child I was that way too. But Americans don't teach their children, and their children don't do any housework. We teach our daughter housework. She listens to us, and she can be useful in the house. Sometimes when I need a glass of water or something, she brings it. She also helps her mother wash dishes. She is only five years old and is too short to reach the sink, but she climbs onto a chair and does the dishes.

Although she is good now, I don't know what my daughter will be like in the future. I think it's important for her to go to school, get a good education, and earn enough money so she can have a good future. I have a hard time here because I don't have much knowledge, and I don't want her to be dumb like me. I would like her to be a doctor so she can help people, but it's up to her.

My main ambition now is to know more English. Some people have no problems speaking or learning English, but because I had little education in Cambodia I find it hard to learn English. When I call someone on the telephone I tell them to speak slowly, and then I can understand. But when I meet people who think I know English and speak fast, I feel embarrassed to tell them I don't understand, and I end up saying "yes" and "no" even when I don't know what's going on.

I am a Buddhist, but when I first came to America I went to church with my sponsor to learn the Bible, because I think it's good to know about everybody's religions. But my mom, dad, and everyone else in my family liked the Buddha's teachings, and I do too. I also believe in kamma, and always try to do good things to people. I think I have a good life now because I looked after my grandmother.

I didn't have parents to teach me these things, but I lived among good people in the village, and I learned how to live by listening to them. They told me that in this life I had to take care of other people, that I should never take things that do not belong to me, because if you steal from others, someone will steal from you.

I still think of my mother. I can never forget her or my father. We have an altar in our home, and we pray to our dead relatives and ask them to help us because we believe that they are the gods who look after us now. Sometimes I go to the temple and give food to the monks and think of my parents and my grandmother. I don't go often because I am very busy, but my wife goes all the time, and when she gives money or food, it comes from the whole family. So when my wife goes to the temple and gives offerings, I feel I have participated in the actions also.

Sometimes I think of becoming an American citizen, but I love my country too. I miss everything I had in Cambodia: my family, my sisters, and the rice fields. Farming was hard work, but we were happy doing it. I would love to go back and become a farmer again, but I worry about returning to Cambodia now because the Vietnamese control our country, and if they remain there, in ten or twenty years there will be no Cambodia. However, the Vietnamese don't kill as many people like the Pol Pot soldiers, and right now, I feel any government is good as long as my people are safe. When we were growing up I could not live together with my family for very long. So I would like to live with my family now, and I wish I could bring them here.

CHAPTER EIGHT

Mum: Dad's Little Girl

"Mum," which means "little girl," is a popular nickname given to Cambodian girls. When I first saw twenty-one-year-old, fair-skinned Mum in her T-shirt and jeans, playing with a beautiful black puppy, she looked more American than Cambodian. Her easy smile and her mannerisms, however, were unmistakably Cambodian.

Mum came to the United States when she was twelve years old and has spent most of her formative years in American public schools. When I asked her if she would tell me her story, I assumed that I would collect the narrative of a rather Americanized Cambodian. A fluent English speaker, Mum began her story on a Sunday morning, sitting cross-legged on her living-room carpet. Before long, I discovered that her use of idiomatic English matched my initial impressions of her.

With shining eyes and lighthearted laughter, Mum recalled the happy times she had when her father, a wealthy Chinese Cambodian lawyer, satisfied her every whim. Her recollections of her father's ambitions both for himself and for his children are perhaps a fair reflection of most urban Chinese Cambodians, who were professionals or acted as middlemen in the Cambodian economy.

Mum related her story effortlessly in her soft voice, until she relived the evening the Khmer Rouge took her father away; then tears began to stream down her childlike face and sobs shook her slender body, betraying immense sorrow. I cried too, and my heart ached as I asked if she wished to stop for a while, but she shook her head, indicating that she wanted to continue.

Mum wiped the tears with the back of her hand, and her sobs lessened. But her plaintive voice echoed the pain that remained as she tried to find answers to the unanswered questions: What happened to her father, and why? Why did the Khmer Rouge force them to endure such pain and terror? As she continued recalling not only the atrocities of the Khmer Rouge but also the traumatic events that she experienced since coming to the United States, I felt anger and indignation welling up: that an innocent child should be punished so cruelly, for no apparent fault of her own. But there was no self-pity or bitterness in Mum's voice or manner; there was only the sadness she felt so deeply, and this only made her narrative more poignant.

By the end of the second long day, I realized that rather than her adolescence, or even the misfortunes she experienced in America, it was the tragedies caused by Pol Pot in her early childhood that exert the primary influence on Mum's current life. The wistfulness in her voice as she answered my questions about the impact of her father's death made it difficult for me to go on; but I persisted because her responses provided critical explanations for understanding her adaptation to the United States.

When I completed my interviews with Mum I was surprised that, based on her outward appearance, I had greatly underestimated the impact her religious and cultural roots have had on her own identity as a person and as a woman. Her discussion of Buddhist concepts shows how they have fashioned her thinking and worldview. Most of all, I was struck by the fact that despite the tragedies that have befallen her, Mum has not sought to escape from her memories by using artificial stimulants, or by turning away from society. Instead, she copes with them by maintaining her faith in humanity, as well as by her own humaneness toward others. Mum's mother's story appears in Chapter 11. ❖❖❖

Dad's Little Girl

When the Communists took over our country, I was eight years old. I was the youngest of four kids, and the only girl. Our dad was a judge and our mom a housewife, and both of them were Chinese Cambodians.

My favorite part of our big two-story house in Phnom Penh was the little wooden cottage that Dad got someone to build for us on the second floor. I loved going up there, especially on warm nights when we would have picnics with barbecued chicken and stuff. Oh, it was great! We had a TV, and got our telephone just before we left our home, when the Communists came. One of our three cars was a Mercedes. In the yard we grew papaya and other fruit trees, as well as vegetables. We had two big gates in front of our house, and three or four dogs as well. I also remember having servants who did the housework, and my dad's friend who lived with us.

We called our dad "Papa" in the French way. He wore a gown and hat when he went to work, and I used to get very excited when I saw him dressed like that. At night, I slept next to him on my parents' bed, so I was used to having a dad next to me all the time. My dad spoiled me a great deal. Once, when I was five or six years old, he took me to his friend's house. His friend had a teenage daughter who played the piano real well, and I loved it so much that a few weeks later, my dad bought a piano and got a teacher so I could learn to play.

Dad really pushed us to study, and sent us to the French school in the morning, and the Cambodian school in the afternoon. Sometimes we had tutors who came to the house too. He demanded a lot from us, and although I was very young at this time, I was able to handle most of the things he expected because I was quick to learn; but I don't think I was very good at remembering what I learned!

We called our mom "Nya," which is a fancy word. I don't know why we were brought up calling her Nya, but that's what we called her. [Nya Madai is a term for mother.] She made sure we did our math and writing before Dad came home, and if one of us didn't do well, Mom told him so and he'd ask sternly, "Why didn't you do this well or that well?" Although I knew my dad loved me, I was afraid of him when he spoke sternly like that. He never spanked me or scolded me, but he beat my brothers with belts and things. My mom always joked that my brothers were afraid of his face; that they probably thought he was a tiger or something. I never thought of him that way, probably because he never spanked me.

I got spanked by my mother. She said that I was a pretty naughty girl, and that I was hardheaded. I believe I was, for I have a mind of my own, and would not do most of the things she told me to do. When I disobeyed her she would say, "I'll spank you." Before she spanked me, I cried anyway. I can't think of many sad things in Phnom Penh except when my mom spanked me. I hated it!

Even though Dad was strict, he loved all of us a great deal. Once he and Mom had an argument, and Mom said she would go back to her father. My brothers and I decided to go with her and Dad couldn't accept that because he just loved the kids too much. He said, "Well, if you are all going with your mom, you will have to walk to school starting tomorrow."

The school wasn't far, but he or his friend always drove us there. I don't think I had ever walked anywhere in the sun until he made us walk to school the next day, and I fell ill with fever. My dad never made us walk to school again.

All four of us went to school together for a few years, but later on my parents sent my two older brothers to stay in a French house, where they spoke French and ate French food. We just ate regular Cambodian food. I remember eating butter, but I don't think I ever ate cheese in Cambodia. We had chocolate once in a while, which my parents bought when they went to France.

Unlike here, we never had birthday parties back home. We had heard of Christmas, but we never celebrated it. I had friends who lived close by, but I was rarely allowed to go out of the house to play with them; I guess my parents were afraid somebody would kidnap me. Once in a while my dad would bring home movies and a projector, and invite the kids in the neighborhood to watch them. He showed the movies in the garage, and all the kids sat on the floor and watched. I remember seeing "Hercules." It didn't have voices or music, but we thought it was great.

My parents were Buddhists, but I don't remember going to temple that often. I guess my dad was too busy to go because besides his regular job, he also had a car business. I think that's why we had so many cars.

Although we didn't go to the temple, we learned about religion from our parents. They never sat us down and said, "Okay, this is what we are supposed to do because we're Buddhists," but if we mentioned we killed insects or stole something, they said, "You are not supposed to do that," and explained why. When we visited our grandma in Battambang, she also said, "If you did this, this would happen to you according to the Buddhist way," and taught us to pray.

Battambang was quieter than Phnom Penh because there were not many cars. It was not as modern as Phnom Penh, and the only thing I liked there was that my grandparents let me do whatever I wanted. I was not afraid of them at all; I was so spoiled then, I don't think I minded anybody. Nowadays, when I hear my grandparents reprimanding my little cousins, I tell Mom, "You know, if they talked to me like that when I was little, I would never even have gone close to them."

I also remember monks coming every morning to collect food from our house. One monk who came to our house liked my brothers, and he often stopped and talked to them and stroked their heads. But he never did that to me, and one day I went close to him because I wanted him to stroke my head too. But the closer I got to the monk, the farther he moved. Finally, I started chasing him down the street, crying, and my mom started laughing. She called me back and explained that monks were not supposed to touch girls. I didn't know that because I was so little; and at that time I thought of myself as one of the boys because we were only a year apart in age, and I always did things with them. Mom tried to stop me from doing a lot of things they did, like running around and climbing trees. "You can't do that, because that's a boy's game," she would say, but I did it anyway.

I don't think my brothers liked having me around because if they didn't give me what I wanted, I complained to my parents. "Why don't you give your sister this or that?" my parents would say, and made my brothers give things to me. But it ruined the game they were playing, so my brothers teased me a lot.

When my parents were away my oldest brother hit me when I didn't do what he said. I remember once he told me to brush my teeth, but I refused to go into the bathroom at night because, like most of my friends, I was scared of ghosts. He slapped me, and I just sat there, crying.

I was always afraid of ghosts, but my parents didn't believe in them. They said, "There is no such thing as ghosts. Once you are dead, that is it."

But my oldest brother and my dad's friend were good storytellers, and told us a lot of ghost stories. One story I still remember was about a pregnant lady who died, and whose ghost came back to haunt people. It was said that when pregnant women died, their spirits were even more mean than other ghosts. I don't know why I was so frightened of ghosts, because I'd never seen a dead body until we were under the Communists.

Childhood Under the Khmer Rouge

The Communists told us to get out of our house the morning they came into Phnom Penh, but we didn't, because my dad had a misunderstanding with my maternal grandfather, who was visiting us. But we packed food and clothes to take in case we had to go.

In the night, the soldiers returned. "Is there anybody in the house? You had better get out now, or we'll start shooting," they shouted.

We were so frightened that we got into the first car that fitted my dad's key, and left our house without even taking the things we had packed, because they were in different rooms. I don't know what happened to our dogs.

In the boulevard my dad had to drive real slow because it was full of people, who, unlike us, carried many things. After we had gone a short distance, a Communist came over and asked my dad, "Do you want to go back and get a few things?" My dad said yes, and the man told us to get out of the car and wait for him. After a while Dad returned. He brought mostly food, because he was afraid to take too many things.

We lived in the car for several days, and at times Dad felt so desperate that he wanted to drive off the cliff with all of us, but Mom pleaded with him not to do so. "Things can't get much worse," she said.

I don't remember for how many days or nights we drove. Eventually we ran out of gas and we walked, carrying whatever we could. On the street, some people tried to make money by carrying evacuees' belongings from place to place. Others killed the pigs and chickens they had brought, and sold the meat for cash.

After several days we came to the countryside, and the Communists gave us a house. I had never lived in the country before, and I had a hard time sleeping because of the disgusting smell of cows and horses. I was not afraid, though, because I was with my dad.

A few weeks later, the soldiers said we could go to our hometowns, and we got on a boat going to Battambang. Along the way, the boat came to a village where my grandpa's relatives lived, and we decided to stop there for a day or two to get some supplies before going on to Battambang. When we were ready to leave, Grandpa said, "I want to stay here because I don't have the strength to walk anymore, but you can go to Battambang." My parents didn't want to leave him there by himself, and decided we too would live there, in the house of a distant relative.

I don't remember ever talking to Pol Pot soldiers when we lived in that village, but my dad did, because they would come and chat with him. They asked what he did back home, and he replied, "I worked as a pharmacist." He always pretended to be nice to them, and even offered them some medicine he brought with him if they ever needed it.

One evening, I sat on my dad's lap while he talked with some Communists when two soldiers carrying guns came into our compound.

"*Bong* [older person]," they said to my dad. "We want you to come with us because we want to talk to you about something."

Dad put me down and left with them without saying anything. I followed him.

The Khmer Rouge took my dad to the third or fourth house, and began to speak very quietly to him. I could not hear what they said because I stood a few feet away, and I don't think Dad knew I was there because he stood with his back to me. I was terrified, but I stayed there until a soldier saw me and said, "You better go back home, your dad will be home soon."

I ran home and told my mom what had happened, and we all started to cry.

Our dad did not come home that night or the next day. We searched around, but we never found out what happened to him, or what they did with him. The village leader, who usually referred to himself as our friend, said the soldiers just wanted to talk to him. I don't think Mom tried to find out much information because sometimes when you asked too many questions, they took the rest of the family away too. I am so lucky that they didn't take me; I was there with him when the soldiers came for him.

I think the Pol Pots took my dad away because the relative we stayed with told the Communists about our background. Nobody else in the village knew us. Although I was very young, I knew when somebody didn't like me, and I don't think she liked us very much because we still had a city look. Also, unlike her kids, we respected our parents; so I think she was extremely jealous of us. The soldiers would have believed anything she said because she was an "Old Person" in the village; and anyway, there was no justice at that time.

It has been years since my dad was taken away, but it hasn't been easy for me to come to terms with it.

I think my dad expected something would happen to him, because he always said to us, "If something happens to me, you guys take care of your mom." Usually the mom takes care of the kids, but he knew that my mom didn't know how to do anything. He taught my brothers to fish and to do a few other things.

After he disappeared, we would ask our mom what happened to Dad, but all she said was, "Don't worry about him. He will be back." I guess she said it to make us feel better; I think we kind of knew that it was never going to happen.

Two or three days after Dad was taken away the Communists evacuated all the "New People" from the village. We had to walk for several days, carrying our pots, rice, blankets, and whatever else we needed. It was extremely hard because we were just four kids and a lady. We came to a jungle where people had never lived before, and the Communists ordered us to build our own houses. My mom didn't know how, and we were too young to do such hard work. Finally, some people helped us make a hut with bamboo and some branches. Although it could hardly be called a house, at least we had a place to sleep at night.

In the jungle the Communists didn't allow us to own anything. We had to give up everything we had, and dye our clothes black by soaking them in a pail of water blackened by some crushed berries.

In the night we slept on the bamboo floor with no mattress, and oh, my back hurt terribly because I have a big mole on my back. My dad had always told me, "You have got this big mole on your back, you need to always sleep on a mattress."

I never forgot that and I would ask Mom, "Why did Papa say I would always be sleeping on mattresses?"

Every year things got worse. The soldiers told us that we couldn't cook our own food anymore, that they would give us food, and that we were all equals. At the beginning they gave us rice, but soon, we got only rice gruel with very little rice, which was sometimes thickened with yam. The Communists, though, cooked and ate in their house, and while we became skinnier, they were plump.

So how could we be equals?

I was always so hungry, I told my mom that if they wanted me to beg for rice, I would. But I knew nobody would give me any.

I'd say, "Mom, how come I never ate back home? How come I never liked bananas, never liked beef, never liked rice? Now I am so hungry. Why didn't I eat back home when we had so much rice?"

Sometimes we asked her, "Why is this happening to us? What's going on?"

The only thing I remember Mom telling us was, "Life is like a wheel; it turns. It never stays the same. Things will get better."

In a way we believed her because we didn't know any different. We had no radio, no lights, and we didn't know what was going on; that was all she could tell us.

The Pol Pots took my two older brothers away to live in the junior camp. We lived with Mom, but she went to work in the rice fields every day, so my third brother and I looked for food, and cooked and ate together.

One day my brother found a very pretty mushroom. We didn't know what kind it was, but I had heard that good-looking mushrooms were poisonous, and I told him, "That one looks suspicious, Brother, don't eat it." But I guess he was too hungry and ate it, because a little later he came outside where my mom and I were trying to grow some yams and said, "Oh, I got a headache! I got a headache!" Then he lay down and never woke up for two days and three nights.

We didn't know what had happened to my brother. We assumed it was mushroom poisoning.

A person who was supposed to be a Pol Pot doctor told my mom to get some leaves from the jungle, and to boil them and feed the water to my brother. My mom didn't know how to find those leaves, and she figured he was dying; so she didn't go to look for the leaves. Instead, she coin-rubbed him [a common home remedy] with a bit of gasoline the Communists had given us to make fires with.

Mom had also heard that sugar helped to get rid of mushroom poisoning, and she went to the place where the Communists made palm sugar and said, "My son has got mushroom poisoning. Please give a little bit of sugar to get rid of the poisons."

They told her, "We told you not to eat mushrooms because you might get poisoned, but you don't listen to us. We don't have sugar to give you."

My mom got mad. I don't know what was going through her mind, but she didn't bother to look for the leaves. She only boiled any fresh vegetable she could find and fed him that, hoping he would get some sugar from them.

When the Pol Pot found out Mom had not given my brother his medicine, he accused her of abusing her son, and gathered the leaves and told her to boil them and feed the water to her son. We fed him the water, and he peed all day long. Every time I looked at him I could see more of his bones. I knew he was alive only because he breathed.

On the third night, we heard him call "Nya!" Mom jumped up saying, "What happened, son, what happened?" But he only said, "Oh, my body hurts so badly!"

Mom wanted some extra light and she flicked the only cigarette lighter we had. It had never worked after our evacuation, but that night, it started. It was incredible!

After he woke up from his coma, my brother became like a baby. He couldn't hold his head up, and couldn't remember what had happened to him. When he ate, he put his hand all over his face, groping for his mouth. He took a long time to eat, and my mom would yell, "What's the matter with you?" I didn't know what to do when Mom got angry; my heart just dropped. My brother was so afraid of her.

One day my oldest brother came to visit us from the junior camp. My third brother looked at my oldest brother with his eyes wide open and said, "Who is that?" Oldest brother asked, "Don't you know me? Can't you see me?"

He said, "No, I can't see you."

For a long time afterward, as my brother recovered from the poisoning, Mom continued to massage him, and he cried, saying, "It hurts, it hurts!" But what she did was the right thing for him, because finally, he was able to walk with a crutch. At that point the Communists assigned Mom to work in a village far away from home.

Since she had no choice but to go, Mom asked the Pol Pots for permission to take my brother with her. She would be living near the sea and she thought that even if there was no rice, my brother would get fish to eat. The Communists gave her permission to take him, but I was not allowed to go with them.

After Mom left, I was supposed to live with the other kids in a Pol Pot school, but often I ran away. I would come back to the house because I didn't want to work for the Communists. I just stayed in the house, looked around for food, and fished by myself. But I was very lucky, because one of the Pol Pot ladies who worked in the kitchen liked me. She knew Mom had gone away, and sometimes she left me a little cooked rice, or some raw rice to cook by myself. I would take a piece of coal from the kitchen and light a fire. I didn't have any salt, which is why we were all swollen, but just plain rice was wonderful!

Sometimes I sat in the house and wondered why Mom didn't try harder to take me with her. Anyway, it was no big deal for me, and I never cried because tears really weren't easy for us then. All I cared about was finding something to eat. Oh, god, I was so hungry, I even walked on dirt piles where they had buried people to find little fruits that grew on them. I would feel a chill going down my back, but I would walk on it anyway, and pick whatever I saw. And now here I am, having enough food in my stomach, and still having that scary feeling about ghosts!

After Mom went away, I had no way to communicate with her. Once I wanted to see her really badly, and I told the lady in the kitchen. She knew a guy who went back and forth in an ox cart, taking food to the place where my mom lived. The lady asked him to take me there and back, which he did. She also gave me some rice to eat on the way.

Another time, I had to see Mom again because I dreamed that my brother who was with her was dying. It's not something I will ever forget; even now, it's hard for me to talk about it. I got very scared, and called another girl to go with me.

We went in a cart, but when we came back, we had to walk through the jungle with some other people. We had no problems walking so far, but we were little, and we couldn't walk as fast as they did. They didn't know us, they didn't care about us, and they got farther away until we couldn't see them anymore. It started to get dark and my friend started to cry, saying, "Oh, we're lost, the wolf is going to eat us!" I was scared too, but what was the point in crying? Finally I recognized the trees around us and knew we had got back home.

I did not go to see my mom again; the second time I went, it was just too much.

One day when I was looking for food, I met an old lady who was the only person left from her family. All her children, their spouses, and her grandchildren had died. "If you come and live with me, we can become a team. I have some rice, and you can catch some fish, and we can cook and eat together," she said to me. Mom still hadn't come back, so I went to live with that lady.

I was so lucky I met her. She had been a city person, too, but I think she was a close friend of the cook because she always got extra rice. Best of all, she gave me a cushion to sleep on! I don't know how she still had a cushion. That lady was old, but she was really smart. She told me what I should watch out for, and that I should not tell anybody what we ate.

I have no idea how many years or months Mom was away because we didn't have a calendar, but after a long time she finally came back. The old lady didn't want me to return to my mom. I was young then, and I didn't know what she was trying to do, but Mom said she wanted to keep me because she didn't have anyone of her own.

When we were under the Communists, I had three friends. One was the daughter of the cook, one was the girl who went with me to visit Mom, and the other was a Chinese girl. We walked to school together—the Communists called it the school, but we didn't learn anything.

One day, one of the Pol Pots' daughters walked with us. For some reason my Chinese friend liked to talk too much, and she said that she wished the Vietnamese would come and take over the country, so we would be free. I was shocked when she said that because I knew the Pol Pot's daughter would tell somebody, and that my friend would get in trouble.

They killed her.

They left her body in the back of the school, but I was afraid to go and see her.

I saw the body of another lady the Communists killed because she wouldn't marry one of the soldiers. They left her body in the rice field, marked with a big knot made with rice plants, so people would see it, but it was so swollen that I couldn't even recognize her. Of course I knew the body wouldn't remain there for long because when it started to smell, the wolves would come and eat it.

In our village, people got punished all the time. I was punished once myself, because I stole some sugarcane the Communists grew in front of our hut. I had not had sugar for years, and I got such a craving for it that I would sneak out and cut some sugarcane in the night. But once I did it in the daytime, and the village leader saw me. He had an ax in his hand, and he beat me on the back and on the butt a lot of times with its handle. It hurt terribly, but compared to what could have happened, it was nothing; I could have been accused of stealing, and been killed.

They killed a lot of kids. They killed my friend. I was just extremely lucky.

I don't know why I was never killed because I did a lot of things that other people did that they got killed for, like the time I had a fight with another city girl. I think she was half-Vietnamese, and she said mean things about my mother.

"You can say anything you like about me, but just leave my mother alone," I told her, but she would not stop.

I didn't want to get into trouble or be killed, but she was just too much, and one night I got so mad I started to hit her. The ladies who were in charge of us came and beat us, saying, "You are not supposed to fight. Only enemies would do that. You are children of Pol Pot."

My mom had told us to pray as Grandma taught us, and at night, I did that, and I prayed for my dad too. I prayed that he would be okay, that he would come back soon. Of course we didn't want the Pol Pot spies to find out that we prayed, when they prowled around our huts at night, just like animals. You would think there were dried-up leaves and branches that they might step on, but we couldn't hear even a footstep, and we really had to watch out for them.

I never fell ill during the Pol Pot time, and again I was lucky. If I had been ill, who would have fed me? Who would have taken care of me? My mom was away. When I lived in Phnom Penh, I was exactly the opposite; I was a very spoiled child. Under Pol Pot, I had to grow up.

Escape to Thailand and Return to Hell

Walking back to Battambang after the Vietnamese came, Mom was yellow and swollen, and screamed at us the whole time as if she had gone crazy.

My second brother was so angry that he wanted to go and kill the Pol Pots.

My older brother and Mom stopped him, saying that we didn't have to kill the Pol Pots because they would be punished by Preah. Preah is somebody like God. So my brother stayed with us, and when we got to Battambang we discovered that Mom's brother and his family had survived too, and a few weeks later, we all escaped to Nong Chan refugee camp in Thailand.

We had been in the camp for only a few days when the Thai soldiers gave us some rice and water and told all the refugees to get into nice air-conditioned buses, because they would take us to a different camp. Some people dozed while they drove us around for many hours.

Finally, the soldiers brought us to a mountainous area. There, they told us to get off the bus, and climb down a cliff, which was like a steep wall. They told us to go back to Cambodia!

People started crying and pleading, refusing to go, and the soldiers began to shoot. We ran and scrambled down trees and rocks, and somehow got to the bottom of the mountain. I think we survived only because we were the third group to be sent down; most of the people who went before us got blown up by mines that were buried all over the place.

The paths at the bottom were only about two feet wide. We could not go to the left, or to the right. We had to walk in single file, and we figured the only way to survive was to walk along the paths where the mines had already blown up.

Once we got to a place where, for some reason, we had to stop for a while, and all around us were the swollen bodies of dead people. Although people's skins are pretty thick, we could see worms wriggling inside. Some of the corpses were all dried out. I had never seen so many bodies, some half-buried, left like that for so long. In the end I closed my eyes tightly so I didn't see them anymore, but there was no way I could shut out the smell.

A lot of terrible things happened while we were trying to get out of the mountains. Some people gave birth, but had to leave the babies behind because it was impossible to take care of them. Besides, people were frightened because when babies cried, robbers would know we were there. Others left old parents up there with some food because it was so hard to carry them along such narrow paths. Another time as we walked someone shouted, "A mine is going to explode! Bend down!" There was an explosion, and a piece of a person's flesh stuck on my aunt, and she started to scream. It was so terrible!

I cannot remember how many days it took us to get out of that area; all I remember is walking through day and night, but at last, we got back to Battambang.

Second Escape to Thailand

We stayed close to our uncle who had escaped with us the first time, and tried to make some money so we could try to get out again, but Mom had become so discouraged, she said there was no point in trying a second time. We begged her to change her mind because we had nothing in Cambodia; whatever we had was destroyed. How were we going to live? We told her we just had to try again.

The second time we escaped, we didn't have enough money to pay the guide to get all of us into the camp together. We got in one by one with other groups of escapees, and I couldn't find my mom or my brothers. So I went to live with a man and a woman who called me to look after their handicapped child, and just stayed there because I didn't know how to find Mom. Anyway, I wasn't really worried, because I thought she'd come to get me. It never occurred to me that she would have a hard time finding me! She had found my brothers within a few days of getting in, but it was several weeks before she found me. It was a terrible experience for my mom.

Rediscovering Childhood

In Pol Pot time, we didn't know what was going on around us, and we didn't know what would happen to us. We were all by ourselves, and we didn't know if anybody would ever discover us. We often thought, "What's the point of living? Maybe we should all eat some poisonous mushrooms and die together."

We didn't kill ourselves only because my mom believed that things would never stay like this. She said when other countries wanted to go forward, we couldn't go backward. She wanted to see what would happen in the end. So we tried to think of the positive side, but often we were so desperate that we felt we could not go on anymore.

When we escaped to camp, it too was like a jail, with gates around it. At night we slept on a sheet spread on the floor in a big room like a warehouse. But I still thought that living in the refugee camp was a lot better than living under Pol Pot, when I had so many lice in my head that I could feel the eggs and scrape them off with my own fingers! In the camp, I didn't have to do that. We had soap to wash our hair so the eggs came off. My grandma who had gone to America sent us money through her Thai friends, and even though we couldn't go shopping in Thailand to buy things, we could get candy and stuff from vendors who sold things outside the camp gate. Best of all, I was not frightened anymore, and I realized I was still a little girl because I started to play again. So with all that, I thought living in the camp was great!

I don't think we lived in the camp for more than a year and a half, but I think Mom would have gone crazy if we had stayed there another six months. Before Pol Pot took over our country, she was a mother, but she didn't really have to do anything. Then suddenly we were under Pol Pot, and they starved Mom and forced her to work day and night. By the time we escaped the second time she didn't know what would happen next, and I don't think she even cared anymore. Just when she was becoming very desperate, we were called for an interview to come to America.

Coming to America

I was really excited when we got into the airplane to come to America because I wanted to go to school real bad! I think we were the only refugee family on that plane because my uncle's family had to stay back when one of my cousins broke his leg. When we came to San Francisco, Grandma was there to meet us.

I was twelve years old when I came here, but when she saw us Grandma said, "You guys did not grow the past four or five years." But how could we? We had been under the Communists!

We lived in my grandma's two-bedroom apartment in a big city because we had no other place to go, but the apartment manager gave us a hard time, saying that it was not meant for six people. So as soon as we received welfare money we moved out to another apartment, and finally, we started going to school.

I went into seventh grade because I was thirteen, but people would say, "You are so small and you're in junior high school? How old are you?" Nobody believed me when I told them I was thirteen.

I had a hard time at school because I didn't know English, and the kids teased me about it. I remember one time the teacher asked why my brother hadn't come to school. I tried to explain to her he was sick and that he was in the hospital, and a kid who was a real jerk made fun of my English. Although he got into trouble for that, I cried because I was very hurt. But it taught me that I had to work hard and prove that I could do things too.

Mom tried to encourage us to do well in school, saying, "I will give you a dollar for every A you get." So I worked hard, but when we got our report cards, I had got all B's, while my best friend got mostly A's. She was a Chinese girl who had come here when she was little and spoke fluent English, and she could not understand why I cried when I saw my grades. Although she liked me very much, I knew she would not understand how I felt, because she had not gone through what I had suffered.

At last I started getting A's, and Mom thought I cheated at school because I did not sit down and study for long hours. When she realized I did not cheat, she said, "Forget about the money, I can't afford it!"

I began to get 4.0 in junior high, so teachers liked me. One day a teacher told me to write an essay. She entered it in a competition, and I won fifty dollars as one of the top ten international students in the school. It was a great honor, and I felt wonderful! With the money I won, I bought a record player I wanted so bad then. I have no idea why I did so well in school. It was probably because the teachers and the principal pushed me, telling me to do my best.

When I started high school, Mom became extremely strict with me.

"You must not have boyfriends. If you have a boyfriend, I will punish you," she told me often.

Even though I did not have a boyfriend, I guess she got worried that I might find one. She didn't want anybody to say bad things about me, and she arranged my wedding when I was in eleventh grade. I was seventeen years old.

Love and Marriage

My husband was 26 years old. I did not know him before the marriage. His parents asked my mom about me, and my mom thought that he would make a good husband because he was a lot older, and would take good care of me. But he was an only son who had been spoiled by his parents.

My husband and I fought a lot because he wanted to control me. He wanted me to stay at home, be a good wife, and help him with his business. But I wanted to finish high school because I thought that even if I didn't continue my education now, I could go back to college later if I had a high-school diploma. So while doing all the housework, I continued to go to school. But it was impossible for me to do well because we moved often, and I ended up going to four different high schools. I finally graduated, but I really felt sorry that I didn't do as well as I wanted.

My husband liked to gamble, and I didn't have access to his money. I worked part-time for him and he paid me. It made me unhappy, but I wanted our marriage to work, and told him, "Money is not important to me. I've been through a lot, and since we are married, why don't we try to work things out?"

Little by little he came to understand me. He even offered to give his paycheck to me, but it had not mattered to me at the beginning, so it was not going to matter now.

I told him, "I just want you to understand me a little, and not always listen to your parents. I am living with you. You should understand what type of person I am, and what I do for you. I can be a good wife, but you also have to help around the house a little bit."

He started to help me when his parents were not around, and things got better between us. But his parents became worried because they thought I was taking control of him.

Our marriage started to deteriorate again, and I asked him, "Is there anything we can do to make things better?" He said he wanted a baby. He was still helping around the house, so I said, "If you would stop gambling, I will have a baby. All I ask is that. I don't want money or anything." He agreed and I got pregnant.

My mom was angry when I got pregnant. She knew our marriage wasn't going to work. She had wanted me to end it a long time before, but I felt I had decided to let the marriage happen, and I had to make it work. If it did not work, I wanted to be sure that I would not have any feelings for him. So I got pregnant, but he continued to gamble. I filed for divorce.

I told Mom I wanted to keep the baby. She tried to advise me against it, but I refused to listen to her. So she asked other people to talk to me. They said, "Your mom does not want you to have an abortion, but she wants you to think about your future. If you wanted to marry in the future, would another person love the kid? If you wanted to go back to school, who would take care of the baby?"

I thought about what they said and realized that Mom was right. Although I would have probably kept the baby if I was older, I wasn't sure that I could take care of financial things as well as the kid at nineteen.

I made an appointment to get an abortion. It was one of the hardest decisions I ever had to make, but I really had no choice. However, I guess by then I was under so much pressure that I had a miscarriage the night before the abortion. I am so glad it happened that way.

Since I had the miscarriage and had to get emergency treatment at a hospital other than the one my insurance company recommended, they refused to pay my medical bills. I couldn't afford to pay those bills and also to hire a lawyer for my divorce. So with help from Mom's friend who was in law school, I figured out certain things regarding divorce. One day I went to the courthouse to file some papers and I got lost. I asked a really hotshot-type lawyer what I should do, and he took me in his car and showed me where to go, and told me what to do, and I got divorced after two years of marriage.

After my divorce, a man who saw me working at my previous office offered me a new job because he liked the way I worked. "I know that you don't get such good pay at the moment, and I'll start you off at so much if you will come to work for me," he said, and gave me his business card.

I thought it was kind of weird, but when I told my girlfriend at work she said, "Give it a try." When I asked my family, they also thought it was a good idea to give it a try, and I went to work for him.

I had a hard time the first two months because I didn't have experience, and other people in the new place didn't want to help me. They would teach me something only once, and expected me to remember it forever! They acted as if they didn't want me to have certain things, or do certain jobs. I suppose they had been there for so long they felt they deserved to get everything. But my boss, who referred to himself as my father, kept on saying, "You will learn; you've got to trust me." Things worked out in the end, and we're all friends now; but sometimes I feel it's still mostly on the surface.

Although I like my work, my ambition is to go to school and study to become a lawyer. But I've discovered that this is not a good time for me to go to school because everything that happened in Cambodia, Thailand, and here is too fresh in my mind. I continued to go to school all these years because I wanted education to be a part of my life, but I have not been satisfied with my performance. I don't expect 4.0, but I expect at least 3.5, and it has been hard for me to achieve it. I don't think I could do it now; I think

I need time to think things out. I hope to return to school one day, but I don't know when.

I think part of the problem is my job. My boss offered me a job I couldn't resist. My salary is good, but I know it's not going to make me rich. But nowadays it's hard to find a place where you make decent money and you can also trust your boss. Also, a degree does not always guarantee you a good job. So I'm kind of in-between; I don't know what to do.

Reflections

If Cambodia went back to the way it was, I think many Cambodians would want to go back because they haven't adjusted to life here. Most haven't learned to speak English, and they miss the foods they used to eat, and the way they used to live. I think some refugees have a hard time because they don't try to adjust, but a lot also depends on what types of backgrounds they came from. Many people, like my grandmother, came from the countryside with no education. They never went to school, and lived all their lives in Cambodia. So it is harder for them to learn new things. My grandmother, for instance, is extremely old-fashioned. She does not like it when I go out on dates, and wear certain clothes. The one thing that she and I have in common is that we are both stubborn! However, while I listen to other points of view and try to understand, she does not, because of the way she grew up.

While they are not used to new ways, some refugees also do not give themselves time to learn, to explore some of the things here. For instance, after coming here, some Cambodians married young, like I did. But while I never gave up on school, they got married and had kids, so they never really got a chance to learn much. You really have to go to school to learn, to be able to grow a little bit.

My family does not want to return to live in Cambodia because what we went through was too much for us. I will not forget Cambodia and I would like to visit my country some day, but I am just too scared to return right now. I don't think I could survive another war; if that happened, I would probably commit suicide.

I am glad I was young when Pol Pot took over our country. I think that helped me to deal with it more easily. But while I don't think I can go through all that again, I never sit down and cry, thinking, "Oh, this happened to me, and that happened to me," because I think my experiences have made me a better person. I could have been a spoiled brat if I grew up in Cambodia, and never know some of the things I know now.

I still have nightmares of the Pol Pot time. They happen unexpectedly, without any reason.

Sometimes I dream that Pol Pot has come, and that I can't run; that is really scary. Once I dreamed that my dad died. I don't know if he was buried under our house, but his bones started coming out of the ground; and my mom woke me up asking me why I was crying and screaming. Now I dream of my dad only once or twice a month, and I always see his face. I ask him, "What happened to you, Papa, and why? Where are you now? Why do you look for us after all these years? Why do you suddenly show up?"

But he never talks to me. He's always sad. I never dream of him laughing.

When I have nightmares I open my eyes hoping it was a dream, and pray quietly to myself. When I dream of my dad I take food to the monks in his memory, whenever I have the time.

We have tried to find out what happened to our dad, and we have heard all types of stories; that somebody saw him and that he was skinny and so on, but I don't know who to believe. I don't think there's any way to find out; only the Pol Pots would know what happened.

Although the Pol Pot experience makes me sad, makes me cry at certain times, and gives me nightmares, it doesn't bother me as much as it used to. I have learned to look at it as an experience; but I don't take what I have for granted, the way American people do. There's more to life, more to families, than money and stuff.

For me, money is no big deal. Of course it's something you always need living in this country, but it's something my family has had, so it is not the main thing in life.

Money comes and goes. I think to me, the main thing is happiness. Happiness is to have a pretty close family, and to have the ability to do anything that I want, and to accomplish anything I want.

I would be extremely happy if I could be an attorney; this is something that's going to bother me for a while. I know I can do it, but after all that happened, I don't know if I am ready for it. I don't want to go to school and not do well.

My marriage too was an experience I learned from. Even though it was a difficult experience, I don't mind talking about it because it was not something I asked for.

If we were in Cambodia I wouldn't have rushed into a marriage because of the power Dad had. Also, my parents would probably not have considered the man I married to be a suitable husband for me because compared to what I had then and what he has now, we would not have been social equals.

Like the Pol Pot experience, my marriage changed me a lot too. Before I was married, I was really a nice girl. But with that guy, the only thing I could do was to tell the truth about everything. I got to the point where everything came to him straight out of my heart, and that made me a stronger person. I don't regret the experience, but a lot of the time I hate myself for being too strong. I don't think a woman should be like that. A woman has to have some weaknesses in her, whether she is Cambodian or American.

Nowadays I don't think of marriage at all. It's not a big issue for me. It is for my mom, though, because she doesn't believe in someone living by herself. I can understand that, but I've been through a lot, and it is going to take a while for me to know what I want in a man, or even what I want in my life. Some men I've gone out with, or who have been introduced to me by friends, have asked if I would marry them, but I sure learned a lot from my marriage, and I think I need time to think about it.

If I got married, I would consider the ability to understand and compromise as most important, because nobody is perfect. I think it's important to explain what's going on to each other, and not have secrets between spouses, or between kids and parents. For example, my mom and I have our differences, but she knows practically everything that's going on in my life. Most of my friends are surprised about our openness, because they find it difficult to talk about their lives with their families. Some parents don't know what the children do, or where they go. I find being honest and open with people pays off in the long run, and it's because I discuss things with Mom that I am able to live at home more easily than they can; they have a lot of secrets. But even though I tell her everything, I don't do what she says all the time. I do what I think is right for me, and what I can handle, because what is important is how I feel inside.

I used to date a fair amount, but now I don't date much because I don't want things to get out of hand. I want to have control of myself. I don't believe in going out with different people all the time, and I don't believe in living together. I figure if you have the freedom to go out with a person for as long as you want, you should know after some years what type of person he or she is. You don't have to be spending twenty-four hours a day to find that out. In a way, I think it's silly to think that because you are an Asian woman, you should not do certain things. I don't believe that is 100 percent correct, but I still would not behave differently because I don't want someone to step on my pride.

If I thought of getting married again, I would try to avoid getting involved with a Vietnamese man because we have always been told of bad things the Vietnamese tend to do, and I find that they say and do things regardless of consequences. I don't think I can marry an American because of differences in our backgrounds.

I respect Americans, but I am embarrassed about some of the things they do. I think that here, kids have too much freedom. I think people have too much freedom. Parents can't tell the kids what to do. Kids don't care about parents. People around my age do practically everything they want to: drink, smoke, go out, and even move out. I see, and I know a lot of people who do those things. None of us in my family will do them. I am going to be 22 soon, but I still don't do the things my mom doesn't want me to do. I will not get a sports car nor will I go out with someone if she thinks it's wrong. If I want to do it and she is stopping me, I would be upset about it, but I wouldn't do it just to go against her or the family because then I would not feel good inside. I understand and sometimes even respect people who go after what they want, but I will not do that. Maybe I still have a little bit of the Asian background in me.

I also think it would be difficult to have a close relationship with an American because I think they are afraid of marriage. I've heard them say that they are not keen to have close relationships with women because they think that women will get pregnant, or at least claim they're pregnant so the men will marry them, and after marriage, the women want to control everything. But all women are not the same, and they should give a chance at least to those who are from different backgrounds. For instance, I would do anything for the marriage to work, for the husband and the kids to be happy.

I don't think I have problems adjusting to anything, wherever I live. But when I am in my house, I don't necessarily do everything the way other people do. I still want to keep my own traditions and do certain things my way, especially as a woman. For example, I figure doing housework is a woman's job, regardless of where I am. It's something my mom taught me.

I know Cambodian women my age who don't know half of what I know about cooking, because they're becoming so Americanized. They're more outgoing and they dress better. Sometimes they look at my closet and

A traditional wedding in America

say, "Oh, you still keep such and such?" Old clothes don't bother me as long as they are not torn, and they fit. Of course I am not going to be dressed in rags, but I don't have to show off all the time. To me, what counts is what type of person you are and what's within you.

In a way I am very Americanized, in a way I am not; it depends on who I am with. If I am with Cambodian people I am 100 percent Cambodian. I get along with older people as well as the kids, and I think that older people respect me because of the way I am around them. With American people, I can be very Americanized. I talk, act, and dress the way they do, but I don't do everything the American way.

I can think of two Cambodian friends who have changed a great deal right now. I was in school with one, and we were the best students back in junior high. She was a good student in high school too, and now she is on her way to college. But if you see her, you would think that she was born here, she is so Americanized. The way she talks, the way she eats, the way she acts, what she wouldn't do is so American. She doesn't know how to cook, or take care of the house. She's a year older than I, but she acts like a kid. When we get together she always fights with my friends. I can't recall getting into an argument with any friends. If they believe in something I do not say, "Hey, that's wrong," even if I didn't believe that. My friend would say something like, "I don't like this. It should have been like this, instead of that."

I think everybody has different beliefs for themselves. My friend really disturbs me, but in a way I respect her because it's amazing to me that someone can change so completely. I could never do that. I wasn't born here, so I can't be so Americanized.

When I get together with friends I don't decide what we do because I am afraid they may not like it. I go along with whatever my friends want to do, if I feel comfortable with it. Some of them like to dance and drink, but I don't drink. I've tried it, but it warms up my body which doesn't make me feel good, so I don't like it. Considering what I've been through, you might think I have to turn to something; most people who have problems turn to something, but I don't drink, smoke, or do drugs. All I know is that they are not going to make things better for me. If anything, they will make things worse.

I've been asked to go to church, but I don't believe in that. We don't go to temple as much, but we believe in Buddhism a lot. I can't think of anything that monks tell me that is bad for me. I would love to go to the temple whenever I get the opportunity because I feel great when I go. But it's hard for my Cambodian Christian friends because they are really into Christianity. If they listen to a tape, it has to be a Christian tape. Before they eat, they have to pray. For me these things are not necessary, because again, what is important is what is within you.

At the same time, if they are so much into Christianity, why do they do some of the things they do? Many of them go to church just to meet boyfriends or other people. They try to force the opposite sex to become Christians, so they can marry, but then those people would not believe in it. People should be aware that if you are not Christian and want to marry a Christian, they'll try to make you become one. I like the Buddha a lot because you can marry whoever you want.

Nobody ever forces you to get into the Buddhist religion. I hate it when people come to our door saying, "You want to become such and such religion?" That really bugs me. I don't believe in that at all, because again, what is important is what is within you.

I like Buddha because you don't have to go to the temple every weekend; if you go, it is fine. If not, that is okay too. In the Christian religions you have to go to church every week, have candles around, give money, pray, and do all that. To me, these things do not make me different. I don't have to show anybody I am listening to Christian tapes or Buddha tapes or whatever. I don't have to show them I am into something, and turn around and do something else. But that's what most of my friends do. The Buddha doesn't require you to do so, and I think it's what you believe in that's important.

I have always thought of myself as a Cambodian, but the older I get, the more I realize I have a lot of Chinese blood, and that I do some things differently from Cambodians. But I still think of myself as a Cambodian, I don't know why. I am living with my mom, regardless of some of the problems we have, because I figure wherever you go, you have problems anyway. So what if we have differences? My family is more important than anything else.

PART III

In Search
of Freedom

CHAPTER NINE

Coming to America

At the end of the 1970's, Cambodia was divided politically and territorially under two regimes, each claiming to be the sole legitimate government of the nation. The Vietnamese set out to tighten their grip on the country from Phnom Penh, while the Khmer Rouge regrouped in remote enclaves near the Thai border to give armed resistance to the Vietnamese.

In the 1980's, a partnership between feuding Communist and non-Communist factions resulted in a government in exile, the Coalition Government of Democratic Kampuchea (CDGK). It consisted of the Khmer Rouge and two non-Communist groups led by Sihanouk and Son Sann, a former prime minister under Sihanouk. Their forces sought international aid to resist the Vietnamese and to win Cambodia back, and they had a distinct advantage in that they were recognized by the United Nations as the lawful representative of the state of Cambodia.

A United Nations–sponsored peace treaty was signed by the warring factions in October 1991. It came far too late, however, to prevent large numbers of Khmer refugees from fleeing their homeland in search of refuge, for the first time in the country's history. They fled in several waves and at different times (Stein 1982; Hamilton 1982).

The first wave, which left in 1975 when the Khmer Rouge defeated the Lon Nol government, included a number of Westernized or educated people who went to Vietnam or Thailand. They subsequently resettled in third countries, mainly in France. The United States received about 6,000 Cambodians from this wave, the first time that such a large number of Khmer came to live in the United States.

When the Vietnamese invaded Cambodia in 1979, the second influx of refugees, numbering about 100,000, fled to the Thai border. They included urban and professional people who had survived the Pol Pot regime by concealing their backgrounds. Also fleeing were large numbers of rural people, and Khmer Rouge cadres and soldiers.

With such an enormous influx of refugees, the Thai government was faced with two major crises. First, they had the administrative and economic problems of coping with a mass of starved and abused people for whom they received little international assistance. Second, a depopulated Cambodia enabled Vietnamese troops to move easily to the west and become a political threat to Thailand. In response, the Thai government refused to accept these Cambodians.

They called these asylum seekers "illegal immigrants" who were "conceived by the U.S. policies during the 1970–75 war, and. . . delivered by Vietnam," and forced large numbers back into Cambodia at various periods (Shawcross 1984: 88). Only when some 40,000 survivors of the holocaust were ordered at gunpoint to climb down a steep precipice, sending hundreds of people to their deaths from mine-filled footpaths or from sickness and hunger, did the Thai government finally receive the world's attention and the aid that they could not get before (see Mum's story, Chapter 8).

A severe famine in 1979 and 1980 and fears of another Communist government forced the third and largest wave of some 500,000 Cambodian refugees to flee. Several refugee camps, including Khao-I-Dang, Sakaeo, Kamput, and Mai Rat were opened in 1979 and 1980. More refugees arrived at the camps established in the no-man's-land along the border. By June of 1980, more than 150,000 Khmer refugees were in holding centers operated by UNHCR (United Nations High Commissioner for Refugees). Thousands of others waited in border camps, either for admittance to Thai camps and from there to countries of resettlement, or for peace in Cambodia so they could return to their homes.

The camp officials provided refugees with food, shelter, medical aid, education, and assistance with resettlement at the camps. But the camps were hardly places of refuge. The residents of the camps were subjected to harassment and thievery by some Thai guards and even by other inmates. Some border settlements were caught in periodic battles between Vietnamese and resistance forces in the region; this caused displacement, injuries, and deaths. The responses of camp administrators to these crises ranged from expressions of concern to hostility.

At the 1988 congressional hearings on Cambodia, the camps where these refugees languished for years before being resettled were described as places where "brutality escalates hopelessness, suicide, child abuse; attitudes and behaviors of a tragic kind have become the norm" (Kitty Dukakis, 1988). Niseth, whose narrative follows, describes best some aspects of the stressful changes in status and identity the refugees endured in the camps, which challenged their physical and emotional resources and resilience. Thousands of Cambodian refugees, of whom approximately 138,000 are children, still live in a state of limbo in such camps, uncertain about their futures (UNICEF: 1990).

Although the United States contributed significantly to the disruption of Cambodia (Shawcross 1979, and Senator Solarz, on the TV program "20/20" January 8, 1989), the United States government was at first reluctant to resettle Cambodians because officials feared that any resettlement program would rapidly escalate into general immigration, given the miserable conditions inside Cambodia. Instead, "the U.S. government had always preferred to focus resources on aiding the politically more important Vietnamese" (Tollefson 1989: 4–7).

Despite the fears expressed by American policy makers, the narrators in this book, like most Cambodians, were unaware of the economic or technological conditions of the United States, or its social or cultural values. Many Khmer refugees came here more or less by accident, when their applications to emigrate to France were rejected. Others came because the United States was non-Communist, or because it was a large country, with more space for outsiders. To date, there are some 150,000 Khmer refugees in the United States, who were admitted only after intense lobbying by the Citizens' Commission on Indochinese Refugees in 1978.

When Khmer refugees first arrived in America, they were a part of a large influx of Indochinese refugees from the neighboring countries of Vietnam and Laos, who also fled when their countries fell to the Communists. Khmer culture and history were distinctly different from those of their neighbors. Furthermore, as noted previously, the Khmer and the Vietnamese have had a long history of enmity and distrust.

Nevertheless, when they first arrived here, the Khmer were treated the same as other Indochinese refugees because refugee service providers knew little about the differences between Indochinese peoples. This misunderstanding resulted in much hardship for all groups. The Khmer, in particular, faced three problems: first, they had no knowledge of English, and so could not communicate their needs; second, most of them had not been exposed to Western behavior, beliefs, laws, or technology prior to their arrival here; and third, they did not have a group of people who had already established themselves in the United States who could provide support to newly arrived refugees.

The narratives in this book provide striking examples of how these three problems affect the adjustment of Khmer refugees in the United States.

CHAPTER TEN

Niseth: A College Student

Niseth, a slight woman, is just over five feet tall. Her assumed name is the Khmer term for a university student, which she is. With short black hair parted in the middle, she looks much less than her 27 years. In fact, she looks almost like a happy-go-lucky teenager, and if I had not listened to her narrative, I would never have guessed that she is a survivor of the Khmer Rouge regime, and of the awful conditions in the refugee camps.

Niseth sat across from me at the kitchen table in her parents' home, gazing at me steadily with her gentle black eyes. She had made tea for both of us, but after three hours of narration, her cup of tea sat untouched in front of her. Her hands remained folded on her lap, and her voice, though emotional at times, remained soft.

In interviewing Niseth, I was struck by her ability to remain calm and collected, and her ability to retain a balanced outlook, even when she described the most horrible events of her life. This enabled me to inquire about her experiences with more ease than I had been able to with any of the other narrators.

When her family was evacuated by the Khmer Rouge, they were sent to live in the wilderness with tribal peoples. Niseth's account of this experience contrasts with Vickery's view about the hostility of tribal peoples to the "New People" (1984). Her family's escape from the country, and the ultimate reunion in the United States with their father, occurred as a result of many remarkable coincidences.

Niseth's memories of life before the Khmer Rouge provide an informative account of how Cambodian children were socialized. Twenty years later, the influence of this early training on her is especially striking in her attitude toward the roles of teachers and students.

When she described her flight to freedom after years of confinement in Cambodia and in Thailand, I could almost see Niseth's wide-eyed wonder as she drank in the sights around her. When they arrived in the United States, however, Niseth and her family were almost back where they started; in a tiny apartment in a crime-ridden neighborhood, like most other refugees. Niseth was luckier than most, however, because her father's miraculous survival enabled them to improve their standard of living. They now live in a spacious home in a secluded, quiet area, and it was here that I met her.

In recording her story, what impressed me most was the fact that Niseth displays no desire for revenge against the Khmer Rouge who disrupted her life. On the contrary, her story is one of coming to terms with the experience through courage and humility. But I believe the most striking thing about Niseth is her efforts to understand others by understanding herself, from the time she lived with the tribal people to her present adjustment in the United States. ❖❖❖

A Veterinarian's Daughter

My parents are ethnic Cambodians who lived in Kratie province near the Cambodia-Vietnam border. My dad was a veterinarian who worked for the government, and we had a house, a gardener, and a chauffeur given to us by the government. My mom was a housewife.

Kratie was a rural place, so before the Communist regime, every time she was pregnant, my mom went to Phnom Penh to have her babies because that is where they had the best hospitals. I was born there in 1962, and when I was two weeks old, Mom took me back to Kratie.

I am the second child in our family. I have an older sister, two younger brothers, and one younger sister. My older sister lived in Phnom Penh, with my grandparents from my mom's side. Because they never asked her to do any work, she became a spoiled kid, just like my brother, born just after me. He was spoiled by my parents because he was their first son. I remember he had all kinds of toys and games, and when he cried, saying, "I don't want to go to school," my parents gave him money so he would go! Only my youngest brother was not born in Phnom Penh. He was born in Preah Vihear during the Communist time. I often forget he is in the family because he was the very last son, the very small, unexpected child.

Though we lived in the town, our house, like all other houses in the area, was built on stilts because the Mekong River flowed through our province and flooded during the rainy season. The Mekong was a very beautiful river, and to get to it, all I had to do was to cross the road in front of our house and walk down the path. But Mom, who was afraid of water because she couldn't swim, forbade us to go near the river without an adult. So although I loved the river, I didn't get the chance to play in it as often as I would have liked.

I think most of the people who lived in Kratie were ethnic Khmer, but I remember seeing a lot of Chinese people too. Our town had one hospital, a paper factory where many people worked, a city hall, a big open market, and one big school. My siblings and I went to that school, which had all grade levels right up to high school in the same compound. We had the French system of education, but I learned all my lessons in Khmer.

I had many friends at school, and I loved to jump rope at recess. Although I was not as good a student as my brother, I never failed the end-of-the-year examination we had to pass to be promoted to the next level. I remember we had to memorize stories to relate in front of the class. I didn't mind that, but I hated it when one teacher made me dance too. I was not a good dancer, but I couldn't refuse to do it because my parents always told us that we should respect the teacher.

"You always listen to the teachers and do whatever they ask you to do," my parents said. "When you go to another place, you belong to someone else. When you go to school, you belong to the teachers, and you must not do anything bad or disrespectful to them," they told us; and that was how Cambodian parents taught their children to behave.

After I came back from school, I sometimes played with a doctor's children who lived behind our house. That was the only place Mom allowed me to go by myself because she didn't like children going out on the street alone. Even to buy candy at the market, I had to go with someone. But since my parents were always busy, I ended up staying home much of the time. I really didn't mind that, though, because when Dad went to the capital, he brought back dolls and toy cars imported from Japan or Taiwan, and my aunts and uncles brought me dolls from Europe, so I had many toys to play with. I also had a lot of inexpensive jewelry, made of stone.

I helped Mom with housework only if she asked, which was seldom, because she thought it was her job to cook and take care of the family. Once in a while she told me to pound lemongrass with a mortar and pestle for a vegetable soup. I disliked doing it because pounding took up too much energy, and I hated that soup too! But Cambodians like lemongrass, because they believe it has medicinal value. When people get a high fever or a bad cold, they boil lemongrass and drink that water.

Since Mom doesn't expect me to help in the kitchen even now, I haven't learned how to cook Cambodian food. Nor do I know how to care for young children, because she never asked me to take care of my younger siblings. Most daughters know how to do these things, and I am embarrassed because I don't.

In Kratie, my parents had friends among other government employees, but we had no relatives there. So we came to Phnom Penh for the New Year, and for other holidays. It took us more than half a day to reach the capital from the province because we had to wait for the ferry to cross the river. The ferries were big, and usually carried about thirty cars, in addition to the people.

My grandparents had a large two-story house with about nine rooms in Phnom Penh. A big kitchen adjoined the house, and next to it was a three-car garage. There were mangoes, jackfruit, coconut, and many more trees in the garden.

My grandmother stayed home all her life taking care of children, but she had a very easy life because she had servants to work for her. Sometimes she did some gardening, but nothing that was really hard work. My grandfather was the mayor of a small city, and he had a smaller house there too.

I loved coming to Phnom Penh for the New Year. On the first day of the New Year all of us went to the temple. My grandparents took food to share with other people who came there, and after we finished eating, we played lots of games.

On the second day, many relatives came to my grandparents' house, and when we finished eating all kinds of delicious food and fruit, my grandmother told many funny stories while all of us grandchildren sat around her on the floor. My favorite was about an old lady and a rabbit. It went like this:

THE OLD LADY AND THE RABBIT

There was an old lady who went to town daily, to sell rice and bananas. One day, as she walked along a narrow path with her basket of rice and bananas on her head, she met a rabbit who asked her, "Can you give me a ride to the city?" The lady said "OK," and sat the rabbit on top of the bananas. But as she got close to the city, the rabbit hopped out of the basket and ran away. When she got to the city, she discovered that the rabbit had eaten all her bananas. She felt sad and angry, but it was too late to do anything.

We all laughed when Grandmother told us these stories, but many of them taught us lessons. They taught us such things as we should not lie or cheat people, and that we should show respect to older people. I think the rabbit story taught us that we should not trust strangers.

I also liked to come to my grandparents' house because they had five dogs and plenty of puppies. They kept all those puppies because when they tried to give them away, no one wanted them. I would have taken them to Kratie, but my mom didn't like animals.

When I was about nine years old the Communists started shooting and bombing in Kratie. Dad said, "It is not going to be easy for the government to win this war."

When the situation began to get really bad, he stayed in Kratie because he had to do his job, but sent us back to the capital. Two weeks after we left, the Communists took over our province and put Dad in jail. However, they soon found out that Dad was a veterinarian who had nothing to do with politics, and that he did not harm people but helped them; so they released him.

After that Dad did not want to stay in Kratie. He asked the government for a new placement, and they moved him to Kompong Cham province, which was a lot closer to Phnom Penh. But when the Communists came closer to Kompong Cham, he resigned from his job and came to live with us, jobless. The government did not like it when he resigned, and announced over the radio: "The veterinarian in Kompong Cham province resigned and went to join the Communists."

Luckily, they didn't mention his name, and a friend found him a new position in a bank. Though he was glad to find work, he now earned a much smaller salary.

The youngest of four children, Dad was raised in Takeo province, very close to Vietnam. His parents were extremely poor rice farmers who eked out a living by saving some of their rice harvest to feed the family, and by selling or exchanging the other part for meat, vegetables, and clothes. Although his brothers and sister grew up to be farmers like their parents because they believed it was enough to have a family and a farm, even as a youngster Dad thought, "Farming is a very poor way to live. It's not enough for me."

Dad pestered his parents to send him to school, so he could get educated and find a different job when he grew up. But they couldn't afford it, and besides, they needed his help on the farm. He next pestered the Buddhist nuns who often visited his house to let him live in the temple with them so he could learn to read and write. He wanted to go with them also because at the temple, unlike his home, there were all kinds of food to eat. He continued to beg the nuns to take him with them, until one day the nun who loved him the most decided to do so. His parents let him go because they knew that if their son became a monk, he would be one of the most educated people in the village, and like other people in my country, they believed that by becoming a monk, he would bring them merit.

The nun looked after Dad as if she was his second mother until he reached his twelfth year, when he left her to live with the monks at another temple.

Dad was a good student, and when he was about sixteen years old, he won a government scholarship that enabled him to leave the village and go to a government school in Phnom Penh. There, too, he still lived a very poor life, though now at the temple of a monk known to his former teacher in Takeo. Later, he won another scholarship and went to live in a dormitory where the government looked after all his needs.

After my dad got his diploma, his friend, who was my mom's neighbor, introduced him to her family. Cambodian girls usually got married when they were about twenty years old, but because Mom had not liked the lieutenant her parents proposed for her, she still lived at home, helping to take care of her younger siblings.

When she met Dad, Mom liked him even though he came from a poor family. Most rich people in the city would not have liked their daughter to marry a poor man, but my grandfather understood that while Dad was poor, he had more gumption than some rich kids; he came from a village to the capital, went to school, and got his degree. So they let Mom marry him.

When the Communists started fighting in Takeo, Dad brought his parents to live in Phnom Penh. So even though I never went to his village, I lived with his parents at my other grandparents' house for a couple of years. Dad's parents were very old, and my mom cooked for them and took care of all their needs. Her sisters looked after her parents, who were younger and healthier.

My dad's parents were very unhappy in the city. When they lived in the village, they got up early in the morning, went to the rice field, and worked until dusk. Now, they couldn't go anywhere and lived in a small room with nothing to do. Often, I heard them tell Dad, "Take us back to Takeo. We have a home there, we have land there, we have children there. We want to go back to the village."

But Dad told them, "You can't go now because the Communists took over the province. It's not your land anymore."

My grandfather died two years after he came to Phnom Penh, and my grandmother died a year after the Khmer Rouge takeover.

I was very happy in Phnom Penh because I had always wanted to live with my grandparents in their big house. I went to school with lots of other kids who had come from provinces that were taken over by the Communists. Of my new friends, the closest was a professor's daughter, but after the evacuation, I never saw her again.

At this time, there were lots of very poor refugees too in Phnom Penh. The kids wore rags, or went naked, and they picked food in the trash heaps, or walked from house to house, begging. Although my grandparents wanted to help them, money had become tight after Grandfather retired, so they couldn't give much.

Schools closed in early 1975 because the Communists started bombing the city, and we stopped going to the beach or visiting people, and only went to the market. But food was scarce and expensive because the farmers were unable to travel. Dad knew that the Communists had a lot of power, and that poor people wanted to be equal with the rich people. He always believed that the people would one day defeat the government, and they did, when the Khmer Rouge took over.

The Evacuations

The day Khmer Rouge came to Phnom Penh, my parents' voices were thick with tension as they repeatedly ordered us, "Stay inside the house and be quiet!" We could hear the voices of people outside on the boulevard that bordered our house, but because of a screen of palm trees, we couldn't see much of what was going on. But we knew when the Khmer Rouge entered the city, because the people started cheering and shouting, "We will have peace now!"

My mom believed that too.

The next morning Pol Pot soldiers came to our door and said, "You must leave your house for three days. We have to check it to make sure it is safe, that there are no bombs. This is a temporary move and you can come back here." But they didn't say where we should go. Dad said, "Well, we'll be back soon, so we will just take a change of clothing and some food for the children."

We packed some rice, dozens of eggs from the chickens Dad reared as a sideline, and a few other things, and we left. Our dogs started to jump and bark because they wanted to go with us, but when we tried to take them, the soldiers said, "You cannot bring your dogs with you." I cried, and I saw my grandparents cry too, because we didn't want to leave our dogs, but we had no choice. I guess we knew in our hearts we would never see them again, but we really didn't know for sure.

The boulevard was packed with people, and cars moved only at something like five miles an hour. Dad drove our car while we walked beside it. As night fell we were still on the road, and because we hadn't brought cooking utensils, we broke into a house and took some pots and dishes. Other people did the same because like us, the owners of those houses had left too. We ate some rice with eggs, and slept outside on the street.

We walked with thousands of others for about a week, alongside a big river called Tonle Thom. The soldiers ordered us to keep to the main thoroughfare, and no one was allowed to step into a side street, even to eliminate. So people eliminated out on the streets, and at night, it was nearly impossible to find a clean space to sleep.

The soldiers eventually took us to a village, where they told us to live under a farmer's house, which was built on stilts. But we had to share the space with the cows that the farmer tethered at one end. Since we had run out of food, the farmer gave us some, but it was not enough for our large family. So even though they were hungry too, the older people gave their food to the children. That night, we spread a small sheet of plastic on the ground, and slept with our heads there, and our legs on the ground, while hundreds of mosquitoes bit us all night through.

Right from the next morning, the Communists put us to work. The old people had to weave cloth or baskets by hand, and people like my parents had to work in the fields of corn, which was the main crop there.

I had to go with a team of children and kill the mice that destroyed the corn fields. To do so, we had to throw sharp tools that looked like forks with long handles at the mice. But I was too scared to do it, because I thought I might pierce my own feet, and I never killed a single mouse. I wished I could, though, because the Communists gave us so little food and I was always hungry.

When we were growing up our parents always told us, "Don't kill animals because you will pay for it in your next birth!" But now we were too hungry to be afraid, and when a kid in my team killed a mouse, he cut its head off, peeled the skin, and took the meat home to cook.

Since people did not grow rice in that village we got only corn to eat, like the animals. But because we were not used to digesting large quantities of corn, many people, including my grandmother from Dad's side and my little sister, became sick with very bad stomachaches and diarrhea. They became smaller and smaller and we thought they would die like other people, but luckily, they survived.

We also killed tiny frogs and crabs that lived in the fields, and whenever my grandparents had a bit of free time, they went to the river and caught a few fish. Life was even harder for them than for us because they were too old to walk far to search for food like we did.

Because they were so hungry my mom's parents often got mad at my mother, and accused her of not supporting them in their old age. It was hard for them to understand that she had to do what the Communists ordered her to do, that there was no way for anybody to help others, and that we had to survive on our own.

After about six months, the Khmer Rouge ordered us to pack our things and walk to the riverbank and wait for the ships to go to another village, but we didn't know where we would go. By now, Mom's parents were so mad at her that they decided they would not go with us to the new place.

"You are not supporting us, so why should we go with you?" they asked her angrily.

Mom wanted them to stay with her, but she couldn't promise to look after them. All she could do was to plead with them, saying, "Please don't go, let's just live together and die together."

But my grandparents wouldn't listen to her. They were so angry they could not bear to see her anymore, and they left on a boat with the rest of their family as Mom watched helplessly, and cried, with nothing to say. Later we heard from other people that my grandparents' ship went to Battambang. We were left with just my grandmother from my dad's side.

We were the last shipment that day, and the Communists shipped us like animals to Preah Vihear province. It was a place where city people did not expect to survive, because it was infested with malaria and other diseases.

The ship took three days to reach that place. We were on the lower deck, and so tightly packed that we couldn't move. The soldiers would not allow us to go to the bathrooms, and for the next three days people urinated and defecated where they sat, but they had no way to change their clothing. The soldiers gave us two meals of rice and soup during those three days, and even though we felt desperately hungry, we were so nauseated by the foul smells on the ship that we could not eat. Oh, those three days were more than hell!

On the fourth day, the Khmer Rouge unloaded us in Kompong Thom province, gave us some food, and kept us there for the night. In the morning, they packed us into big trucks that usually carried troops, and we stood for four or five hours until they finally let us out near a temple. We didn't know where we were, and we stayed in the temple for the next three days. At least this time, they gave us food on all three days.

When they were ready to move us again, the soldiers brought an oxcart for each family and told us to put whatever we carried inside. It was the rainy season, and the floodwater came up to my waist, but we were told to walk. Fearing that Grandmother and our little sister would drown, we put them inside the cart along with our things. We had to walk all through the night and I kept stumbling because I was so sleepy. I held on to the cart tightly until we got to the next village, about twenty kilometers away.

The Communists placed each new family with "Old People" in the village. We were not assigned to work, however, because the soldiers did not know where they would be taking us next. We got enough rice and salt to keep us from starving, but we were terrified to live in that village because it was full of leeches, which we had never seen before. Every time we got into the water, they clung to our bodies and sucked our blood until they became bloated and fell off.

After a month or so, the Communists walked all the "New People" back to the temple and loaded us into five trucks and took us deep inside the jungle where there was no village, or even huts. Wherever we looked, there were only trees. "This is your place. Make a village and live here," the soldiers told us, and they drove away, leaving us there.

The next day, some village folk came down to the jungle. When they saw us they said, "You can't live here. You go to the village." We felt very happy to hear that we had a village to live in. The people brought us there and gave us a very good lunch of nicely cooked rice and some beef soup. It was the best meal I had in all those years!

When we finished eating, however, they walked us about thirty kilometers into the countryside, far from the highway, and left us near a building in another village. Soon, a group of children who spoke a different language surrounded us. Some of them were naked, and others wore only shorts. Some girls wore tiny tissues wrapped around their bodies. Their skin was whiter than ours, and I think if they had dressed in a civilized way they would have looked like city people. I didn't know who they were, but my dad knew. He said, "These are Pnong—the mountain people."

I had heard about mountain people but had never met them before. I suppose one can say they are Cambodian, but except for a few old people, they didn't speak Cambodian.

We lived with the Pnong for more than a year. They were not Khmer Rouge soldiers, but they had power over the "New People." They made small huts for us, and when we came back from the fields they gave us food. But instead of rice, their main food was meat. They killed deer, buffalo, tigers, snakes, and all kinds of other wild animals to eat. So although I didn't hunt, I ate wild animal meat, and became like one of them too. If they couldn't find any meat, we didn't get food.

At the beginning we were really scared of the Pnong. I remember thinking, "Oh my God, how can I communicate with them, how can I ask them anything? I don't speak their language!" We thought they were very mean because when they didn't ignore us, they kept interrupting us or imitating our speech. They also made fun of the way we did farm work. The first time I dug potatoes, I dug them sitting down because I had no energy. But the mountain people were very strong, and they dug potatoes standing up, and when they saw me, they crowded around me and poked fun at me, saying, "Look at this girl. She is doing it like this!" They really hurt my feelings.

After a while, the children started to pick up some Cambodian and we began to know them a little better. Then we discovered the Pnong were very good people. Compared to some city people, they were very hospitable and honest. They shared even the smallest piece of meat, and if we lost something they helped us find it. It was as if they had become very close friends.

At that time, I discovered that if you know a little psychology, you understand people. I realized that the Pnong were mean to us at the beginning only because they didn't understand the way we spoke. I can say that we were lucky to be with them rather than in another village with city people who might have treated us differently.

Teenage Years Under the Khmer Rouge

After we had lived with the mountain people for a few months, the Communists sent my brother to a boys' camp, and my older sister and me to a girls' camp, where we had to work with other girls between the ages of twelve and eighteen. They called us the "front-line workers," because we were the strongest people. We worked hard building dams, and planting corn in faraway places. Sometimes we spent days in mosquito-ridden jungles, cutting down trees.

I had never been separated from my parents before, and I yearned to see them. But I saw them only a few times, when our leader permitted us to visit them. I never went to visit my parents without permission, because I had to walk about 40 kilometers through thick jungle to get to their village, and if discovered, I could have been killed. Every time I saw them, I thought my parents were lucky to be alive; so many people had died, and my mom had been so sick, she too had nearly died.

We had lived in the mountains for about a year when the Communists said, "This village does not produce anything. No rice, nothing. We will destroy it."

They moved everybody, including the Pnong, to another village. It was the first time the mountain people had to move from their home, and they were very upset and homesick. But we, city people, didn't really care where the soldiers took us anymore. All we wanted was food to eat.

Our new village was also in Preah Vihear province, but it was in the valley. There were no Pnong there; instead, we now lived with people who practiced true communism. They gave us more food and better clothing, so our living conditions were much better. But they also killed a lot of people who previously had high social status, and many people who came on the trucks with us were killed.

We were again separated from our parents and sent to work at the front line. But this time they made us work much harder, like sixteen hours a day, building dams and planting rice. Usually in Cambodia rice farmers planted only one crop of rice per year, but we had to grow two crops a year, one in the rainy season and another in the summer. So in the summer we planted rice and also built the dam. The dam was about ten feet high and we had no machines; we built it with our bare hands. All the time we built that dam, I was really frightened because if the floodwater had come hard and strong, the dam would have broken and all of us would have drowned.

Once in a while our parents were also sent to the front to build dams. At other times the soldiers let us go to see them for a few hours or to stay with them for one night. Once when I went, I found Mom terribly swollen, and fluid oozed out of her hands. She told me that it was because she didn't get any salt, and that she really craved it. She had once stolen a bit of salt from the kitchen, but a soldier who saw her warned her, saying, "If you do that again, you will not see your children." So she never did that again.

After that, whenever I was sent to the kitchen, I stole rice and especially salt, and hid them till I got a chance to take them to her. Mom cried whenever she saw us, saying, "You take care of yourselves. Don't think much about me."

I always feared that my mom might have died. I knew she was alive only because someone would come from the village to work with us, and tell me how she was. Although I worried about her and Dad, I was too tired and too hungry to miss them too much. All I wanted was enough food and enough sleep. Those were my only wishes.

I never thought I would die of starvation, because even though we didn't get enough to eat, we had more food than my parents. My biggest fear was that the Communists might discover that our dad had been a government worker, and kill all of us. I often thought they suspected him, but they couldn't be sure because Dad was dark-skinned like the farmers. Furthermore, from the beginning of the Khmer Rouge rule, Dad changed his name, and told the soldiers that although he lived in the city, he had worked as a shoemaker. He told us to change our ways too.

"Call me 'Pok' instead of Papa, and call your Mama 'Mai,' because that is what farmers' children call their parents," he told us. The first time I called them Pok and Mai I felt very embarrassed, but he insisted that we do so, especially when he discovered that soldiers spied on us the whole time.

In the new village, the Communists decided when people should marry, and who they should marry. They never ordered me to marry because not only was I young, I was always sick with malarial attacks, and physically small. The Communists made fun of me, saying, "This kid looks like a skeleton!" But my sister looked healthier, and they ordered her to marry one of their people. She didn't object because she didn't want to die, but she was devastated. Luckily for her, the man they ordered her to marry didn't like her, so she was free, at least for a while.

With time, the old leader of our village became very fond of my sister. He wished to have her as his daughter-in-law, but he wanted to wait until his son was a little older. In the meantime, he looked after us well, and gave us things that we hadn't even seen since we had left after the evacuation: nice clothes, shoes, and even toothpaste and toothbrushes! Till then, we had cleaned our teeth with ashes. Even though the shoes were the black sandals the Communists made from old tires, we were very happy to get them, because they protected our feet from splinters in the jungle. I am sure the other girls in the group felt jealous of us, but what could they do? We were all under the Communists.

Although we cheated at times just to survive, my sister and I usually did whatever the Communists asked us to do, and the Communists made me a group leader, responsible for six other girls. My job was to hold meetings to tell them about communism. Instead, I told them, "If you will not let anybody know, I am willing to use this time to find something to eat." They all agreed, so we never had a meeting. We were very lucky, because nobody found out about it.

All the time we were under the Communists, I was very angry and longing to fight back, but of course I didn't because I did not want to sacrifice my life! By now, of the people who came on the trucks, there were only three families left. One was a policeman's family, one was a soldier's family, and the other was our family.

The next time I saw Dad, he told me that one day, the policeman and the soldier complained at a meeting, saying, "When you say we have enough to eat, what do you mean? Only the 'Old People' have enough. They can grow their own food and eat it. We grow the food, but we cannot eat it. We have nothing, nothing at all."

When they finished, the village leader said, "Two people have spoken out. There is still one more. If you want to say something, just say it."

My dad knew they were talking to him and he felt really frightened, but he said nothing. The next day the two who spoke up disappeared. Fortunately for us, two or three months after that incident the Vietnamese took over the country and everybody was released.

The Vietnamese Liberation

We never expected the Vietnamese. One morning we woke up to find that the Pol Pots had disappeared, and other people at the dam site told us that they ran for their lives because the Vietnamese came.

"Let's get back to the village," said my sister, and we left immediately. When we reached our hut we found that our brother too had come back, and Dad, who was with the fishing team, returned in the afternoon. At last, our whole family was together again.

Everyone in the village rejoiced that we were finally free from the Khmer Rouge! But Dad was worried about what the Vietnamese would do, because they had always been our enemies. He decided that we should escape into the jungle. He said to other villagers, "If you live in the village, the Vietnamese might come and kill you. We are going to the jungle, and if you come along, you might survive."

The people listened to Dad because he was one of the few older people left, and about twenty families came with us to go to the jungle.

On the way there, Dad said, "We might not find food and water in the jungle. Why don't we go down to the rice field? It's harvesttime, but there's nobody to gather the crop." So we went to the rice field.

Next morning, Dad, who spoke simple Vietnamese, decided to go back to the village to see what was happening there, and to get some sugarcane for the children. He tied a white handkerchief on an ox cart to show he had surrendered to the Vietnamese, and left with my sister.

On the way, he met some Vietnamese troops who told him, "We have defeated the Khmer Rouge. People are now free to return to their homes." So he came back and said, "The Vietnamese have changed their policies, and we can now go back to the village." We all gathered our things and returned to the village.

Mom obtained a temporary hut for our family, and we tried to grow some potatoes and other vegetables to make a living. But Dad could not trust the Vietnamese. He always expected they would harm us because that is what had happened throughout our history, and he was also afraid that if the Communists knew this village belonged to the Vietnamese, they would come and kill everybody. We were between the two enemies.

The Vietnamese chose Dad to be the new village leader, but he said he didn't want the job. So they gave the position to his friend, but brought Dad to the Preah Vihear town and made him the leader of the whole province. But something inside Dad told him he should never trust the Vietnamese. He told them, "I want to help you, but I do not want a position in the government." The Vietnamese let him come home, but Dad began to fear that they would hurt him because he refused to do what they asked.

About two weeks after he came back he said to Mom, "I want to escape from this place, but I don't want to take the family because it's too dangerous. I am not sure that I will survive, but if I do, I'll get you out too. In the meantime, you must take care of the children."

Mom was really upset, but there was nothing she could do. She had nothing to give him, except the only picture we had left, of my brother.

"Why don't you take this with you? If you survive, send the picture back as a sign that you are alive," she said, and gave it to Dad.

He left the next night. We didn't want anyone in the village to know that he had escaped, but we couldn't stop crying. It was such a hard time for our family!

We didn't know what had happened to Dad. It was as if he had just disappeared into the night. Soon everybody in the village knew he was gone, but when people asked, we said, "We don't know what has happened to him. One day he went to the jungle to find some food, and never returned."

The villagers were suspicious, though, because at that time the Sereika freedom fighters had started fighting near the border, and they thought he had gone to join them (see Chapter 1). The Vietnamese soldiers also suspected that, and two soldiers followed us around to find out what had happened to Dad. They even slept under our hut at night. We pretended everything was normal, and that we were just trying to get by, like any other family. When they couldn't discover what they wanted, they finally left us alone.

A month or two after Dad left, Mom found out she was pregnant. There was not even a nurse in the village, and she really couldn't face it.

"Why did he leave me like this?" she cried bitterly every night. My older sister tried to console her, saying, "Mom, this was unexpected. You can't blame him. If he knew he wouldn't have gone, and we all agreed to let him go."

When Mom became stronger, my sister asked the Vietnamese if she could become a nurse. They said yes, and sent Sister to a school in town for six months. After she came back she helped other sick people in the village, and when Mom went into labor, she delivered my youngest brother—the first baby she ever delivered.

I didn't help my sister because I was afraid to stay in the room, but I watched through the bamboo slats. When the baby came out he didn't cry, and Mom thought he was dead. But my sister took him by his feet and spanked him! I saw water come out of the baby's mouth, and he started to cry, and I heard Mom say, "Oh, he is alive!"

I never expected the baby to survive, though, because my mother had no nourishment when she was pregnant, and he was so tiny, he was even smaller than a chicken! And now, Mom was upset because she didn't have enough milk for him.

Return to Phnom Penh

Two weeks after the baby was born, Mom decided she wanted to return to Phnom Penh, but we didn't know how we could do it. We were far away from the capital, and only my sister knew the way from Preah Vihear to Phnom Penh because when she went to the town to learn nursing, she saw the highway going there. We didn't want anybody in the village to know about our plan to escape, but it was impossible to leave secretly, because of the baby. While we were wondering how we could go, some Vietnamese soldiers that my sister knew came to the village in a truck.

"We want to go to Preah Vihear town to visit friends for two or three days," Sister told them.

"Is your whole family going? Do you need a ride?" asked one soldier.

"Yes, we're all going."

The soldier said he would take us to town. We took just a few things because we didn't want to arouse suspicion, and we all got into the truck. When they saw us with the soldiers, the village people were curious. One old lady climbed into the truck and asked my sister, "Where are you going with the soldiers? Aren't you afraid? And your mom has a small baby too." She was worried because she didn't trust the Vietnamese.

"Oh, we're just going to the next village to get some medicine from a friend," Sister replied, and said goodbye to her. Nobody knew we left the village that day hoping never to come back.

My sister had made a few friends in town, and she went to one family and confided that we wanted to go to Phnom Penh because we had relatives there. They understood because they were also city people like us. They said, "You can spend the night here, and try to get a ride from someone taking food to Kompong Thom in the morning."

Next morning Mom took out some gold she had managed to save from the Pol Pots and paid a bit of it to a truck driver traveling to Kompong Thom, to take us there. In Kompong Thom my sister located another friend, and she too helped us to get a ride, this time to Phnom Penh!

We were so lucky, every step we took turned out to be right, and we got back by truck to Phnom Penh, in just three days! It's still like a dream. Had we tried to walk, I don't think we would have ever made it because of the baby. And we would never have escaped from Preah Vihear, if not for Sister.

I saw my birthplace again after more than three years. The city was a shambles, and my grandmother's house that I had thought was so big did not seem very big anymore. Parts of the roof and walls were gone, and some strangers lived in it now. I didn't feel I belonged there anymore, and neither did my family. We looked at it a while, then left without going in.

My sister had heard that my mom's aunt had survived the Communist regime too, and that she had returned to the capital, but when we hired a cyclo and went to her house, that too was occupied by strangers. We did not know what to do. The driver, who must have felt sorry for us, said that he would take us anywhere we wanted to go. We told him to drive around the city, hoping to find someone we knew, and suddenly, we saw our great-aunt, who we called Grandmother also, sitting on a bench by the roadside! We couldn't believe our luck!

Grandmother took us to a room she rented in a small building nearby, and the Vietnamese guards gave permission for us to share it with her. Her husband worked for the Vietnamese. Mom's younger brother had survived and lived with her too, but he told us that Mom's parents and five of her brothers and sisters had died under Pol Pot.

Grandmother had a lot of contacts in Phnom Penh, and she found me a job in a nearby factory, where I had to produce about 38 bicycle tires a day. I earned 24 kilos of rice and 100 riel a month, but things were so expensive that all we could buy for the 100 riel was 2 kilos of beef. I got very tired doing my job because I had to stand all day, but it was still better than working in the "front lines"!

My sister sold some jewelry belonging to my mom, and bought sugar, condensed milk, and other foodstuffs and sold them in the market.

We survived in Phnom Penh for a year, but every month, we spent all our earnings just to buy food. Mom was really worried, and kept on saying, "We can't survive like this. One day we will run out of money and die because we have nobody to help us."

The Escape

We didn't know who he was. A man, carrying a tiny picture, had come to Mom's friend's house and asked, "Do you know anything about this family? I heard they are living in Phnom Penh now."

It was my brother's picture that Mom had given Dad, the night he escaped! Mom's friend recognized my brother, but she didn't want to bring the man to us at once, in case the guy had come to say our dad had died. "Why do you want to find this family?" she asked, but he refused to tell her. Because she wanted to protect us she said, "If you don't tell me the reason, I'll not let you meet them."

The guy told her, "I want to meet them because their father survived!"

My sister and I heard the news when we got back from work: Dad had survived, and we had a chance to escape! Oh, we were so happy and excited. Mom wanted to leave that very minute, but the guy said, "Don't be so rushed. Escaping from Cambodia is very risky. It might destroy the whole family." Mom disagreed. She said, "We must escape tomorrow. It's the first day of New Year, and everybody will be celebrating. There will be lots of people on the road, and no one would care about people traveling." The guy agreed, and said he will try to hire a truck to take us to the border.

Mom asked her youngest brother if he wanted to escape with us but he said, "This is a very risky thing to do. You don't know this person. Don't trust him."

"I don't think that the guy would lie. He has the proof, the one and only picture. If you don't want to go, you can stay, but my family has to go. We can't live like this, not knowing what will happen tomorrow," Mom replied. Finally, Uncle decided to come with us.

That night we could hardly sleep. We felt so happy, and yet so frightened. We planned to do something nobody should find out about, not even Grandmother, because her husband worked for the Vietnamese.

The next morning, Mom told her that we would celebrate New Year at her friend's house. Grandmother asked, "Why don't you celebrate here?"

"Well, their house is a little bigger, so the children can have more fun. And my friend will bring the monks to her house."

"OK, you can go, and I will take care of things here," Grandmother said. We left without even saying goodbye to Grandmother properly.

We stayed the night at Mom's friend's house, waiting for the morning to come.

At four o'clock the next morning, we walked down to the truck-parking place near the train station to hire a truck going toward the border, but there were none. With every ray of sunlight, Mom began to panic. "When morning comes we cannot leave from here because people will see us," she told the guy. "Why don't we go by train to Battambang?" The guy thought it was a good idea. We bought tickets and got on the train.

When the train reached Battambang, we hired an ox cart to get to the border. When we had got quite close to the border, two guys stopped our cart. One of them pointed a gun at us.

"Put the baby down, and give us everything you have," he said. We were very frightened.

"This family is poor. They have nothing. They just want to go to the camp because they have no money to live in the city, and the camp provides food and clothes," Dad's guy told the robber. But he paid no attention.

He ordered us to pull our clothes down, and began to check Mom to see if she was hiding anything on her body. She had only two diamonds left, and she had hidden them in the baby's diaper. But the diaper was stinking so much that the robbers never asked to see it. While he was still checking Mom, there was a sudden burst of gunshots in the distance, and the two men fled, taking with them a small bag in which we had put some clothes.

Along came two Vietnamese soldiers, shooting at the air; they were patrolling the border. When they saw us they asked, "Where are you going?" Dad's guy said, "Oh, we are going to the camp to get some food. We thought we could also get some milk for the baby." My mom thought they might order us to go back home, but they said, "You can go, but be careful. There's a lot of shooting going on and you might get killed." We thanked them and went on our way.

My dad's friend didn't take us to a normal refugee camp. Instead, he took us to a Sereika camp, saying it had more protection. The soldiers gave us a place to stay, and said that Dad would come but they didn't know when.

We lived there for three months waiting for our dad, and although he sent us letters he never came. The soldiers looked after us well, and gave us space in the trenches to sleep at night. But during the day there was so much bombing and shooting that we expected each new day would be our last.

The first time I saw him I ran across the field to meet my dad, but when I reached him I was crying, and didn't know what to say. We were meeting for the first time since he left that night in Preah Vihear, and everyone, even Mom, ran out and dragged him and pulled him inside the hut. We had so many emotions, but we didn't have enough words to express our feelings, and for a while, we just hugged him and cried. When we settled down, Dad gave us all kinds of very delicious Cambodian foods he had brought, and the whole family shared them. While we ate, my dad told us what happened to him after he left us.

Dad had joined the Sereika freedom fighters, just as everybody at Preah Vihear suspected. Their mission was to bring supplies to the Cambodian soldiers, and Dad asked one soldier who was going deep into Cambodia to look for us. He went to the village where we lived, but we were gone. When Dad heard that, he had first thought that the Vietnamese had killed us because he left the village; but he had not wanted to give up hope that we might be still alive.

When Khao-I-Dang camp opened in Thailand, Dad posted our names there, hoping we might have reached the camp. In the meantime, Mom's sister had escaped to Khao-I-Dang camp, and she saw his notice, and contacted him. But she didn't know what had happened to us. A few months later my aunt met my mom's friend's son at Khao-I-Dang, and he told her that we had come back to Phnom Penh, but he didn't know where we lived. So Dad sent the guy who helped us to escape to look for us.

Dad wanted to come to see us from the time he heard we had reached a refugee camp, but his leader refused to give him permission to cross the border, saying, "Your family is in a camp, and they are being cared for. You have nothing to worry about." Dad kept trying, and finally, he gave permission for Dad to stay with us for one night. So the following morning, he went back to his group.

A few days later, Dad returned to take us to another camp. It took us half a night to walk to the first resting place because of the baby, and Dad was really worried in case one of the kids stepped on a mine and blew up the whole family. The second base was at least another three nights' walk, and Dad didn't want to risk it. He appealed to a Thai colonel, "Please find a truck to take us to the next resting place." The colonel, who treated my dad well because Dad spoke Thai, did so.

The truck took only five hours to get us to the second Sereika base camp. The soldiers there treated Dad with a lot of respect, and their families cooked us a special dinner. That night, for the first time since leaving home in 1975, we slept peacefully, and we even got nice mattresses! The next day, we said goodbye to all those people and left for Suren camp in Thailand.

Suren camp was controlled by Americans, and refugees needed permits to enter it. Without them, the Thai soldiers said they could not admit us to the camp. Since we did not have permits, Dad knew he had to give the guards a large enough bribe. But Dad, who worked for the Sereika, didn't have a lot of money. "Why don't we sell the two rings I have and get the money?" said Mom. One was the wedding ring Dad had given her. But because there was no other alternative Dad sold the rings and got just enough money to get us into camp. And once we had got in, nobody could force us out.

Refugee Camps

The people who lived in Suren were mostly those who had escaped from Battambang before Pol Pot took our country, and many had lived there for a long time and spoke Thai and Cambodian. When they saw us the next morning they crowded around us asking, "Where have these people come from?" The soldier who was taking care of us explained that we escaped across the border, and asked them to help us. So those people helped us to get food, as well as the permit to live in the camp.

We got into that camp just in time, because about three weeks later, the Americans decided to move the refugees elsewhere and close it down.

Mom decided to apply for resettlement in a third country, but we didn't know where to go. First, Dad told us to go to France because he had a friend there, and a lot of Cambodians went there. But then he heard about America, and he said it was a good place for his children because it had better education and opportunities. Mom said, "This is our lucky time; the right time for us to secure a good future," and she applied to come to America.

Dad would not come with us because he still had to serve our country. He told Mom, "Right now, all I want is the family to be safe. I will come to America later." We got ready for our interviews, memorizing information such as our dates of births, and our parents' and grandparents' names. When the Americans called us, our interpreter turned out to be the man who first told my dad that we had escaped to Phnom Penh! He was very happy and surprised to see us, but pretended not to know us because he didn't want his boss to get us another interpreter.

We passed the interview, and the next day we got our pictures. Soon after that, we were moved to Chunburi camp to wait for resettlement in a third country. "This is it," we thought excitedly, "We're on our way!" But we felt sad because Dad wasn't coming with us.

We expected to remain in Chunburi for only a short while, but we ended up living there for six months. Though better than Pol Pot's camps, Chunburi too was like a jail. We couldn't do what we wanted, or go anywhere we wanted; instead, we had to live in the small room that each family was given in a bamboo building.

Living in the camp was terrible! We could see people fighting and crying through the bamboo slats, and babies cried all through the night. The restrooms were so dirty and smelly that we had to force ourselves to use them, especially to take baths. Day after day, the camp workers gave us the very basic foods: rice, salt, and *kratu* fish. Some refugees had relatives in third countries who sent them money, so they bought food from other vendors. But Dad made just enough money to support himself, and we had no relatives who lived in third countries. So every day we were stuck with eating that fish that nobody ordinarily ate because it was so tasteless. We tried to have some variety by making fish soup one day, and fried or curried fish the next day, but they always tasted the same! In a way, it was better to be poor in the camp: many refugees were robbed in Chunburi, but nobody bothered us because just by looking at our clothes, they could see we had nothing.

The only good thing in camp was that we learned English two days a week. I learned to say a few sentences like, "Hi, how are you?" On days I didn't go to school, I cleaned our room, and learned how to crochet from a lady in the next room. I made a small pillow cover, but it took me four or five weeks to finish it because I never learned quite how to hold the needle, and I quit learning crochet.

When Mom's sister went to America and sponsored us, the officials moved us to a transit camp. After two weeks, our name was called to get on the bus going to Lumpini camp in Bangkok, from where refugees were put on planes to leave for their new countries. We were told that we would stay in Lumpini for a week, and that we would go directly to the U.S.A. without going to the Philippines like some other refugees.

But the night we were supposed to leave, my baby brother got a fever, and the guards gave our seats to the family who lived in the next room, even though we still wanted to go. That family probably bribed those guards, but since we were too poor to do that, we had to stay back.

Lumpini camp was infested with mice, and we could see them running all over the sacks of rice. At Lumpini, unlike Chunburi, other people cooked for us. I don't think they ever even bothered to wash the rice before they cooked it, because when we ate, the rice smelled of mice. Sometimes we even found mice feces in the cooked rice. It was so gross! But we had to eat it because we had nothing else.

"Oh God! If we stay here for one more week, we are going to get so sick that we will never be able to leave. We will be sent back to the other camp," Mom kept crying every day.

We got some new neighbors who had money. They must have felt sorry for us for they gave my brother bananas and other food they bought from the vendors, and he began to recover. At last our name was called to get on a plane to America, and we said goodbye to all the miserable suffering we had gone through, and began to look forward to the new things that would happen in our lives.

Flight to Freedom

It was only when we went by bus to the airport that I first saw the big Thai city. It was so beautiful, with big buildings, hundreds of lights, and a big airport! We got to the airport about eleven that night. We were very tired, but nobody could sleep because we were so excited!

When the morning came the people who were taking care of us gave us some food, and at last we climbed into the plane. I was crying again because I was so happy; it was like saying goodbye to a bad dream.

There were about 100 refugees on the plane. Some were Vietnamese and Laotians, and when the plane took off, many people, including my older sister, got sick. "I am so out of breath, I can't breathe," my sister kept moaning. I tried to encourage her, saying, "Just hold on, you'll be okay. Try to sleep." But she was very sick.

It took two days for the plane to reach San Francisco. As it came lower and lower, we could see the whole city, filled with lights. I will always remember that beautiful sight!

We landed about 5:30 in the morning. It was dark and raining, and the wind was very cold. We put on the big jackets people had given us before we got on the plane, and got off.

"Wow, what a big airport, Mom!" I said, as we walked to the building, where we hoped that Mom's sister would be waiting for us. We didn't see her. We waited all day. Many families came to meet their relatives and friends, but nobody came for us.

In the evening, the people taking care of refugees brought us to a camp on top of a hill in Oakland, and gave us some very tasty soup and bread sandwiches. The soup was Cambodian because the older people liked that, but the sandwiches were American. I ate a big sandwich with different meats in it. I had never tasted food like that before, but I loved it. It was so good!

After we ate, the people took us up to a large room on the fifth floor of a very tall building. It had two big beds with nice mattresses, and my family went to sleep.

I stood near the window, and looked at Oakland city lights until it was like 3:30 in the morning, when Mom woke up and said, "You didn't go to sleep?"

I said, "No, I feel so excited, Mom. I've never seen a view like this from the top of a building before; it's like looking down from heaven!" Mom called me to sleep, and I went to bed, feeling really happy.

In the morning we had a shower in a nice restroom, and went back to the airport because the people said from there we could get another bus to San Jose, where my aunt lived. We waited all morning, and at lunchtime, the people gave each of us a piece of sandwich for lunch. But it was so little that when the bus came in the afternoon I was still hungry.

We were the only refugee family going on the bus. The driver asked my uncle, "Where are you going?" My uncle said, "Go to San Jose," but he said it like the way you would pronounce it in French, and the driver said, "San Jose? I don't know where that is. Can you repeat?" My uncle repeated it two or three times and by now we were all laughing. At last the driver understood, and he said, "We pronounce it *San Hosai.*" We got to "San Hosai," and my aunt was waiting there to meet us, because the people who look after refugees had called her.

My aunt and uncle were on welfare, and lived in a two-bedroom apartment with their three children. We too lived with them until Mom also got welfare and rented the apartment downstairs.

A few months after we came here, a Cambodian worker at the refugee service place fell in love with my older sister. The guy had not even finished high school, and she was only a sophomore in high school, but she wanted to quit school and marry him. Dad wrote to her, saying, "I sent you to that country so you can have a good education and good opportunities. You should go to school," and Mom said, "You are too young, and he's really not the type of person I want my daughters to marry." But my sister would not listen to Mom.

My sister grew up with my grandparents, and perhaps because of that, she was never very close to Mom, except when she delivered my brother. Even then, there was still something inside them, some differences that made them distant. I think Mom is a good mother and my sister is a good daughter, but when we came here she never got along with my mom. She always got mad and said things my mom didn't like. She insisted on getting married. Mom let her go. After the marriage, her husband moved into our apartment, and he helped us a lot.

My mom applied for my dad to come to America as a political refugee. As we went to the airport to meet him we felt very happy and safe, because this time, we were meeting Dad forever; nothing was going to break us apart again.

When he came, Dad had to find work immediately, because when Mom sponsored him she promised that he would not accept welfare. He found a job picking fruit and vegetables on a farm for 35 cents an hour, and soon our whole family, like most other refugee families, picked produce too. Though fruit picking was not something we would have chosen to do if we had even a little money, farm work here was much better than what we had to do in the Pol Pot time! We all worked hard, and after a few months we had saved $1,000! With that, Dad bought our first car, a very old Pontiac.

We continued to work, and started to get good offers from the farmer. Once he gave us a big field of cucumber to pick, and paid $25 for each bin we filled. The bins were very large, but if we filled four bins, we got $100! Everybody except my youngest brother worked from early morning until dark, and little by little, we had enough savings to buy a second car and to search for new jobs.

Dad got a small job at a veterinary place that paid $4.50 an hour, and Mom and I found assembly-line work in two electronics companies. Mom liked it because she did not speak English, and nobody expected much from her. I began working part-time because my parents would not allow me to work full-time. They told me that right now I had to concentrate more on getting good grades at school.

Although there were three people earning, we still needed more money for our large family. So when Dad realized this place was good for electronics, he got a loan and went to a private school to learn electronics work.

After he got his degree, Dad got a very good job in an electronics company paying $10 an hour, and we all got very excited! Dad worked there for one month, and realized that even though he knew the theory and knew how to fix things, he couldn't do the work because his fingers were too stiff, and his eyesight was too poor. So he was forced to give up that job and take another, lower-paying job, and he is still paying back the loan for his college education.

After we got new jobs, the first thing Dad did was to move the family to a new apartment, away from the place we first lived, where we could almost feel the crime in the air. I don't think Mom could have ever got us out of that place if she was here by herself, because except when we were under the Communists, she had never worked. She had always been a housewife, and she wasn't used to public life. Even now, she doesn't like to go out and meet new people. She just wants to stay home, cook, and take care of the children, because that's what she did all her life.

Dad, on the other hand, dealt with all kinds of people from the top of society to the bottom when he worked, and can handle any type of situation. So I think we are really lucky to have Dad here.

Schooling in America

When I started going to school I didn't know any English, but I was admitted to grade ten and given five classes: PE, science, English, ESL, and the most basic math class.

When I went to my first class, the teacher said, "Let me see your schedule," but I didn't know what a "schedule" was. So she looked through my stuff and took it from my pocketbook. There were some Cambodian students in the class, but the teacher did not ask them to help me. I think she wanted to see how much English I knew, but I didn't understand a word.

After she checked the schedule, the teacher said, "OK, you can find a seat." I just stood there, looking at her. Again she said, "Find a seat," but I still did not understand. Then a guy at the back told me "Find a seat" in Khmer, and I finally got the seat, but I was most embarrassed.

At school, I picked up math faster than English, because even though I had had no schooling since the Communist time, I remembered from my previous schooling how to do addition and subtraction. I also remembered how to do word problems in Khmer. I could already read and write Khmer and French, so I learned English faster than other kids who didn't know those languages, but I still found English difficult. I worked very hard that year, but except for a C in math, I got all D and F grades, all because they put me in classes that required the English knowledge that I didn't have.

During my second year in school, I began to help other Cambodian kids who had problems. Some of them had turned eighteen, and their benefits stopped. Their parents wanted them to quit school and go to work, to help the family. I explained to parents their children would have a better chance to get good jobs if they completed high school, and helped them to apply for scholarships so the kids could complete their education. I also translated for American people who worked in the school, because though they wanted to help Cambodians, they couldn't explain things in a way the Cambodians understood.

I enjoyed helping people at school. The best part was that I realized when I helped other people to solve their problems, I understood how to solve my own too.

I am now in a four-year college, but because I came to college with very little background knowledge, I need extra help to understand what I learn in class. I find General Education classes very difficult because I don't have the necessary background to understand varied subjects. I have fewer problems in my major classes.

Even after four years, I still find English grammar confusing because it is so different from Cambodian grammar. For example, I mix up the tenses especially when I talk, if I don't think consciously about what I am saying. Sometimes I write down the rules, but if I am in a hurry I forget them, and at other times, I have difficulty understanding the rules. Because of these problems, good tutors are among the most important people in college for many Cambodians. But when we go to the tutorial center, we get different tutors every time, which does not help.

I continue to work hard to learn English, and although most professors in my college are considerate about our English language problems, a few don't care about our difficulties. Once I had a professor in a General Education class who knew that I was learning English as a second language and shouldn't have expected me to write perfect English. But she gave me an F for a very long paper I wrote and said, "You have to deal with your grammar."

I said, "I am an ESL student, and my grammar contains so many mistakes because my own language is different. As I learn more English, I will try to correct my grammar."

"When you come to a four-year college I expect you to do better than this," was all she said. She was so mean. Finally, I got out of that class with a D+ because I gave a speech for extra credit.

I didn't complain about this incident to anybody because I thought that I may have been at fault; because of the way I was brought up, I think the teacher is always right. I've gone through high school and college in America, but I've never believed it's right to complain about the teacher, even if I may feel the teacher has done something wrong. I don't know if this is the right way to think, but I believe most Cambodian students are like me.

I chose to go to a four-year college instead of a two-year one because I knew I wouldn't stop going to school after two years, and because I didn't want to be left alone when my Cambodian friends from high school came here. I don't meet them in all the classes because we have different majors, but I get together with two friends almost every holiday, and we usually barbecue some food and eat together. Like me, they too have the passion to work hard, and are doing well in college.

I also have American, Chinese, and Vietnamese friends in college. We sometimes do projects together, and all of them are good friends that I can count on. When I make new friends, I tell them a little bit of my story so they know where I came from. They do the same, and that way, we begin to know each other better.

My grade point average is 2.0, so I am barely surviving. But I know I have such a low GPA because I don't have the background knowledge, and there's nothing I can do about it. When I don't understand what the instructors say, I try to memorize what I have to learn. So sometimes I pass examinations because I memorize the work, and not because I understand it. Sometimes I misunderstand the examination questions, so I fail my examinations.

Right now I am just trying to survive so I can get the degree. I've always wanted to have a degree, so I can become a good citizen, and people will say, "You can count on this person." But getting good grades is very difficult for people like me, who have nothing when it comes to previous education.

Love and Marriage

My older sister and younger brother are both married, and my parents are worried because I am 27 and still single. "Don't wait until you're too old to marry," Mom reminds me often, because Cambodian girls usually get married in their early twenties. "Well, the age is not so important here as in Cambodia. I want a little freedom to make my own choice, and I don't want to get married right now," I tell her then, and she and Dad accept that.

When I am ready to marry, I will not marry an American because of cultural differences. I dated an American once, but not for long, because Americans have a different pace of life and different ways of thinking. For example, I save money, but the guy I dated just was not into saving. I know he liked me, because he was willing to learn the way I lived, the way I ate, and the way I dressed, but I don't have the time to teach him so many things. I think I can be very good friends with him, but I don't think I can live with him or get very close to him.

I have tried to pick up some of the good things from the American culture. For instance, now I shake hands with people, sit and gesture with my hand the way they do when I want someone, and hug people, and those are big changes. We have also started to eat some American foods, which are more nutritious and better for our health than Cambodian foods.

Since coming here, I've also become more open-minded about people. When I was small, I always thought that the Cambodian nation was the greatest. Although I played with Chinese kids, I used to think "Oh, they are Chinese and Chinese are nothing!" While I still do a lot of things with other Cambodians, I now have friends of different nationalities, and who came from different schools. So I am more liberal now.

However, there are many differences between American and Cambodian cultures, and I can't switch myself from one to the other. I don't think that I will ever change the way I believe in the family, and the way I treat people or talk to people. So if I marry, I would prefer a person from my own race because I think it's much easier for people who came from the same background, and who know the culture, to live together.

Though I expect to marry some day, I don't date much because I don't have a lot of free time to go out, or to feel strongly about another person. I am too busy with my schoolwork to hang around, so dating is a secondary choice. Right now the most important thing is to get the degree, and dating will interfere with my ability to concentrate on my education. My future goal is to have a small, but very good CPA firm. To achieve that, I first have to learn the basic things about living here, so I can have a good foundation to rest my feet on, and start to move on.

Reflections

I don't plan to go to Cambodia to live, but if the country went back to the way it was before Pol Pot, I would go back to meet some of the family I've only heard about. I would also like to see the big house that belonged to my grandparents, the one about which I have a lot of happy memories.

I don't know why nobody in my immediate family did not die under Pol Pot. Maybe it was luck; it's like destiny, we never know what will happen. We can't say that we did the right things, and that was why we survived. We wanted to survive and we did, but we can't tell how it happened.

I don't believe in kamma or anything, but sometimes when you have no explanation, it's the right word to use. I remember my dad said the same thing.

My parents, my grandparents, and my great-grandparents were all Buddhists, and my dad lived in the temple for years, but he really doesn't believe so much about any religion. I have been to the temple only twice, with my grandparents. My parents never taught us to pray. I know a few prayers from Grandmother and Grandfather.

Still, I have some understanding of Buddhism because of the way I was brought up, but I cannot say I am totally, 100 percent Buddhist. I am not American, I am not Christian, and I am not Buddhist, but I have some kind of an image. Buddhism teaches us not to kill, not to steal. We think these are good things, so we follow them for our own good.

Sometimes we talk about religion, and I ask my mom, "You are getting old, and you have no religion, what's happened to you?" I even ask my dad, and he says, "Well, sometimes you think that you have to believe in something or somebody, but religion is in your heart." I think so too.

Once I asked my dad how he feels about what happened to us and the Cambodian people. He said Cambodia did not fall because it was the fault of the Cambodian people, or the government or the king, but because of international politics. He said that when bigger countries like Russia, China, and America play games with the politics of small countries, small countries like ours could not survive. He believes in the domino theory: that no matter how strong our government was economically or politically, when one country in Southeast Asia collapsed, our country had to collapse. He hates Pol Pot because Pol Pot killed millions of people. He thinks Pol Pot is a crazy person. But he blames international politics because that is what enabled Pol Pot to gain control of our country. Finally, though, he looks upon all that happened as experiences to learn from.

My parents and many other people have nightmares about the Khmer Rouge time, but I don't, probably because I was young when everything happened. But I still feel very angry with Pol Pot, and my whole family hates him.

I don't want to take revenge on all the soldiers or the Communist people, because most of them were uneducated, and even if they didn't want to kill or steal, the people behind the scenes forced them to do so. They had no choice. I know this because I was there too; the Communists forced me to be a leader, so I became a leader. If they forced me to say bad things, I probably would have said bad things while knowing it was wrong, because I would have had no choice. So it's not right to hate all people, because they are like us. I hate only a single man—Pol Pot.

But one cannot erase the past; it is part of your life. Under the Communists, we lost some of our family. We lost property. We never thought or imagined that we would ever become as poor as we did. Sometimes I get depressed when I think of all that happened. But as Dad says, you can learn from difficult experiences, and suffering under the Communists was a strong experience for me to go on to the future. I now see the future as brighter than the past.

In my family, we save money together, and when we had $5,000 in the bank, Dad suggested we should invest it in a house, but Mom was not so sure that we should put all our money into a house. Dad said, "House prices will only increase, and if we buy one now, the money we invest will make more money in the future."

The house we liked was very costly, though, and we didn't have enough money for a down payment. Dad decided to take the risk anyway, and borrowed money from some friends to make up the down payment. We didn't know that family in Cambodia, but they trusted my dad and gave us a loan, and we bought the house. As it turned out, Dad was right about the investment. We were able to purchase a doughnut shop for my sister and her husband using the equity from this house.

We still owe money on this house and all of us work hard to pay it off, but it's the base that enables us to move on. I think this is our prize for all the effort we've put in together. Our home is not just for living—it makes our life a little more stable, and we can move on to make use of the opportunities we see ahead for education and for having small businesses.

I don't save my money individually because I live with my family, and I know the family is needy. I think the family and I are one unit. When I am wealthy, the family is wealthy; and when the family is wealthy, I am also wealthy. That is how I always think.

My dad makes the most important decisions in our family, but before he goes ahead, he always consults my mom and me. My parents have very different personalities because of their backgrounds. The only thing they have in common is, Dad loves Mom's food! But he knows that although Mom did not get an advanced education, she has her own special identity. I think they get along really well. They have a lot of conversations, but I can't tell you how much they love each other because they never show their feelings in front of the kids. I have never seen them fighting, though, and they are always very respectful to each other.

I have a very warm, close life with my family. I have no problems getting along with anybody because I always listen to people before I say anything, or make judgments. Maybe it's just my character, but I can say I am the most moderate person in my family. My brothers and sisters tell me that even when I was young, I never argued with my parents. When my mom and sister couldn't get along, they would talk to me, and then I talked to one or the other.

Even though I have a warm relationship with my parents, Mom and I have a certain distance. When I was small I was close to my mother, but when I was about six years old, she wanted me to be more independent. For example, if I wanted to cuddle, she would say, "No, you are a big girl now, you go and play." Cambodian parents expect respect from their children, and as children grow older, they become less physically close to children. Americans hug and kiss, but Cambodian people don't express their love like that; it's all inside. When we get close to them it's in the proper way—with respect. For example, before we go to school we go to them, put our palms together, and we say, "*chumriep lieh* [goodbye]." When we return, we go to them and say, "*chumriep sova* [good day]." We don't just go "Hey Mom, I'm back!" and hug them. That would be very disrespectful. Now that I'm grown, Mom never hugs me. But my dad still does, and therefore I think I am closer to him in some ways.

I don't know whether it's better to do things the Cambodian way or the American way. I think it's important for children to know how much your parents love you, and because I don't know how close I can get to my mom, I always think that she expects more from me. I think Americans have an advantage because they have closer physical contact between parents and children.

On the other hand, Americans think Cambodian children don't have their independence. They believe that we should be on our own and have our own lives. I agree that you have to develop your own way of life, but I also believe that you can never guarantee that you can become so independent you will never need somebody's help. My sister, for instance, wanted to be independent, to get out of the family and make her own life. But she always needs us, and often comes back and asks for help. And my parents help her because they are always behind us. No matter what we do, they will always look after us. They will never turn away from us. That is how I think most Cambodian parents are.

I don't know much about Americans, but the way I see it, they believe that they are behind their children; but the first thing they want is for their children to be independent. They let the children have their own ways of thinking about life, and don't want to have a strong bond with their children. That's why most American children leave the house when they turn eighteen.

I don't know whether the Cambodian way or the American way is better, but I think for the family to be one unit is good, and for me, I think the Cambodian way is the right one. But if the Americans think their way is better, then that's what is right for them. Some Cambodians say that the American way is not good for the family. But I say, "Independence is important for an individual's life, but you always have a need for other people also."

CHAPTER ELEVEN

Nya Srey: A Widowed Single Parent

When I clasped my hands together and greeted Nya Srey in the traditional manner at our very first meeting, she seemed surprised at my familiarity with her customs, but she reciprocated without hesitation. After introducing me to her children, Nya Srey led me to the kitchen table, where I requested her to begin her story with her childhood. "But my childhood was so dull that no one would want to hear it!" she exclaimed. Once she started, however, she needed little prompting from me to continue. It was not until about four hours later that Nya Srey stopped to get some refreshments: English muffins, liver paté, and tea.

I had only had Cambodian food at other homes, and while I very much enjoyed the food and drink served by Nya Srey, I was surprised by her enjoyment of such Western flavors. Even the decorations and furnishings of her home were unusually Western. While statues of graceful Apsaras, or dancers, and framed posters of the Angkor Wat conveyed her fondness for her heritage, the elegantly pleated drapes and a tall vase filled with pink, blue, and cream-colored dried flowers that grace her living room struck me as typically American.

As I became better acquainted with Nya Srey through her narrative, I realized that she was unusual in the Cambodian community in the United States; unlike many others, she had traveled to Western countries such as France and Switzerland long before she was forced to seek refuge here. As she herself says, this early exposure to the West opened her eyes to a new world.

Despite her outward adjustment to the United States, Nya Srey has enormous problems in coming to terms with the Pol Pot experience, and in coping with her new life in the United States as a widowed single parent. This is evident not only in her narrative but also in the manner in which she related it.

Like Look Tha (see Chapter 3), Nya Srey was reluctant to talk about the Pol Pot years. I requested her to tell me only as much of that experience as she wanted to, since it was the central cause for her arrival here. As she recalled the evacuation and the painful events that followed, sometimes she cried, and at other times she burst out in anger. When memories were too traumatic to relive, she left them unsaid. I know of these incidents because they appear in her daughter's story in Chapter 8.

Because relating her story was such a traumatic experience for her, after I completed recording it I asked Nya Srey why she chose to do so. "I want the world to understand what happened to my people," she replied.

Nya Srey means "married lady of ordinary status." She chose this term in preference to my original pseudonym for her, *Look Srey*, which means "lady of higher status." But the more I think about her, the more extraordinary she seems to me. In the face of the most adverse circumstances, Nya Srey, like many other Khmer Rouge survivors, displayed, and continues to display, an inner strength that saved not only her life but also the lives of her family. ❖❖❖

Early Years

I was born in 1945, in Battambang province during the Second World War. I had a younger brother and a sister of the same blood [siblings]. My mother was ill when I was born and didn't have enough breast milk to feed me. She could not easily obtain baby milk because it was wartime, so unlike my siblings who were strong and healthy, I was a sickly child.

I also had three half-brothers from my father's first marriage who lived with their mother. I seldom saw my father's brother or sister because they lived far away, but we frequently visited my mother's sister who lived close by. I never knew my grandparents—they had died before I was born.

We called our mother "Mai" like the Cambodians, but we called Father "Papa" in the French way. He worked as a politician in Phnom Penh, and he had a house there too. Because my father had been educated in a French school, he was more fluent in French than he was in Khmer.

Although my parents were Chinese-Cambodians, we lived in town among Cambodians, and we grew up speaking Khmer. I think we got along better with Cambodians than the Vietnamese did; I remember a lot of half-Chinese, half-Cambodian people, especially in the town. There were very few half-Cambodian, half-Vietnamese people. The farmers in the country-side were pure Cambodians. They had problems with the Vietnamese all the time, I really don't know why; but the way the Vietnamese lived was completely different.

I don't know how much you had to have to be middle-class or rich, but I think my parents were middle-class because my mom didn't have to go to work to get money. She inherited a lot of rice fields from her father, which she leased to other farmers. At harvesttime, she collected the rents and spent that over the whole year. Some people paid her in money, but others paid in rice, which she sold to the rice mill.

When Mom went to the rice fields she stayed there overnight or about five days a week at harvesttime. She had a fairly big house near the fields. People didn't have two houses unless they had rice fields, like my mom. Sometimes I went with her, so I came to know the farmers. I never worked in the rice fields, though—I just played around.

Mom never visited the farmers, but they came to visit her; they considered her to be a person who was socially higher. In addition to working on her land, they sometimes asked her for loans. If the people were very poor, she didn't charge them interest; instead, they gave her a young girl, like a granddaughter, to help around our house. Even if the people were not so poor, she didn't charge a lot of interest because she was really a Buddhist, and believed that it was very bad to charge people a lot of interest.

My mom owned a few ox carts too, but she usually hired trucks to bring the rice to the mill because she felt it was bad to use the oxen both to work in the rice fields and to pull the cart. I understand how she felt; I felt like that too.

My parents never agreed on anything, so they didn't get along. They never shouted at each other, and my father never hit Mom; he was not that type. Much of the time they just kept quiet and didn't talk to each other. When Father came home from Phnom Penh to stay for any length of time, Mom went to the rice fields and left me alone with Father. Sometimes she would be away for about two weeks or so. Since they didn't get along, she didn't care.

My father was more affectionate toward me than my mom. He spoiled me, and hardly hit me. Whenever I did something for him, he would say, "That's good, Daughter, that's the way to do it!" which made me feel really good. So I was not afraid of him at all, but I was afraid of my mother, because she spanked me.

Mom liked my sister more than she liked me. "Oh, your sister is so much smarter; she does everything better, and she even talks better than you do," she would say. I think it was true that I was not as smart as my sister, but it didn't help when Mom kept on saying that.

I know Mom loved me, but she was not an affectionate person. She didn't show her feelings, or talk about how she felt; she didn't get close to anybody. In fact, I think it would have been better had she been a father instead of a mother!

When I was young, Cambodia was still a French protectorate, so even though I went to a Cambodian school, I learned a lot of French. With time, however, they taught more and more in Cambodian, and students who were younger than I knew less French. In my school there were only girls. Although I had close friends in school, I was always shy and hesitated to talk to people. I was a good student, but I was not very smart or intelligent.

Because of my upbringing, I don't remember having any ambition to become somebody other than a mother and a housewife when I grew up. Not only my mom, but most people at that time were very strict about how they brought up children. I just went to school, came back home, and did housework. I couldn't go out, and I couldn't have a friend over. Sometimes I wanted to go out to eat in a restaurant or to see a movie like everybody else, but I couldn't because my mother would not go. My sister was too young to go with me, my brother always played by himself, I couldn't go with the helper, and I couldn't go alone; so it was only once in a great while that I went out with my father, or with my aunt.

Mom taught me to cook, to take care of money, and to take care of the house. We lived in the town, and I often walked with the woman who helped Mother with the housework to the nearby market to buy food. My mother lived a Buddhist life, so when I went to the market I could not buy live fish; it had to be already killed. She ate eggs only if they were cracked before I bought them.

Although we are Buddhists, my brother didn't go to a temple school. I think only poor people went to temple schools because they got a free meal there. My brother also went to a government school like I did, but he was raised completely differently because he was a boy. He went out a lot and played around; he was not a scared girl like me. My sister too was different from me. She was more intelligent, and didn't get sick a lot as I did. I was scared to talk to people, and because my parents raised me in an old-fashioned way, I became worse. Even now, I am uncomfortable going anywhere by myself, and I hate myself for being like that.

I don't believe my mother ever had a happy life. Her mother had died when she was born, and she had been raised by her stepmother. She didn't even have a happy marriage, so we did not have a happy time at home.

When parents have a broken marriage, it affects the children. My brother would do wrong things, and at one point Father took Brother to live with him, saying to Mother, "You don't know how to take care of him. I can bring him up better." But after a short time, Brother said, "No, I cannot live with Father," and came back to Mom. Since he could not get a steady education like that, my brother quit school after something like high school and became a farmer.

When parents don't get along or separate, it affects the children; I hate that. I was so young when I realized my parents didn't get along, and from the beginning, I felt sad and uncomfortable.

Love and Marriage

I got married young, when I was just sixteen; but I don't feel bad about it. When you don't have a good time at home why should you want to stay at home?

My husband was 22. I knew him a little before marriage because he was related to my mom, but it was like an arranged marriage too. I was aware that other people also considered me a suitable wife for their sons, because sometimes when people came to our house or were standing around outside, I felt that they had come to observe me. But when Mother asked me if I would like to marry someone else, I did not say anything because even before I married him, I liked my husband. Although she always found fault with me, I did not believe Mom would ever force me to marry someone I disliked.

In our country people don't date, and I was not supposed to go out with my husband before marriage. But I did sometimes, along with my brother, sister, and anyone else who wanted to come; so we always went out in a group. Although I had no boyfriends before marriage, I knew my husband had had girlfriends. But I did not worry too much about it because in Cambodia, wives were treated differently than girlfriends.

I did not know about sex until I was married because nobody talked about sex with young people. I was young, and my husband was young too, and we didn't know about contraceptives because in the old days nobody taught you about those things. There were clinics, but I do not know if they taught about family planning.

I got pregnant right after marriage. When my son was born, Mom sent me a helper. I breast-fed my son for three months, and then Mom said, "I think you are too young to know how to take care of the baby," and she took my son to Battambang. I didn't mind it because I really didn't feel very attached to my son; perhaps I was too young at the time.

I became pregnant again after three months. I was not happy to be pregnant so soon, but I didn't know what to do about it. I didn't want to have an abortion because it is a big sin for Buddhist people to have abortions.

Each year for four years, I had a baby, and when they were three months old, Mom exchanged the new baby for the older one, which helped me a great deal. After my fourth child was born, I heard people talk about family planning. We went to a doctor who had just finished school in France, and he told us about family planning methods. My husband had no objections because we had four children, which was a lot.

When we got married my husband had just finished high school and entered the law school in Phnom Penh. Until he graduated five years later, he taught French in a private school for two hours in the morning, and went to law school from four to eight in the evening. I stayed home, cooked, and took care of everything. When he returned at night we just talked, and sometimes I helped him with the students' tests. During weekends we usually went for a drive and ate out in restaurants.

I can't say my husband and I were rich, but we had enough money to have a good time. At that time I didn't think I needed to save any money because I thought that later on we would be rich, since my husband would have a good position in the government. Moreover, when he was a student, my father paid our rent for the whole year. Mother sent us rice, dried fish, and other food, and we never bought any rice. I did not pay Mother for the food because she really didn't need anything from us, and it was her way of showing she loved us. Besides, it was the way in Cambodia; most people helped their children.

In our country people didn't have to take a bar examination to be a lawyer. Because Cambodia was an underdeveloped country there were not too many educated people, and right after he graduated, my husband began to work as a lawyer. He gave me all the money he earned, and we spent it together.

My husband usually let me have anything I wanted. Both times he went to Europe to study juvenile law, I went with him. The first time, we went to France, Holland, and Switzerland. We visited various places in those countries, and walked around looking at clothes and other things in the stores. Our children stayed with my mom, and she loved to have them. She was not strict with them as she was with me, but then, they were small at the time.

When my husband got the second chance to go to Europe he really didn't want to go because our country was beginning to have problems. But I told him, "Oh, I want to go again; I had such a good time over there. I would like to have a short vacation." So we went for two weeks to Paris, and two weeks to Geneva. People in Geneva asked my husband if he wanted to stay and work there, but he said, "No, my mother lives alone, and I must return to look after her."

We came back home in December, just before Christmas. I remember that because people asked us to stay for Christmas. I too didn't want to stay in Geneva for a longer period because our country was having a lot of trouble by then, and I had all my children in Cambodia. I went to Europe only to take a vacation.

When our country was at war during Lon Nol's time, the people were scared. Nobody wanted to go to the movies, or even to the market, in case bombs exploded. Many intellectuals who were dissatisfied with the government formed various groups, and my husband also joined one. But his group did not work against the government.

During the war, Battambang was quieter than Phnom Penh, so I left my children there. I stayed in Phnom Penh with my husband. He asked me, "Wouldn't you also like to live in the countryside?" But I loved him, and I didn't want to leave him. I said, "No, I don't want to leave you alone, I don't want to go anyplace without you."

I don't remember having a happy life when I was young, but I had a really good time with my husband, who had a nice personality and was a happy guy. He was nice and polite in the way he talked and in the way he acted, and he was also very kind to people. For example, when he met a friend on the street, he never hesitated to give his friend a ride in the car. Not everybody offered to give people a ride in their cars. My husband was not shy like me, and he was also very smart. That's why my first son and my daughter are very intelligent. When the country's troubles deepened, he wanted to have all the children back at home, so we brought them to live with us in Phnom Penh.

Surviving the Khmer Rouge

Before the Communists came, I kept asking my husband, "Aren't you afraid of the Communists?"

He always replied, "Oh, I don't care that much. I am not afraid because I am not one of those corrupt people, and anyway, I believe the Communists will need educated people to build the country."

My husband never thought the Communists would take over the country and kill people. Instead, he expected they would perhaps try to brainwash people, and change the government by getting rid of corrupt people. If he had thought otherwise, we would have left the country with our whole family.

Then all of a sudden, the day Pol Pot came to Phnom Penh, the soldiers ordered us out of our house. They came in the morning and ordered us to leave, saying the Americans were going to bomb the city. We decided to spend the night in the house, and go early the next morning.

Right before we went to sleep, soldiers shot two guys in front of our house. They then said, "If you don't leave the house now, we will kill you too." We fled, and we took nothing with us, not even any food.

Out on the street, we saw that other evacuees carried all sorts of things and I told my husband, "I don't know what to do. I didn't bring anything, not even my jewelry." He tried to pacify me saying, "Oh, don't you worry about it, we will be all right," but before we had gone very far, a Khmer Rouge soldier told him to go back home and get a few things. I suppose that soldier felt sorry for us because we had nothing. We crossed Tonle Sap river by boat and arrived in a place where my husband had relatives. We decided to stay with them.

One night the Communists came and took away my husband, to kill him or to put him in jail, nobody knows. I didn't even see him go because I was in another part of the house, but my daughter, who always stayed close to my husband, saw the soldiers take him away. My daughter heard her father ask, "What do you want from me?" A soldier said, "We just want to talk to you." That was all she saw and heard because when she followed them, a soldier told her to go home.

When she came and told me what had happened, I thought my head would blow up. The next day I got a severe migraine headache, but there was not much I could do or say to find out what had happened to my husband. In many places the soldiers took whole families away; we were just lucky that they didn't want all of us.

The Pol Pots evacuated us again a couple of days after they took my husband away, and this time they sent us to the jungle. The Pol Pots took my two older sons away. I lived with my two younger children, but I had to work every day, planting rice from morning till night.

The regime became stricter and stricter with us each day. We got less and less food until we were nearly starving to death, and all the while I worked, I only thought about food. I even dreamed about food. We were so hungry, we ate anything we could find. When my older son came home, he taught his brother to catch fish. My daughter went digging for food and sometimes she dug lotus flower root. At night when she couldn't sleep because she was so hungry, she crept out and caught grasshoppers or a frog, and cooked it over a little fire we kept going to keep us warm. She would eat one leg, give me one, and give her brothers some. When they managed to steal some rice, my son ground it secretly, and my daughter winnowed it with her hands. Oh, we were so hungry! I survived only because of my children. Everybody helped me, and helped each other to survive.

My third son lost his sight to the Communists, and the soldiers beat one of my sons so badly with bamboo poles that he still has scars. I too was once beaten, by a woman boss. I felt very angry and revengeful then, but there was nothing I could do; I didn't want to be killed. All I knew was I didn't want to die, like my sister. She was studying chemistry in the university to become a pharmacist when the country fell and we all got separated. I think she was killed by the Communists because it has been a long time since the country was liberated, and we have never heard anything from her or about her. I lost two half-brothers in Cambodia too.

I wanted to keep myself alive to bring the children out of the country, and to send them to school. "Oh, I want to go to school, I miss it so much!" my oldest son would say. I felt so bad then because I could not see how he would ever go to school under the Communists. Just to make him feel better I would say, "Be patient, things will work out and you will go to school."

"When, when will that happen?" he would ask, but I didn't know. All I knew was that we could not have Communism forever; the way they treated us was so horrible! If the Khmer Rouge had changed things a little and told us to work more and not get too rich, it would have been all right. But they treated us like animals. What we went through was so horrible that if it had not happened to me, I don't think I would ever believe it.

I didn't want to give up to the Communists, and I had to hold onto some idea to survive. I knew there were Cambodian people in France and in the United States, and I believed that they would do something to help us.

Looking back, however, I think I survived largely because I was so angry. I wanted to feel I was the winner. And I always expected to see my husband. At that time I never thought he would be killed or that anything would have happened to him.

In late 1978, we began to hear rumors that Vietnamese were coming, so we just waited for our time. I wanted to see the Pol Pots' faces when the Vietnamese came, but one morning when I woke up, all of them had run away. There were a couple of families left, but they did not try to do anything, and we just walked out of that place.

When I came out of the jungle I felt as if I had gone crazy; I couldn't think, or remember anything. I was badly swollen and my tummy was really big, but I was so hungry that I thought I would never make it back home.

When the Vietnamese came we were pretty far from Phnom Penh, and I never thought of going back there. Who knew when the Khmer Rouge would come back? I only wanted to get away from Cambodia.

We walked to Battambang to find our relatives. I found some, including my brother, and we decided to go to a refugee camp with his family.

A Single Parent in America

Although my father was under Pol Pot for four years, my mother escaped the regime. Right before the country fell, she and my aunt went to Thailand to see a doctor. When the country fell they couldn't get back. They were so lucky! My aunt's husband died in Cambodia.

My mom had a lot of Thai friends and relatives she used to help, so they helped her now. They gave her some money and she did a little business just to survive, but because she was not Thai and did not have a Thai identity card, she had a hard time in Thailand. When the refugee flow started the Thai government became strict about Cambodians living there. So Mom went to a refugee camp and a friend who had already come to the U.S. sponsored her to come here.

After we escaped to the refugee camp, we found out Mom was living in the U.S., and my brother and I wrote to her. She wrote to me, saying, "I cannot believe you are alive! I thought all of you would have been killed because your husband was a lawyer."

My mom sponsored us to come to America. When we came to San Francisco we were so overwhelmed with everything that had happened, all of us were crying. But Mom only said, "Why are you crying? We are together again." She is such a strong person!

I came to America with bare hands, not knowing anything about this country. When I decided to leave Cambodia, my only thoughts were to get away as far as possible from the Communists, and to send my children to school. I didn't know about welfare benefits in America; I don't think anybody knew about that. After I came, though, I liked America better than France because this is a richer country with more opportunities, and it is not overcrowded like France.

When I first came everything was different, and I had to find out how to live in this country. At the beginning, a Buddhist monk helped us a lot, and he even bought us clothes from the Goodwill store. I soon realized that I didn't want to remain in the big city where Mom lived, because there was so much crime! It was a terrible place to bring up children.

I wanted a job. I was on welfare, which I couldn't stand, and I also didn't want to go out and spend food stamps; it made me feel terrible. But before I could do something for a living, I first had to learn English.

I had gone to a private teacher to learn English for just a month or so before the country fell, but I had not made a serious effort to learn. I went to that class not because I thought I needed to learn English, but because my husband let me do anything I wanted, and the only word I remembered when I came here was "water." So I went to adult school and learned English for about a year.

I had a hard time learning English because the Cambodian language has a lot of vowels and consonants that you don't have in English. I felt that when you speak English you use your tongue a lot more than you do when you speak Cambodian. Reading English was easier because I know French. I recognized words like "amputate" and "intellectual" which are similar to French, but I didn't know how to pronounce them in English.

My biggest wish still is to learn more English, but it's becoming harder for me because I am getting older, and because I have so much work to do by myself since I don't have a husband. I have to take care of all the payments, paperwork, cooking, and housework, and I also have to care for my mom. So I always have something on my mind, and very little time to study.

I like to read, and I think I can improve my English if I read, but I don't have the time. So I speak to my children in English and tell them to correct me when I make mistakes. My aunt dislikes it when I speak in English because she doesn't understand it. She asks me, "Why do you speak in English? You don't know how to speak Cambodian anymore?" I understand how my aunt feels. I too think it is important to keep our language because we are Cambodians. But I also wish to speak English really well, and that is why I speak to my children in English.

After I learned some English, I studied computer data entry and got a job that paid pretty good money. I was unhappy, though, because I had too much pressure at work from my supervisor, who was too bossy. I got laid off from that job after some time, and I moved to a new city. But again there were a lot of drunkards and thieves there too, so I kept moving. Once I found a house in a small city I liked, but even though I worked ten hours a day, I could not afford to buy it.

I worked hard while my children came home from school and cooked. After about three years, we managed to move into a better area. I still have to work very hard, but I don't mind that as long as the people in the workplace do not treat me badly.

When we arrived in America, my children had a hard time too. My oldest son was admitted to a junior high school, but because Mom made a mistake about his birthday when she registered him at school he had to go to high school after three months. He was terrified to go to high school because he did not know English, and he cried for days, saying he didn't want to go. He had no choice, however, and now I feel proud of him because he was ambitious and he worked hard. After a year or so, he started to get straight A's.

After he finished high school, my son went to college, and he wanted to study law. But I didn't want him to be a lawyer like my husband. I think my husband got killed because he was a lawyer.

I told my son to be an engineer. My son tried engineering and said, "I don't like it because I don't use my mind enough," and changed over to business. He reads the business news in the newspaper and wants to keep up with everything. He is the one who suggested we should move to our present house.

Sometimes, though, my son pushes me too hard; he tells me to wear makeup and so on, and it makes me angry and then we have problems. But I really care about my children. I thought only about them all these years; I never thought about myself. I think I should do so now, before it's too late.

I should think especially about my social life, and everybody, even the monks, tells me so.

Reflections

I think our country fell because of too much corruption, but I think Sihanouk is mostly responsible for what happened. He was the king, but he didn't do anything to improve the situation. Corruption affected us too. Even if you had a good education, you couldn't get a good position in the government unless you had connections.

I thought I had got over Communism, but I haven't. For the first time since Pol Pot, I read a book about Communism two years ago, and I had nightmares. The next time I tried, it was the same. I remembered how people suffered in the evacuation; the patients in the hospital—the man whose legs had been amputated dragging himself on the road. . . Then one night there was a thunderstorm. I was sleeping, but it was as if I didn't sleep. I felt I was in my country, listening to the rockets; it was the same sound. I was so upset the next day that I couldn't go to work. I called in sick, and stayed home.

Once a year I go to the temple and give food and money in the Buddhist way, in memory of my husband and all my relatives who died. I really want the children to go to the temple, and they often go with me.

Although I have changed somewhat after coming to the United States, I still believe in kamma: that if I did something bad in my last birth, then I will suffer. This belief has helped me not to go crazy. I know some people who lost their minds. They were Buddhist, too, but I don't know what they believed in.

A lot also depends on how far you can control your mind. When I was young, I tried meditation. My mom meditated, and she taught me to just stay still, and to put my mind on one thing. I think it helped me to control myself a lot after what happened. Remember, Buddha said, "Always control yourself; don't be too happy or too sad." I try to follow his advice.

It is hard for me to live here, but it's harder for older people because they don't speak English. When you are seventy years old, I don't think you can learn a foreign language. My father knew a lot of French, but although he learned to read English, he just couldn't learn to speak English.

Mom lives with us. She is old and sick, and when everybody leaves for work and for school, she gets thoroughly bored. She does not want to go out of the house at all because she is afraid she will fall, so even though she wants to go to the temple, she can't go. My aunt has knee problems, but she's a lot healthier than Mom, and sometimes she stays here during the week, to keep Mom company. She really helps me to take care of Mom.

I don't spend a lot of time with other Cambodians. I think I have a different mentality, because I am from a different social class and because I had visited other countries. The first time I went to France, it opened up new ideas for me, and I learned a lot. I want to go back to Paris with my daughter, and I want my second son to travel a little too. He works six days a week, and I always tell him that just going to work, coming home, and making money is not enough.

Money is important, but education is more important. I want my children to go to school and get a degree. Before I came to America, I used to think education was better than anything else; but now I am not sure. This country has kind of confused me because here, even if you don't have much education but you do good business and have a lot of money, you are an important person.

I think my children should learn as much as possible about America, but everything depends on how they act. I think the way one treats people is important; one should talk to people nicely, and be honest with them. In a way I want the children to be like the Cambodian people; not dress like a punk, cut their hair funny, or exaggerate things. So far my children have been pretty good, compared to some children.

I don't want my children to be very rich, but they should be happy. When they marry, they should have a nice family and get along with their husbands and wives. They should not be like American people; Americans divorce and separate very easily. In Cambodia divorce was not common. It was legal to have two wives, but it was not common.

I feel so sorry that my daughter got divorced. I gave her in marriage at a young age because I didn't know what else to do. I didn't have a job, and my parents put a lot of pressure on me about my children's future. "You don't have a husband, and your children don't have a father. So why keep your daughter for so long?" they asked, over and over, and I arranged a marriage for her.

My mother used to be bossy and tell me what to do, but after my daughter divorced we had a long talk. I told her not to get involved with my children and not to run my life. It so happens now when I get upset with things, I get upset with my mother. The best for her wasn't the best for me. Sometimes I want to show affection to my mom, and I can't do that. I feel sorry about it, but I can't do anything now.

I changed a lot after my daughter's divorce, because I don't want to have similar problems with my children. I became closer to them; now I am like a friend to them. We talk and discuss things. I wasn't strong enough before to do what I should have done, but now I do what I want to do. Therefore I feel I am somewhat different from other Cambodians. Maybe I have more modern thinking, become more Westernized. Maybe I am stupid, too proud of myself, I don't know.

I think my sons should marry who they want, and I do not want to arrange marriages all the time, but I would like a good Cambodian girl for my son. I don't care much for white girls because they don't know how to cook, how to save money, or how to care for a family. But I don't blame them; we have different customs. I feel we are completely different. We like to take care of our families. I don't like people living together without being married. Dating is okay with me, but I don't want the children to have real close relationships unless they are sure.

Compared to American children, my children are more mature; they can take care of themselves. Maybe that was a good thing they got from Communism! So far they haven't got into big trouble. We just disagree about normal things. They know what to do, and how to make money. They also know they have to help me. My oldest son has always earned, and he gives me money. The second one has no degree, but he maintains a job, and he gave me money to buy this house. I feel sorry for the third one. He is very nice, but the doctor says his optic nerve is damaged and that they can't do anything for him.

I feel so alone here. I have nobody to count on. I don't want to ask my children for too many things because I don't want to be a burden to them, but it really hurts when I can't get any support or help when I am alone. When my children were young I felt I was important, but now they are big and they can take care of themselves. They have their own lives and I feel I am not needed.

I wouldn't worry like this if I had my husband. In Cambodia I didn't need to work. I had my husband, I had everything. My husband spoiled me a lot. I feel so bad because I lost him. I never thought I could be by myself. I had such a good time with my husband, but unfortunately it was too short for me.

Since I lost my husband, I have made myself stronger and I can do many things I had never done before, but life is still very hard. However, things are not going to be the way they were before. Since we had Communism, I don't want to be Cambodian. Why should I want to be like those people, those crazy people who killed my husband, my sister, their own flesh and blood? I just feel bad, sick, and tired, and it's not great to be like that.

I would like to marry again, but it's hard to think of a second marriage. It's hard to be with somebody when you have been alone for so long; it's been thirteen years since I was separated from my husband. Also, I don't meet many Cambodian men from my background because a lot of them got killed. When you are young and you marry for the first time, you don't worry much about getting along with your husband. But the second time, you think of everything. My friend asks me, "Why don't you want to go with some other Asian man?" But I don't want to because an Asian man will make me think too much of my husband.

It's about time for me to go out and find out a little bit more about American society. I find it easy to go out with white men, but not with Cambodian men because I feel guilty that I will betray my husband. I hope to find a good man I can marry, so I don't end up like Mom—a burden to my children. It's not that I don't want to look after her, but she is always on my mind, something to worry about.

What do I do besides housework? I don't know anybody, and it's hard for me because I want to forget the past. I want to forget my husband. I want to become like Americans, and start all over again; but I feel shy. I don't speak English well. I feel shy about having conversations with people. I don't know how to act, how to dance. I don't even know how to begin to learn to have a social life. As a woman, I think even if you wanted to, you cannot chase a man, the way a man can chase a woman. Even in this country with equality, I don't think you can be equal in that. I would like to find somebody who can understand me, who is like me. I don't mind if he is old or poor, but I want someone I can get along with. I don't think it will happen, I am just hoping. I am not sure I can live with another person again after being alone, though; I don't trust myself.

I feel angry with myself, I don't know why. Why can't I be like other people? American people go out, have fun, and forget what's on their minds. You don't have to worry all the time. Why not just have fun sometime? It's better than staying home and feeling sad all the time. I had an idea of going out and being crazy like Americans; that might make me forget, I thought. I think the most important thing is to go out and meet people, and maybe I will start to go out with co-workers. I don't really want to blame her [nodding her head towards her mother], but it's harder for me to change now. I am too old-fashioned.

CHAPTER TWELVE

Apsara: A Cambodian Wife

As I walked up the steps to Apsara's home one Saturday morning for our interview, I heard laughter and chatter through the open window. The aroma of spices I had smelled almost as soon as I got out of the car became stronger when Apsara's five-year-old daughter, who was standing near the window, spotted me coming and opened the door. In the kitchen, Apsara was preparing delicious-looking Cambodian pancakes, meats, and vegetables for friends and relatives who had arrived unexpectedly that morning.

Since I could not record her life history while visitors were there, I asked Apsara if I should return at a later date. She assured me that I should stay, and that she would talk to me after lunch. I sat at the dining table at one end of the small living room, above which hung a thriving houseplant in a basket. The wall facing me was adorned with photographs of Apsara and her husband, taken on their wedding day.

A framed picture of a Buddha in repose sat on a small shelf fastened on another wall. In front of the picture lay a plate with two bananas and an orange; Apsara had offered them in memory of her deceased relatives. She tells me that every time she buys groceries, she first offers the best fruits to the Buddha and prays for her relatives' souls.

Although I joined in the conversations of Apsara's family and friends, I was much more interested in observing the hostess herself as she moved around the kitchen. A very slender, petite woman, Apsara has an oval face and large expressive eyes. As I watched her reaching for dishes and spoons, and pouring spoonfuls of pancake batter into the hot pan, I was fascinated by the way she stretched her arms and curved her fingers. I felt that I was watching not a woman cooking in her kitchen but a ballerina. Never before had I seen a person who was as lithe and rhythmic, and so full of grace. Everything about her, even the golden-colored pancakes she folded in half and arranged on a platter in the shape of an open fan, looked like a work of art.

Later, when she told me her story, I discovered she had indeed been an artist. She had been an Apsara, or dancer. Even though her carefree dancing career ended abruptly when the Khmer Rouge took over the country, Apsara will always be an artist and a dancer; it permeates her whole being.

I first met Apsara at a Buddhist ceremony in the temple, where, dressed in a beautiful *sampot* (traditional dress for women), she looked every inch a Khmer. The next time I met her outside her workplace, she was clad in a sweater and a skirt, and looked strikingly Western. While her spirituality provides an interesting contrast to her unusually independent nature, her blending of the East and West is reflected particularly in her views of marriage and women's liberation. While it is clear that Apsara has made conscious choices about her role as a wife, her reflections also give us a glimpse of the gradual process of change that newcomers go through as a result of being exposed to a new culture and customs. ❖❖❖

Dancing Through Childhood

"Here is my child who came so fast that I didn't even have time to go to the hospital for her birth!" my mom loved to tease me when I was a little girl. Of her eight children, I was the only one to be born at home, in Phnom Penh, in 1960.

Even though I was born in the capital, my parents, who were ethnic Cambodians, originally came from Kompong Cham province, where my dad worked as the manager of the train station. It was an important job with a good salary, but my parents were poor because they had a lot of children, and Mom didn't work. They moved to Phnom Penh, hoping that Dad could earn more money. Dad was an educated man, and he did find a new job with a higher salary as a clerk in the army; but when I was young, I remember my family still being poor.

Our two-bedroom house had a thatched roof. We had wooden chairs and a dining table in the living room, but we didn't have sofas. Only rich people like Dad's sisters had them. They also had servants, but my mom cooked every day for our family on her clay stove, using coal for fuel. My older sisters helped Mom in the kitchen, but Dad liked to eat only what Mom cooked, so she cooked all the main dishes.

In Cambodia, some people built their kitchens adjacent to their houses, but our kitchen was inside the house. Since we didn't have running water, we connected a hose to a neighbor's faucet and filled up the big tank in the kitchen every day. We paid our neighbor five riel for the water. During the rainy season, we collected the rainwater that came down the gutters and used it for washing and bathing.

Although Cambodian girls were supposed to help with housework, I did not have to do any, because my older sisters helped Mom. My job was to fatten the pigs she raised to sell, and to keep them clean. I also loved to play with the pigs. Sometimes they would roll over on their backs and lie with their legs up in the air until I stroked their tummies. Those pigs were like family, and I missed them badly when Mom sold them, but I knew she did so because she needed the money.

My mom got married when she was sixteen years old. She had never gone to school, and when I was little she started going to adult school. But when she tried to read, Dad made fun of her, saying, "Look at her, she is learning A B C!" and she quit going to school.

Although Mom could not read or write, she was a good talker, and she began selling diamonds and houses that belonged to her friends, for which she earned a commission. I loved watching her get ready to go out in a nice sampot and a lot of jewelry. She looked real nice then, and I felt proud of her. "Mom, let me come with you," I would pester her, but she wouldn't, because I had to go to school. My mom earned a lot of money from her business, and with her earnings my parents built a new house.

Our new house was much taller and bigger than the old one, and it had a clay tile roof. It had two living rooms, three bedrooms, a new kitchen with a faucet and a sink, and a bathroom inside the house. Now we were able to bathe inside the house, and other neighbors bought water from us.

The new house was so big that my older sisters and their husbands also lived with us after they were married. Mom did not want them to separate from the family after marriage, and besides, it was cheaper for them to live with us because though they bought their own food and cooked separately, they did not have to pay for other utilities. We all got along well with each other, and I loved having my sisters living at home because if I didn't like what Mom cooked for us, I could eat with them.

My sisters' marriages were arranged by my parents. My parents had known my brothers-in-law since they were young, and it was almost like my sisters were marrying relatives. My oldest sister's husband worked as a security guard for a Chinese business company, and my second sister's husband was a teacher. He taught agriculture, and often went to the countryside to teach farmers. I don't remember my oldest sister's wedding at all, but I remember the beautiful red, frilly dress my aunt sewed me for my second sister's wedding.

I was about eight or nine years old when my third sister got married, but I missed her wedding. I was very sick at the time with a lot of pain in my throat and ears, and the doctor told my parents that I needed to have a throat operation. So about the time my sister was getting married, my parents sent me to stay at my uncle's house, which was within walking distance of the hospital in Phnom Penh.

My uncle, who was Mom's brother, owned a small grocery store in which he sold dry goods such as rice, fish, pepper, onions, sweetmeats, as well as all kinds of fruits. My grandma, who lived with us, went there almost every Saturday to help him. I too went with Grandma to Uncle's store because he let me eat anything I liked.

When I went into the hospital for the throat operation, Grandma came to stay with me. But I felt lonely because my parents and my brothers and sisters did not come to visit me, and after the operation I was even more miserable because I was hungry, and the nurse would not give me food. When I asked her for something to eat she said, "You cannot have anything because hot food will hurt your throat. You'll have to wait for a couple of days until you feel better." But I was too hungry to wait till I got better, and I told my grandma, "I want some rice, Grandma, but the nurse won't give me any. Why don't we run away from the hospital and go home?" So that's what we did. Without telling the doctor, we first went back to my uncle's house to say goodbye, and then returned home in a taxi. I was afraid that Mom would scold me because I ran away from the hospital, but though she was surprised, she did not get angry. She only said, "You should have stayed there until you got better." I got better anyway, at home.

Although Mom loved to talk, Dad didn't. He smiled a lot, but said very little, even to the children. After he came home from work he sat with his books or listened to the radio. Mom took care of everything. She cooked, looked after the children, and went out to sell things. When she went out, Dad looked after the house, and made sure that we behaved properly. If we misbehaved, he spanked us with a piece of wood.

The only time Dad spanked me was when I refused to go to the market in the evening to buy cigarettes or fish sauce because I was scared of ghosts. I had never seen a ghost, but people in my country talked about them a lot. I had heard those who had seen ghosts say, "They look so frightful! They have long matted hair all over their faces, and tongues hanging out of their open mouths!" So when Dad told me to go to the market in the evening I refused because I was scared that a ghost would grab me when I went down the steps, and he spanked me because I disobeyed him.

When Dad spanked me I shut myself in the room, and cried and swore, saying, "I don't like you, and I will never ever go to the market again to get anything for you." Of course, I never said that loud enough for Dad to hear, but I got so angry and hurt that I refused to eat dinner when my sisters called me, and stayed in the room for the rest of the evening. Later on, though, I felt ashamed about my behavior, and stayed in the room only because I didn't want anybody to see me. After everyone went to sleep, I sneaked into the kitchen and ate whatever was left.

Even though I got angry with Dad when he spanked me, I know he loved me because he often bought me things, and when Mom was away, he cooked my lunch and wrapped it so I could take it to school.

I never told Dad why I refused to go to the market, because I didn't think he would believe me. Mom, though, knew we were afraid of ghosts, because in the night, we all wanted to sleep with her on her big bed in the living room.

I don't know how my parents met, but I think they were very happy together. They were Buddhists, and we went to the temple often with Mom and Grandma. In the temple, the monks told us stories, and sometimes, Mom and Grandma made us sit on the floor and listen quietly while they explained to us the events from the Buddha's life that were painted on the temple walls and roofs. I was bored sitting there listening to them, and all the while I wished I could buy ice cream from the vendors who honked their horns and played music outside on the road! And as soon as they finished telling stories, that was what we did.

Dad prayed a lot, and often told us also to pray and to think of our deceased relatives so they would help us. But he didn't go to the temple as much as Mom, because he didn't like visiting places, and sometimes, instead of taking food to the temple, we invited the monks to our house and offered them food.

Like my Dad, I am a quiet person. My sisters and brothers liked me because I seldom argued with them. My nieces and nephews liked me too, because unlike others, I didn't check on them or spank if they misbehaved.

The only time I fought with my older sisters or brother was when they wouldn't let me go to play with the neighbors' children when Mom was away. "You have to stay home, look after things, and do your studies," they would tell me. I argued with them, but obeyed them in the end because they were older than me.

The only person I didn't get along with was my youngest brother, because Mom gave him whatever he wanted and he did as he pleased. He never listened to me or anybody else. He lives with me now, and he is still like that.

When I was seven years old, I started going to school, which was about three kilometers away from home. I liked Khmer, French, and math, but even more, I loved to dance. My third sister liked dancing too, and she took a test to enter dancing school, but because her body was not straight and soft, she did not pass. I was skinny and straight like Dad, and when I was about ten years old, my sister told me to try out for dancing school. At the test, I had to clap and dance to music. Two hundred or so girls and boys took that test, and only about sixty had the makings of a dancer. I was one of them, and I left my old school and went to dancing school, where we learned to dance for four hours in the morning and had regular lessons in the afternoon.

My dancing teacher was a man, and he taught us folk dances, such as the coconut dance and the fishermen's dance, that depicted our culture. After I came home I practiced in front of the mirror to make sure I danced the way the teacher taught us. But I was too shy to dance in the presence of my family, because if ever Dad saw me, he kicked me lightly in the back and teased me. So I practiced only when they were not around. But I loved it so much that I danced in the kitchen, and even on the road when I went to the market.

I became a good dancer and was always chosen to dance for the president or other important people at the concert hall in Phnom Penh. The concert hall was very big, and it was surrounded with beautiful flowers. Many tourists came to see us perform there, and we also performed for other students in the school. The school paid 30 riel to each dancer, and sometimes visitors for whom we performed gave us money too. With the money I earned I bought makeup and the clothes I needed for dancing. Sometimes our dance troupe visited other cities, and once we traveled by a special bus to Kompong Speu to dance for government officials. Another time we flew to Battambang for two weeks.

When we went on tour we stayed in guesthouses, where we were treated like kings and queens! Before the performances the people who looked after us ordered all kinds of special foods for us, and after we ate they put on our makeup. Then we dressed in our beautiful costumes, and started dancing.

When I danced, I was no longer a part of this world. Moving my body gently and rhythmically to the music, I felt completely free; I forgot reality, and I had no worries. I was happiest when I danced, and I loved my life in Phnom Penh.

Sickness and Death Under the Khmer Rouge

I was fifteen when the Communists came. We had seen other evacuees carrying their belongings and trudging past our house, and Mom had already packed rice, fish, clothes, and other things to take if we had to leave too. When the soldiers ordered us to evacuate, we tied some of the bundles on our bicycles, and carried the rest by hand, on our shoulders, or on our heads. My younger brother and I carried two buckets of water, and we took Grandma on a bicycle because she was too old to walk.

My sisters had six children between them, and we had a terrible time trying not to lose sight of our large family, as we walked with thousands of other people. At night we tried to sleep in temples because we knew they were safe places. Also, temple compounds had lots of fruit trees, and if the monks had food, they gave some to the people.

We walked for about a month, and when we reached Prey Veng, we stopped there, because that was the village where my sister's mother-in-law lived. We had hoped she would let us live with her, but because her family was also large, she could not take us in. The Communist leader of the village said we could live under her house, which was built on piles, and since we had no other place to go, the floor of her house became the roof over our heads.

Our food ran out soon after we got to Prey Veng, so before the Communists put us to work, my older brother walked to faraway villages and traded our clothes for rice, yams, salt, and other food. But after about five or six months, food became scarce, and everybody, even relatives, became mean. When we asked for food, they would say, "Oh, we don't have any food even for ourselves. So how can we give you some?" But we knew they had food because they were the "Old People." They just wanted to save what they had for their own families.

Soon after food became a problem, the Communists separated our family. They sent me away to live with other girls who planted rice. A few days after I left, a soldier came and told me, "Your grandma has died. If your group leader gives you permission, you can go and see her." My leader gave me permission to go, and I discovered that my grandma had died of starvation.

At that time, the Communists were still not too strict, and they allowed us to burn her body in the temple grounds. But they did not allow Mom to build a small monument near the temple for my grandmother's remains, as was our custom. So we collected her bones into a bag, which my mother carried with her wherever she went. Every night, we prayed, "Grandma, please help us and take care of us." We know she saved my brother when he almost died from malaria.

Since we had relatives in Prey Veng, the villagers knew that Dad and my brothers-in-law had worked for the Lon Nol government, and we lived in constant fear because we didn't know when the soldiers would come to take them away. So when the soldiers asked if any families wanted to leave Prey Veng and relocate to a new place to live, we decided to leave. Even though our parents did not originally come from Battambang, we decided to go there because that's where they grew a lot of rice.

The Khmer Rouge packed us into trains and buses like animals, and took us to Battambang. There, they divided families into different work groups and villages, and gave each family a hut. Fortunately, they assigned all my family members to one village, but my married sisters were put into different work groups. Only the unmarried children lived in the parents' hut.

We came to Battambang hoping to get enough food, but there too, only the "Old People" got enough to eat. They had rice, fish, and salt in their own homes, but the soldiers gave us only rice gruel to eat, just as before. We foraged for mushrooms and tamarind and whatever else we could find in the jungle, but we never had enough for our large family. So we began to steal food from the "Old People," and we also stole banana and papaya leaves from the community farms, which we boiled and ate.

We always shared any food we found with the family, and looked out for each other when we stole things. But one day, I didn't see a chlop watching my younger brother stealing rice, and after he caught my brother, the soldiers beat him with bamboo poles until his skin split. I felt terrible because it was I who told him to steal the rice, but my brother never told them.

Two or three months after we came to Battambang, the Communists sent my older brother to another camp and ordered me to join the "front-line workers," far away from the village where my parents lived. There were about twelve other girls in my group, and we had to plant rice for at least sixteen hours a day. We worked in the pouring rain or under the blistering sun. The soldiers supervised us and told us where to plant the rice, and I just pushed the rice plants in wherever I was told to. I was too hungry to care whether they grew or not; my only aim was to find anything to fill my stomach. On good days I found tiny shrimp or small crab in the rice fields. I could eat the shrimp alive because they had no blood in them, and they tasted sweet. But I had to cook the crab, so I killed them and hid them in my pocket until I could roast them over a fire later on.

In 1977, I was stricken with malaria, and the Pol Pots gave me some medicine they made using plants and leaves. But it only made me worse, and I became so sick that one day my group leader told me to go back to the village. I do not recall how I managed to get back to the village by myself, but when I got there I found only my father and younger brother and sister in the hut, and they looked so very thin, I hardly knew them. "Your mother is in the hospital. She is badly swollen and very ill," Dad said.

A few days after I got back a soldier came and informed us, "We need this house for Angka. We have assigned you to live with another family."

We had to live with some "Old People," who lived nearby, and they did not like me. The man of that house told me, "Your family can live here, but you will have to live in that empty house at the edge of the village." But I couldn't live by myself in an empty house, and I had no other place to go. So my dad and my younger siblings moved into that house with me.

After we moved to that old house, Dad became too exhausted to work. We had nothing to eat except the watered rice the Communists gave us. My sisters lived nearby, but they didn't care about us anymore. They were hungry too, and they wanted to keep any food they got for their families.

Because Dad couldn't work in the rice fields anymore, the soldiers cut his ration of rice gruel in half. Soon, he became so weak that he could no longer even walk. One day Dad became desperate for rice. He said, "If I don't get some rice, I will die. I will go to live in the hospital because I might get some rice there." I couldn't help him to go to the hospital because I was sick too, and with great difficulty, he dragged himself there.

A few days after Dad went to hospital, I dreamed that a blackbird sat on the roof of the house in which we lived, and cawed. I woke up feeling terrified because I knew that when the blackbird cried, it was taking a person's soul. The next morning, a soldier came to our door. "Your dad has died," he said.

My younger sister had gone to see Mom in the hospital, so I went with my brother to bring my dad's body back to hold a small ceremony so he could have a good life in his next birth. But the nurse in the hospital would not let us bring him back. She wrapped him in a sheet and said, "You go on home. We will take care of everything." So we had to leave our dad there and go back to the house.

I don't know if Dad got any rice to eat in the hospital, but when the nurse wrapped him up in the sheet, I saw a mandarin orange under his back. He must have hidden it there to eat later. My dad looked so skinny, tired, and sad. I don't think he wanted to die.

After Dad died, the villagers told us that the house we lived in was haunted, and that whenever people lived there someone died. We got so frightened that we asked the village leader for permission to live with our second sister, and moved there.

About a week after Dad died, Mom came back from the hospital. When she found out he had died, she cried bitterly, blaming herself and us for his death. "If I had not fallen sick he would not have died," she wept, and kept on asking us, "Why did you go to live in that haunted house? Why didn't you stay in the hut?" But we had had no choice, no other place to live.

I dreamed of my dad almost every night after he died. He looked so sad, and he would say, "I am cold. Can I have my clothes?"

Soon after Mom got back from the hospital the Communists sent me to the front line again; this time, our group had to build dams. It was even harder than planting rice. And then, the leader of that camp assigned me to work in the kitchen! Everybody liked to work in the kitchen because then they got food to eat. As a kitchen worker, I even got to eat real rice instead of rice gruel, and soon I became plump like the "Old People." But I was still sad because my friends were hungry and skinny, and I stole food and gave it to them whenever I could.

After I had worked in the kitchen for two or three months, the Khmer

Rouge sent me to look after about five hundred pigs that were kept in a big business building in the town. I lived there with five other girls and two boys, and we had to take turns to go to the countryside and cut banana trees and leaves to feed the pigs.

My new boss was a woman, and I was like her right hand. She told me a lot of the things that went on, and I remember once she said, "The Angka want the Khmer to be a white-skinned race, so they are killing the dark-skinned people. Cambodian girls must now marry Chinese people because the Chinese are whiter than us." I never saw anyone being killed, but my leader told me that one man she tried to kill was so strong that he did not die even after she had hacked him with her ax many times. So she had left him on the ground writhing with pain to die.

I was very frightened. I did not want to be killed by this leader. So I just agreed with everything she said, and did what she told me to do; I knew that was the only way to survive.

The Vietnamese Liberation

When the Vietnamese came I was still looking after the pigs. I didn't know that the Khmer Rouge had been fighting with the Vietnamese. I knew things had changed only when I woke up one morning and there were no Khmer Rouge to be seen, until my leader came on a bicycle and said she was leaving the house. "Will you come with me?" she asked. I didn't want to go with her; I wanted to find my family, but I didn't want to tell her so. I just told her that I will stay back. She took her gun, and looked me straight in the eye. "You must go with me," she ordered. I decided to do as she said. We rode into town on a bicycle. She told me to drop her off near a trench, and then, without any explanation, said I was free to go!

I didn't know if my family was still in Battambang. I rode around trying to find them, and I met a Pol Pot soldier who often came to eat lunch with us when we looked after the pigs. I liked him because he had been kinder to us than the other soldiers. "Where are you going?" he asked, and I replied that I was trying to find my family. "It's difficult to find anybody with so many people traveling. Why don't you live with my wife and me until you find your family?" he said. Since I hadn't found my family and had no other place to go, I lived with them for a month or so. Then one morning, my third sister came to that house looking for me! Someone who had seen me living there had told her I was alive.

I thanked the soldier and went to live with my sister and her husband.

We didn't know what had happened to our mother and the rest of our family until one day, a man we knew said that our mom was living in the nearby town of Sisophon. The next morning my sister and I hired two bicycles and rode to Sisophon. We didn't know where to look for Mom, so we rode down the main street, hoping to find someone who knew her. Suddenly we heard someone shouting our names. It was Mom!

That night Mom cooked the best food she could find, and we sat and talked all through the night. Of all her children, only my second brother was still missing. No one knew if he had survived. My two older brothers-in-law and my dad's sisters had all been killed by Pol Pot, and three of our six nieces and nephews had starved to death like Grandma.

My whole family left Sisophon and came to live with my sister. There was still a lot of fighting in Cambodia, and the Vietnamese were everywhere. We had no way to make a living, so Mom traded the gold and medicine she had managed to save from the Pol Pots and got food for the family. When we found stray cows, we killed them and shared the meat with our neighbors.

Mom kept saying, "I don't see how we can ever build a life again; we have nothing left, and things are not getting any better." Finally, she decided that we should leave Cambodia. While we made plans to escape to a refugee camp, my second brother, who had heard from a friend that we were living in Battambang, came looking for us. Mom had found all her children. "Maybe we did something good in our last life; that's why we are all living together again," she said over and over, crying with happiness.

A few days after my brother came back, I was walking along the road when I saw a man who looked like my dancing teacher from Phnom Penh. I went closer and looked, and I discovered it was him! He had even started another dancing school in Battambang and had about twenty new students, and he asked me if I too wanted to join. I rushed home and told my mom that my teacher was alive, and that I wanted to go back to dancing school, but she would not hear of it. She insisted that I should escape to the refugee camp with the family. But my ambition was to dance again, and when I couldn't persuade her to let me go, I decided to leave home on my own, even though I hurt Mom and made her angry.

I didn't worry about leaving my family because I had already lived by myself under the Communists, and I knew I would not bring disrespect to the family by having a boyfriend. Also, unlike my mother who had a hard time finding food for us, my teacher got free rice from the Vietnamese because he worked for them.

In 1980 my family left for the refugee camp, and I stayed in Battambang. I had expected that the country would get back to normal and that we would be performing in many places as before. But we couldn't travel to other places because of the war, and we only danced for the Vietnamese soldiers, who paid us with rice. We didn't get any money. I began to miss my mom. Once or twice she sent me some clothes through people who traveled back and forth between Battambang and the camp, but I had no way to contact her. Soon, I began to wish I had gone with her because I got a big sty on my left eye. Though it didn't hurt, it looked terrible. I couldn't go to a doctor because I had no money to pay. I didn't want to bother my teacher about my eye, so I kept it covered with my long hair. But oh, how I wished I was with Mom, so I could get some medicine for it!

About five months after my family left, Mom sent a man my family had known well in Phnom Penh to bring me to the refugee camp. Since she didn't know I was longing to go back to her, she had sent some nice clothes to persuade me to go. I was really happy, and I said goodbye to my teacher, and left with Mom's friend.

We joined a large group of about two hundred people who were escaping from Cambodia. "Be very careful when you travel, because Vietnamese soldiers are raping unmarried women," people warned us along the way. So even though the man who took me was already married, I pretended that I was his wife. We walked for two weeks, and we were very lucky because we had no problems with soldiers or robbers. But we had little food or rest, and I was very, very tired. I told the man many times that I did not want to escape anymore, but he kept on encouraging me to go on, and at last we reached the camp. I think Mom paid some money to the man to bring me there, but if he had not come I doubt I would have ever left Cambodia.

We lived in Khao-I-Dang refugee camp. At first I thought living in the camp was like living in Phnom Penh again because we had food and clothes, and there were hundreds of people. But after a few days, I began to feel like a prisoner because we had no freedom to go anywhere, and we had to wait until the camp officials gave us food, water, or anything else we needed. At night, it was terrible because the one room given to our whole family was so small that it was nearly impossible to sleep.

I became friendly with a Cambodian man who spoke English, and he introduced me to a doctor in the camp hospital. The doctor gave me a job helping children whose arms or legs had been amputated because of injuries, or who were so weak that they could not move or walk. My second sister got a job as a secretary to a teacher. So even though we still could not leave the camp to go anywhere, we became less depressed because we could at least go to work. Also, we now had money to buy things from the vendors who sold goods around the camp grounds, and I think my family was luckier than most other refugees who were there.

Until we came to refugee camp we had not heard about a country called the U.S.A., but in the camp, we heard people talking about the U.S.A. Many Cambodian people who lived in the camp went there to live, and when our uncle too went there and sponsored us, we decided to make the U.S.A. our new home. American people working in the camp taught us how to live there. They taught us how to buy things in a supermarket, how to use a stove, and how to turn the heat on and off. They said we had to unplug appliances before we went to sleep. They showed us how to use flush toilets. I knew some of these things because I had lived in the city, but they were new things to many people who had lived in villages in Cambodia.

Coming to America

We arrived in Oregon, which was bitterly cold! Even more than the cold, our problem was learning to cope with the snow, which we had never seen before. It took us some time to get used to the new weather, but once we settled down, my younger brother and sister started grade school, and I joined a community college to learn English. I am the smartest person in my family, but I had a difficult time learning English because I had always spoken only Cambodian, and had a lot of problems with English pronunciation. It took me about a year to learn enough English to find work in the refugee office as a clerk, and till then, I picked mushrooms and strawberries with the rest of the family to earn some money.

After a couple of years, I got married to a Cambodian man who also came to Oregon as a refugee. He was sponsored by an American, and although both of us are Buddhists, we also went to church to please his sponsor. The Americans who came to church in Oregon always spoke to us nicely and slowly so we could understand them, but when we moved to California, we had problems because some people speak to us too fast, as if we were born here. And when we don't understand, they look at us as if we were a different species. If people speak slowly and clearly we can understand because when we don't follow their speech, we can still read their lips, but if they speak too quickly, we have problems in understanding them.

I've lived in America for almost ten years now, but though I can speak

English, I can't read and write it well. Because of this, I can't work as a secretary, as I would like to; instead I work on the assembly line in an electronics company. I have worked at this company for two years. I know my work and I was quite happy at my job until a Vietnamese who also works there fought with me. My supervisor told her to do some work with me, but when she needed to ask anything she always went to another person. Maybe she thought I was not a good worker. One day she was talking to somebody else and seemed to be having a good time, and I thought maybe that was a good time to get to know her. I asked her what she was talking about, and she said, "It's none of your business, f--- you." I was so embarrassed. No one in the company had ever talked to me like that or fought with me before. People have always treated me nicely because I am nice to them, and I am honest and I keep my promises. But since she spoke to me like that, I don't feel comfortable working here. I would like to move to a new company.

Although some Americans treat Cambodians nicely, others are jealous of us because we have jobs, new cars, new clothes, or our own businesses. They say that we take their jobs. But it's hard to get jobs because we don't speak good English, and when we find jobs, we work very hard to keep them. We're able to buy what we have because when we get our paycheck we spend a little for food, and save as much as we can. Some Americans don't save, so they can't buy what they want, and it's wrong for them to feel upset with us.

A Cambodian Wife in America

If we lived in Cambodia I would have behaved differently toward my husband. Over there we have to always try to be nice to the husband. Wives don't talk back, but sometimes I do that here a little bit, because I have more freedom to say what I think here. However, I am careful not to speak too disrespectfully to him, and in that way, I think I am different from the Americans.

I am unlike Americans in other ways too, because I always look up to my husband as the person who takes care of the family. I want my husband to be in a higher position at work than myself. If the woman earns more money, she becomes stronger than her husband, and I don't think that is good because then she might always speak harshly to him and make him feel bad.

I want my husband to learn a lot so he can teach our daughter, but when I say to him, "Will you go to school and learn more? I will look after the kid," my husband says, "I will go if you go too." I don't know why he wants me to go as well; maybe he feels lonely if he goes by himself. But both of us can't go because we have to look after our child. If he will not go, I will go to school and he can look after her. I will learn to type and do secretarial work, so I can get a better job, but I will always respect my husband and look after him because he takes very good care of my daughter and me.

My husband treats my family well, and my Mom and my brothers and sisters like him too. The only thing I don't like about him is that, like my dad, he does not like to go out to visit people; he especially dislikes going to parties. I am a dancer and I like going to parties, but because he doesn't go I have to stay at home too. But I feel very close to my husband and we trust one another. We are always honest and don't hide anything from each other. He told me that before we got married he didn't have any girlfriends, and I believe him because when I married him he didn't know much about women. I wouldn't have married him if he had another girlfriend because he might still be in love with her. Now he has no other woman and I have no other man.

Some Americans who are married still go out with other men, or leave their husbands. Although I have more freedom to go about here, I will not do that. I will stay married to one person. I think that is better, because when two people are used to living together, one person will feel sad and lonely if the other leaves. When you have family around you, you feel happier. Here, both marriage and divorce are easy, and while I don't think that is good, I also don't think I should criticize Americans because they think their way is good too.

My daughter is a very nice girl. She likes to sing and dance, and I hope she will have a happy life, like the one I had in Phnom Penh. Sometimes I think she could become a model, but whatever she does, I want my daughter to marry one day. I know girls have more freedom in this country, but she is a Cambodian, and my husband and I hope she will listen to us and get married one day. We, her mom and dad, wait for her to get married, but if she decides not to marry we will not force her. It is her life, and she should do what she wants, but we will feel sad that she does not listen to us.

Whether our daughter marries or not, she must not think of having boyfriends until she has finished her studies and got a college degree. I know that thirteen- and fourteen-year-old girls have boyfriends here, but that age is too young for that. A child is supposed to study until she is much older, and all I ask is that she be a good student and not think of having a boyfriend while she is in school. She can take care of herself after she gets her degree, and that is when she should think of love and marriage.

Reflections

I miss everything about Cambodia: weather, fruits, flowers. The weather was hot in Cambodia, but we also had a lot of rain, and even in the hot season there was a nice fresh breeze in the evening. Around my dancing school there were so many different kinds of beautiful flowers, and when the wind blew in the evening, the fragrance of fresh flowers spread all over the city. Over here, the flowers don't have a nice smell. Here, you see only cars, and you smell only the gas from them. At work I breathe the smoke from the soldering iron, and when I come home I breathe the smoke from the cars, and then I wish I was back in Cambodia, dancing in Phnom Penh. That's still what I wish I could do! When I was a child I always thought about food. My favorite pastime was eating, and when school was over, I bought all kinds of sweetmeats from women who sold food outside the school compound. At weekends, after a cool shower, I got some money from Mom, and walked over to the market, which was not too far from my home, and bought slices of young mango sold with a bit of salt and hot pepper. If Mom wouldn't give me money, I picked fruit from our own trees. In Cambodia people owned their homes and they grew whatever they wanted. There were no landlords to say you couldn't do things. Over here, some people can't grow what they want, and the fruit we buy from the supermarkets doesn't have that fresh taste.

If there had been no war and if Pol Pot had not taken over our country, Cambodia would have only improved. When I think of what Pol Pot did, I feel sad. Sometimes I feel mad and wish that I could kill him. I think I would feel better if I could kill him. I know it's not good to kill anybody, but this is different. But I know I can't do that because I am a woman, and I am not strong enough to kill a man. What would happen if Pol Pot didn't die when I tried to kill him, and lay there only half-dead?

We can't go back to Cambodia right now because there are Vietnamese all over our country, and there is the war, but we must go back to our country when we are old. Over there old people have a much happier life. Here the old people have to stay by themselves, and when a person dies, relatives have to pay a lot of money for cremations.

I try not to think about the past anymore. But sometimes I dream of my dad. He says he's hungry and that he needs food. Then I go to the supermarket and buy beef noodles, which used to be his favorite food. I cook the beef the way he liked, and offer it to the monks and pray for his soul.

I feel happy when I go to the temple. I can meet friends, I can pray that my father will have a good life in his next birth. When I pray, it helps his soul, and it gives my mind some peace to know I have helped him. I also tell the god who takes care of this house to help my father, and to take care of us. My mom and the old people tell us to do that. But I feel a little scared when I dream of my father at night. I usually wake up after a dream. Although I keep my eyes closed and try to go back to sleep, I am unable to do so.

I am pregnant now and I dream of my father often. Once I saw him with a baby. I can't remember if he was carrying a baby, or if he was the baby. I asked a monk about my dream and he said this baby that I am expecting might be my dad being reborn. I will be very happy if it is true.

We lost so many relatives during the Pol Pot time, and in that time we always worried about the future. Now I think it is best not to worry about the future. We should just live a good life while we can. Even here, it is so easy to die; you can die by getting electrocuted. You can never predict what will happen. Today I have a good marriage, but tomorrow my husband might not like me anymore. That's one of the reasons why I want to learn to be a secretary. If he left me, I think I could get a better job more easily if I was a secretary.

I think that in America people have too much freedom; this is why there are more killings, robberies, and drug problems. Here, people don't trust each other enough. For example, if a car hits someone, the driver gets sued for insurance money, but drivers don't mean to kill people. I think it's better to trust people and live a good life, wherever you are.

CHAPTER THIRTEEN

Koun Srey: A Teenage Daughter

At fifteen, Koun Srey is a pretty girl with long black hair, unusually long eyelashes, and a slender figure that looks equally good in skirts, jeans, or a sampot, the traditional dress for Khmer women. I came to know Koun Srey and her mother Pu Ma at least a year before I asked them if they would relate their narratives. (Pu Ma's story appears in Chapter 6.)

My acquaintance with Pu Ma's family began when I met her at another refugee's house, situated in a destitute part of town. When Pu Ma took me to her apartment across the road, Koun Srey was sitting on the couch, playing a board game with her older brother and her uncle. When they saw that Pu Ma had brought a visitor, they quickly picked up their game and got off the couch, so we could sit. Other than a small stool and an old television set standing on a coffee table, the couch was the only piece of furniture in the room.

When her mother introduced me, Koun Srey gave me a shy smile, and went into the kitchen. A few minutes later she returned, carrying a glass of

Coke and a plate with a bunch of bananas, which she placed on the small stool, close to me. Obviously, Pu Ma had trained her well in looking after visitors.

Soon, I became a regular visitor at Pu Ma's house. Pu Ma and I often discussed her concerns about her children or family back in Cambodia, when we walked her younger daughter to the nearby school, or chatted while she cooked, folded laundry, or did some other chores.

Pu Ma's training has ensured that Koun Srey is both a good hostess and an able cook. If I dropped in during the weekend, Koun Srey never failed to give me a bowl of noodles or soup she had cooked. She showed me books about her country, and when I told her that many of the tropical fruits found in Cambodia grew in Sri Lanka too, she brought me various combinations of foods that brought back wonderful memories for me. Once, when she presented me with a plate of sliced raw mangoes accompanied with salt and chili pepper, I remembered how, as children, my friends and I once plucked some mangoes from a tree growing near our school without the owner's permission, and hid them inside the hole of another big tree until the following day, when we could bring the salt and pepper to go with them!

Koun Srey takes such good care of her younger siblings that Pu Ma often laughingly tells me, "She is their second mother!" Koun Srey also has a warm relationship with her older brother and her uncle. Her uncle is only two or three years older than she. I often see them helping each other with schoolwork, or learning Cambodian together. One of their favorite pastimes is printing Cambodian proverbs in decorative writing to hang on the walls of their two-bedroom apartment, along with glossy posters of Indian movie stars and modern motor cars, family photographs, and posters depicting the life of the Buddha.

Koun Srey related her story in English so she could improve her language skills, and her poor grammar and pronunciation made transcribing somewhat difficult. Now, two years later, she has improved her auditory and linguistic skills by employing various innovative methods to learn English. For example, she listens to popular American songs and writes them down, and often asks me to correct them.

I admire Koun Srey for her many talents and qualities, but what has impressed me most is her care, concern, and respect for her widowed mother, who came from a poverty-stricken background, and exists on welfare here. It is for this reason I have called the narrator of this life story *Koun Srey*, which means "daughter."

Since Koun Srey was only two years old when the Khmer Rouge took over her country and her recollections of the Communist regime are sketchy, I was interested to find out if her mother's acute posttraumatic stress affects Koun Srey's outlook and adjustment. I found that they indeed have an influence on her.

As I came to know her, I was particularly struck by the fact that although she now lived in the more permissive American culture, Koun Srey appeared to adhere to her mother's traditional views of conduct without resentment. In my interviews with her then, I attempted to find out how a teenage refugee daughter growing up in the urban United States responded to her mother's traditional perspective on life. Koun Srey's narrative is a good example of how the pre–Khmer Rouge norms of behavior are passed down from one generation to the next, and how they are internalized. ❮❮❮

A Toddler's Memories of the Khmer Rouge

I was born in 1973, two years before Pol Pot chased people away to work in the countryside. My mom is not sure if my birthday is in January or in July. She thinks I was born on the first day of July.

I don't remember anything about myself before the Khmer Rouge took over my country, but Mom says I was fat and short, and that my father called me. . . [Koun Srey would not say the nickname because it is funny]. Mom still calls me by the nickname my father gave me, which means "fat and short." My real name was used for the first time only when I went to school in the refugee camp in Thailand.

While I can't recall the faces of the Pol Pot soldiers who occupied Cambodia in 1975, the birth year of my younger brother, I remember their black clothes, and the scarves they used to wear around their necks. I also remember that they didn't let me eat when I was hungry. They only let me eat at a particular time.

During the Pol Pot time, I lived with my grandmother, parents, uncle, and two brothers in a small camp in the mountains. My parents had to go to work every day. I can recall Grandmother's face a little bit. It was skinny. I don't think she looked normal because she always looked so worried. I also remember my little brother who died. He was such a smart talker! One time, my parents went away to another village to give some rice to my relatives who were starving even more than us. Then the Pol Pots put me in the cafeteria with all the children who had no parents, and I saw a lot of yams on the table. I was very hungry and I wanted to eat one, but I didn't, because my parents had told me over and over, "You must not take anything from the cafeteria because the Pol Pots would beat you hard." My parents had also warned me not to run away. They said that if I did, the Pol Pots would put them in jail.

Although my uncle, my brother, and I ate with the other children in the cafeteria when Mom and Dad went to work, in the night we came back to our hut to sleep with Grandmother. I remember one night when I was walking back, my eyes kept closing because I was so sleepy and I bumped into a cow. The owner of the cow must have felt sorry for me because he took me home. Another time, I stepped on a baby chicken, and it died. I got so frightened, I ran away. That chicken belonged to a girl called Nyar Dey.

Every night, I waited for Mom and Dad to come back. I didn't want to sleep without seeing them first, and I wouldn't go when Grandmother called me to sleep. Once I saw a man and a woman coming from the jungle and ran to meet them, thinking they were my parents. But when I got closer I realized they were some other people, and I started to cry.

I also saw a ghost during the Pol Pot time. One afternoon I went to bathe with my brother at a lake far away from my house. When we were coming back home, I saw a woman going up a tree. She had long hair and wore a white cloth. When she was at the top of the tree, she just disappeared. I ran home and told my parents about the woman who disappeared, and my parents said it was a ghost. I wasn't frightened, though, because I never saw the woman's face; I only saw her back.

The Pol Pots were very cruel and ignorant, and they killed a lot of people; especially the famous and rich people with an advanced education. My father and grandmother were not famous, but the soldiers just took them away and murdered them.

Running Away to Thailand

When I was six years old, I ran away from my country in the middle of the night to Thailand, with my mother, brothers, and my uncle. My father, grandmother, and younger brother had died.

When we were escaping, the Vietnamese soldiers followed us and shot at us, but luckily we managed to escape into the jungle. I helped my mom carry some things. At night we slept in the jungle. My uncle and brother fell asleep quickly, but I couldn't, because I was unhappy; I knew that Mom was awake, worrying about the children and about the future.

When we had almost reached the camp, I saw a man selling water and I asked him for a drink of water. He said, "One bowl of water cost one baht." But my mom didn't have any money to pay him. The man was nice and just gave us some water. He was Cambodian too, but he had come to camp a long time before.

We lived in the same camp that he did, which was called "New Camp" by the Khmer people who lived there. We lived there for several months, and then we left because there were bomb explosions around the camp. Many people died, and a lot of people were wounded.

In 1980, the Americans brought us into Khao-I-Dang camp. The houses in the camp were not yet fixed, so my family lived in a small house that had a wall on one side and a broken roof. After some time we were moved to another house in a different building. The houses in that building were new and a lot of people lived there. Other people died there [from starvation and other abuses suffered under Pol Pot]. Americans gave us rice and meat.

Khao-I-Dang camp was small and surrounded by barbed wire fences, like a jail. It had a big market. My mom said it was like the market in Battambang. She planted things to sell there.

When I was eight or nine years old, I went to school with my uncle and my brother every day except Sunday. I learned how to read and write Cambodian. We had only one class a day, from eight to eleven in the morning. We didn't move from class to class like in high school here.

When we came back from school we had to work in the garden, which was a bit far from our house. So I studied only at night. On Sundays, I went with my family and my neighbors to the mountains to collect firewood, and sometimes we bathed in the river. During the Cambodian New Year, we went to the temple, and we played a lot of interesting Cambodian games like pulling the rope and throwing water balloons. Every year, that was the only time I had fun.

In 1984, my family and I went to the Philippine camp and lived there for six months. The Philippine island was big, and surrounded by the ocean and big mountains. It was a wonderful place and much nicer than the other camps I had lived in. The people there were very polite and nice, and I wanted to stay in that camp forever, but I had to leave because I came to the U.S.A.

Though I live in the U.S.A. now, I will never forget my life in the refugee camps, especially the one in the Philippines. Even though I lived there for only six months, it seems like I lived there ever since I was born. It was a great place where I had freedom to play, and I made a lot of friends. I also went to school, and had enough food to eat every day. So I have a lot of happy memories of the Philippine camp.

A Teenager in America

We arrived in San Francisco in January 1985, when I was about twelve years old. I don't know if we arrived in the morning or in the evening, but I remember it was very cold! After we left the airport we had to ride a bus for a long time to reach our new home. That was my first bus ride. I was very tired and so was my mother. I sat quietly, gazing at the American landscape. The weather looked very cold. As I looked at the sky through the windshield, I noticed that it was not blue, but green. I remember thinking, "Oh, in America the sky is green; it's not blue like in Cambodia and Thailand." Later, I realized I had been looking at the sky through the green-colored part of the windshield, and that was why it looked green.

When we reached our destination, we were met by my uncle. I think he and his family came to America in 1983. My uncle came in a car to take us to his house, but I didn't know how to ride in a car. It went too fast, and with it, the landscape went fast too. I felt very dizzy. We had never traveled by bus or car in Cambodia. We had just walked there. The only time I had traveled in a vehicle in Cambodia was when Americans brought us from the border camp to Khao-I-Dang camp in a truck. Then too, I felt sick. For a long time after coming to America, I felt dizzy when I took the bus to school.

We lived with my uncle in his downtown apartment. There were seven people in his family, and five people in mine, and the apartment had only two small bedrooms and one living room. In the night while the moms and children slept in the bedrooms, the men slept in the living room.

The downtown streets were very narrow, and full of houses. There was no place for us to play, and when I came back from school I had to stay in the house. Most of the time I just stayed in our room, which was very dark. It made me sick and I got headaches. Finally, about a year later, my family moved to a better apartment in a different part of town. I liked the new place better because there were children downstairs I could play with, and the bedrooms were a bit bigger than in my uncle's apartment.

When I first went to school in America there were lots of Vietnamese and Hispanic students, but there were only five Cambodians. At the beginning some children were very mean. They teased me and my friend, and some of them pulled our hair or our hands. Some even jumped over my head. They joked and laughed at us until the teacher came. My friend was so upset that she cried. I was upset too, but I didn't cry. I felt angry, but I couldn't say anything because I didn't know how to speak English. When I knew a few words of English and spoke up other students laughed, and I was embarrassed and afraid to speak up again.

After we had been here for a while, Mom bought me a secondhand bicycle to go to school. One day I found that someone had broken it. After we repaired it, someone stole it. I felt so unhappy that I didn't want to stay in America anymore. I wanted to go back to camp.

My religion tells me that I should do good things to other people. But in America, children did bad things to us, and I thought that here, people did not have a religion. Now I know they have a religion.

I've gone to school now for four years, but I still have problems learning English. I can look up new words in the Cambodian-English dictionary because I know how to read Cambodian, but English has long, hard words I don't know how to read or to pronounce. I find it difficult to understand the meaning of words even after my teacher explains them to me, until she makes sentences with them. When I have trouble remembering English, I worry that there is something wrong with my brain. I worry because we can't speak English well. I am now a freshman in high school. I hope I will have improved my English when I graduate after four years; otherwise it will be difficult for me to find a good job here.

I enjoy school, but I dislike sex education. I find it embarrassing, but we have to do it for science. Once the teacher showed a movie in that class. My friend had already seen it, and she said it was not a good movie. So I didn't watch it. I just put my head down on my desk and waited until the movie was over. The teacher didn't say anything to me.

My mother knows very little English, so we speak Cambodian at home. If I speak in English with my friends, some older people think I wish to forget my language. While I want to learn English, I think it's important to remember my language too, because when I go back to my country I will not speak English again. Some people know many languages, but they don't forget their own language. I hope my little sister who is in first grade now will know both Cambodian and English when she grows up.

I worked in the assembly line in the summer. That was my first job in this country, and I thought going to school was easier than going to work! At work I stood almost the whole day. It made me very tired and I felt sorry for some of the workers who are old; they must find it very hard to stand all day. There were five other Cambodian workers, and since none of us speak

English well, it's hard for us to find good jobs in this country. If we had stayed in our country we would've spoken Cambodian, and it would've been easy for us to find the jobs we'd like to do.

Whenever I work, I give all the money I earn to my mother, because she has to buy food and clothes for us. Sometimes she gives me five dollars, but I don't spend it. Occasionally my friends borrow money from me, but if a person does not give it back, I don't let them borrow again. If they ask me, I say I don't have money. When I go to the store I never buy anything. My mom buys me the things I need, and I let her know what type of clothes and things I want.

My summer job lasted only six weeks. After that I stayed home every day until school started. I was so bored, but there was nobody to drive me anywhere. In the four years I've lived here, I've gone once to San Francisco, once to Oakland, and twice to Stockton. I have cousins in Stockton and sometimes my uncle goes there for a few days. Stockton is a very narrow place. I wish I could go there just for the day. I don't like to stay there overnight because there are lots of children in the area where my cousins live, and it is very noisy. My cousins never open their windows because they don't want any mirrors and things broken when the children play ball around their house. Their house is always dark and gloomy and it makes me feel depressed.

Love and Marriage

There is a boy who likes me, but I don't want to have an affair with him. My mom didn't go to school when she was young, but she advises me to get a good education before I have boyfriends. She says if I'm educated, I will be able to judge if a man is good or bad when I want to get married. She says, "If you have boyfriends and girlfriends, you forget about studying. You will think only about writing letters." I will do what Mom says, and keep studying.

Some fourteen- or fifteen-year-old girls in America have boyfriends. They get pregnant before they marry. When girls meet guys at parties they fall in love, elope, and get married. After some time, the guy doesn't love that girl anymore. He leaves her, and she comes home, but her parents don't take her back. The girl has a baby, that guy has another girl, and she is alone. My mom and other old people say that's no good.

When my mom was young, a lot of men liked her but she didn't have a boyfriend. She met my father at work. They were just friends at first. Mom liked him because he was an honest man who had a good sense of humor, and when Dad said he wanted to marry her, she told him he must first talk to her mother of his intentions. But until they were married, my mom had not gone out on dates with my dad.

I avoid a lot of problems by not going out at night or going out alone; I go with my mom or stay at home. I studied in America for three years, and I've gone to birthday parties and on picnics with teachers and friends where I have a lot of fun, but I've gone only in the afternoon.

In my country, until they get married, children live with their parents. They go out, or move out to live by themselves, only after they marry. Until then, they stay at home, especially if they are girls. Boys have more freedom because they go away to work. In America, young girls can go anywhere without their parents. I think their religion says it is all right to go out. In the movies when eighteen- or nineteen-year-old American children go out with their boyfriends and girlfriends their mothers don't say anything. They don't seem to care about their children. They seem happy that their children have boyfriends and girlfriends. In my country it's not like that. Cambodian parents care about their children. I know it because they tell their children to be good. They want the children to have only one spouse. If the spouse dies, they can marry again if they want to. I hope to get married when I go back to my country. In this country, both American and Cambodian people marry fast and separate fast too.

Parents should take care of you, and advise you, so you can be a good person. I will tell you a story about what happened to a parent who did not do that. It's from our history, and it was first told a long, long time ago.

THE HUMAN BIRDS

Once upon a time there were three girls. Their father had died, so they just had a mother. After some time, the mother married again. Now she only liked her new husband and did not care about her daughters. She often went out with her husband, leaving the kids alone. So her husband said, "You take care of the kids. I will go out with my friend." But the mother did not want to take care of her kids. She took them to the forest and left them there. The children were lucky; good angels in the jungle looked after them. After three or four years, however, the three girls became like animals.

One day, the woman's husband stole some money and he was put in prison. So the mother was alone. She missed her kids. She went to the forest to bring them back, but it was too late. By now the kids had wings, and they flew away. So the mother lost her kids because she did not look after them.

Old people tell us this story. I think sometimes the old people who have come to live here look sad. They want to get back, but the young people want to live here. The young people know only about this country. Many of them don't know about Cambodia or its culture. I have a cousin here. He drives a car. He is a guy, but he has long hair. Once when he came to my house, he brought lots of girls in his car. My mom and my great-aunt advised him. He listened to all that they said and didn't say anything, but I think he was angry with them because he didn't come again.

Reflections

I always think about the past, especially about living in the camp. Over there I grew vegetables: potatoes, onions, tomatoes. Here, we don't do any physical work and we eat a lot of food, so we grow up too fast. I think in this country even the days go faster.

I would like to live on a farm. I haven't seen Phnom Penh or Bangkok, but I think all big cities are the same. In the city we just ride in cars, but on a farm we can walk, or go fishing in the river. I think walking is more fun than riding in a car. If you walk slowly, you can see things. If you're lucky you can find something. My brother found a small statue of the Buddha in the Philippines.

Although I prefer to go back, there are some things I like about America. I think most people in this country are kind. There are some who are mean, but it's the same in my country too. I have good teachers and lots of friends in school. Some of my friends are Cambodians and others are Vietnamese. I have American friends too, but they are friends only in class. I just go to PE and math classes with American students. Some Americans come to me for help with their math homework, and I go to them if I have problems, but at recess they go with their friends and I go with my friends. I don't know what to say to American people. I have never been in an American house, and no American people have come to my house.

Many Cambodians do not like Vietnamese, but the Vietnamese in my school are kind. They play basketball with Cambodians. The only thing that I don't like about them is that at times they are noisy in class. Some Vietnamese students work quietly, but some people are modern. They have new ways; they are aggressive and say "shut up." I don't talk like that. At times I ask people to be quiet, but if they don't listen, I don't continue to ask them. I never fight with anybody, I just make friends. Some Cambodian boys have problems with Spanish people, but I have no problems with anybody.

I am so disappointed that I lost my father, grandmother, and my lovely young brother. I go to the temple and I pray for them and all the others who died. At New Year time we offer food to the monks in memory of all our dead relatives. We believe our dead relatives also come to eat the food, and it makes my family feel at peace. But some of the young Cambodian people living here don't want to go to the Buddhist temple. They only want to go to parties.

I learn Buddhism from my mom. The older people know a lot of things because they were born a long time ago and the younger people must learn from them. The Buddhist religion says that young people have to respect and be polite to older people, friends, neighbors. I show respect to those who are older by using a kinship term like "Aunt" or "Grandmother" when I talk to them. I call only people who are young like me by their names.

I think it's important to help people. My religion says "Do good things, kind things, to people." Before the Buddha was born on this earth people killed and did other bad things, but the Buddha taught people to do good things. The old people say that if people like Pol Pot followed our religion, they would never do what they did.

Sometimes my mother talks about my father, and she cries. She talks about Pol Pot not giving food to my father. She talks about how my father got burnt when Pol Pot threw coals into the jail, and coal fell on father's leg. When I see her suffering because of those memories, I feel very angry with Pol Pot and I would like to kill him. Even though my religion says it is not good to kill, I think it's good to take revenge for a parent. But in America I can't kill Khmer Rouge people. This country is different from my country. In my country people wish that the Pol Pots would die, so if someone kills Pol Pots, people don't care. In this country, if I killed them I will go to jail.

I am happy in this country, but I have never really seen my country. I have only heard a little bit about it from my mom and my great-aunt. So I want to live in my country too. I want to go back to see my uncles, aunts, and cousins. I listened to a recorded speech by Sihanouk in which he said that Cambodia will be free from the Communists in 1991 or 1992. I would like to go back then.

I don't know what I will do in the future if I stay in America. I don't think much about my future, about going to work and having lots of money to buy a house or cars. I think I will go to college and then go to work, but I don't know what type of work I will do. In this country it is hard to think about my future. If I go back to my country I will work in a factory like my mom, or on a farm. I will grow vegetables to sell at the market, like we did in Khao-I-Dang camp. Growing vegetables is hard work, but I will feel happy, so it will not seem like hard work. Although I would like to return to my country, I will never forget that I lived here. I have a lot of friends here, and many happy memories, and I will come back to visit America.

PART IV

Interpretations:
Beyond the Killing Fields

CHAPTER FOURTEEN

Life, Death, and the Holocaust

People tell me America is the Freedom Country,
but in my heart there is no freedom.
— Pu Ma

One day, a woman in whose house I was teaching English to a group of adult Khmer refugees received a letter during the lesson. She read it, leaned against the sofa, and stared into space, clutching the letter. I continued teaching until I noticed that she was crying softly. I asked her what was wrong. She looked at me with tear-filled eyes and replied, "Teacher, my uncle, who looked after me when my father was ill, has died in the refugee camp!" She was concerned because to die in a camp might not have been peaceful; she hoped his death had been an easy one. I understood only too well how she felt; a few weeks earlier, I had received a letter informing me that my uncle had died. While I was saddened, my uncle's death did not upset me because I knew he had lived comfortably, and, according to my sister who sent me the news, he had also died peacefully.

Because of its cyclical view of life, death is as important as life in Buddhist philosophy. Theravada Buddhists (such as the narrators in this book and myself) believe that people continue to be born either as human beings, or as higher or lower forms of being, until they rid themselves of worldly desires and reach the state of enlightenment, known as Nirvana. As Look Tha explains, meritorious actions, particularly that of preserving life, enable one to attain good lives; rebirths are determined by one's karmic actions and by the purity of one's mind at the time of one's death.

Based on such norms, it was the respect for the living and the dead that made people civilized and human in pre–Khmer Rouge Cambodia (Ngor 1987; Yathay 1987). Family members had been bound by emotional, religious, and legal codes to care for their families during their lives and deaths. Social and cultural life revolved especially around the sharing of food; this was an expression of love and concern for the well-being of one's fellow beings.

During their revolution, the Khmer Rouge regime violated every Buddhist precept. The Khmer Rouge especially showed contempt for the first and perhaps the most important precept: that one should not kill. Life, other than their own, held little value. The Angka forcibly separated nuclear families, friends, and communities into age- and sex-graded work camps where thousands died from starvation, sickness, or deliberate killings by the soldiers.

Like other victims of the regime, Pu Ma was forbidden to care for or save her husband, who was kept in chains in a filthy temple, while the soldiers starved, tortured, and ultimately killed him. Pu Ma also was not allowed to help her old mother, also taken prisoner and probably killed by the Khmer Rouge. Apsara, herself stricken with malaria, could only watch as her father, too weak to walk, dragged himself to the hospital in a desperate attempt to find some rice to eat. Bun Thab could not save his grandmother from starving to death, or his friend who was hacked to death while escaping with Bun Thab. Similarly, other survivors frequently could neither save nor even offer meager help to their loved ones who died under the Khmer Rouge.

Look Tha says he did not want to die under Pol Pot because he was not in the right state of mind to die. His heart was filled with fear and hatred for the Khmer Rouge, and if he had died then, the impurity of his mind would not have enabled him to have a good rebirth.

Thus, in addition to the deaths of their loved ones, the violent and tragic way in which these loved ones died bears significant implications for the survivors.

Not only were the survivors unable to help those who died, they also could not perform the proper funeral ceremonies that would enable the deceased to acquire merit and attain good lives in their next births. Following from the belief in reincarnation, such rites were historically required by law. But under the Khmer Rouge, monks who performed these rites were unfrocked or killed. The soldiers killed many of their victims secretly, and Pu Ma and Nya Srey did not see their husbands die, or even see their corpses. In fact, one reason for Nya Srey's survival was her belief that she would eventually meet her husband, although this never occurred. Apsara went to the hospital to bring back her father's body to give him a proper burial, but the nurse did not allow her to do so. Therefore, neither she nor many other narrators and survivors could transfer merit to their loved ones who died under the regime.

In Cambodia, Buddhism was entwined with folk beliefs, and the above norms and rituals were connected to folk beliefs about ghosts. Pu Ma starts her narrative with an incident regarding her mother's dead husband, which illustrates her fear and belief in the reality of ghosts. She now fears that her own husband, murdered by the Khmer Rouge, might not be reborn. Although she has never said so directly, she may fear that the soul of her husband might be wandering about, perhaps as a ghost, unable to be born because of the manner in which he died. If so, the fact that his soul is not at peace will greatly disturb Pu Ma, and hamper her emotional well-being. Such fears and beliefs are not limited to refugees with little education. Haing Ngor, a doctor trained in Western medical practices, writes about his wife and other relatives who died in the holocaust:

> Someday, when Cambodia is free, I will return to the leaning *sdao* tree on the hillock in the rice fields. With me will be Buddhist monks. We will hold a ceremony and build a monument for her next to the temple on the mountainside. We will pray for Houy and her mother and my parents and family, and for all those who lost their lives. Then maybe their souls will be at peace. And maybe mine will be too. (Ngor 1987: 466)

For the Khmer refugees, then, freedom from worldly suffering means freedom not only for themselves but also for those who have died.

The Khmer Rouge stole material goods from their victims, but they also stole their lives and minds by denying them basic human needs. They carved out and ate livers, breasts, and other human organs from live or dead victims, and they removed fetuses from live pregnant women, leaving them to die a slow, lingering death (Ngor 1987). To loosen their inhibitions when committing these crimes, the Khmer Rouge soldiers consumed alcohol until they were intoxicated.

Although rape and other sexual misconduct by the Khmer Rouge soldiers appears to have been rare and usually done as punishment, victims were forcibly married to partners chosen by the regime, and denied relations with their own spouses through separations, lack of privacy, and lack of desire owing to starvation. The people were lied to, from the beginning until the very end of the regime. Thus the Khmer Rouge violated all five Buddhist precepts: that one should not kill, steal, lie, misbehave sexually, or consume intoxicants; they instilled fear in people and caused suffering at every twist and turn. Through their words and actions, they completely desecrated the Khmer culture that had evolved over 2,000 years.

Even more important, the Khmer Rouge also forced their victims to violate Buddhist precepts in order to survive. The victims killed animals, stole food, and lied. Perhaps the only precept the victims could not violate was the consumption of intoxicants, which were not available to them.

In recounting social, cultural, and religious violations committed both by themselves and by other victims of the regime, every one of the narrators justified their own actions as deriving from desperate need; the guilt and remorse they feel are betrayed by their voices and words. In recounting the brutal acts of the regime, they could not withhold their anger and tears.

Understandably, the Khmer Rouge atrocities have far-reaching consequences for refugees' well-being and adjustment. Among all the Indochinese refugees, the Cambodians suffer the highest levels of depression (see Asian Health Assessment Project of Santa Clara and IHARP Study of San Diego).

While I am not a psychologist, as a Theravada Buddhist, I believe that the posttraumatic stress suffered by the survivors is magnified first by the extremely distressful manner in which their loved ones and fellow human beings died; second, by the inability of the survivors to provide care and support for those who were sick or were tortured and denied food by the Khmer Rouge; and third, by their inability to perform religious rites and transfer merit to their deceased relatives at the time of their deaths.

As the narratives demonstrate, the horrors of the Pol Pot experience affect the normal daily life of Cambodian refugees in various ways.

Bopha obviously became deeply disturbed with the letter written in blood by her friend who contemplated suicide because she saw no future as a prisoner in a refugee camp. The hopelessness of relatives and friends trapped in refugee camps continues to traumatize Cambodians in America, even though they now live thousands of miles away from the "killing fields."

Although Bopha has been told her five-year-old sister was killed, she still harbors a faint hope that her sister might be alive and scans every picture of refugees, hoping to find her. Mum's father, and Pu Ma's husband and mother, disappeared under the regime. Though they believe the regime killed them, they have trouble accepting it, because they cannot understand or make sense of the Khmer Rouge actions. Pu Ma says: "My mother and my husband were very polite people who never fought with anybody. I don't know why Pol Pot killed them. I want to know why. I think if they could have come with me to this country, I would have been happy here."

Many refugees are plagued by nightmares; almost always they return to Cambodia in their dreams, which they find particularly distressing. For Nya Srey, thunderstorms evoke memories of bombardments of their country, and she is incapable of going to work after a particularly bad night. For Bun Thab, reflecting on the holocaust often triggers nightmares. Look Tha says that his head feels very tight and his chest hurts when he reflects on the Pol Pot holocaust. Pu Ma's parenting capabilities are disrupted after she dreams of Pol Pot. Even if they could somehow stop reflecting on what happened, the nightmares are simply beyond their control.

The Khmer Rouge experience influences decisions made by refugees in the United States. Nya Srey stopped her son from choosing a career in legal studies here in America because she believes her husband was killed by the Khmer Rouge only because he was a lawyer. She gave her daughter, Mum, in marriage, thus disrupting Mum's promising academic future, because she feared that Mum would go astray in permissive American society.

Like many other Khmer refugee women, Nya Srey is desperately lonely and wishes to find a husband, but the problems she faces are a direct consequence of Pol Pot's actions. She does not meet many men who are compatible with her educated, middle-class upbringing, since most were killed by the regime. She believes that she is unable to find companionship among American men because her knowledge of English and her Western social skills are inadequate. At the same time, she believes that she must marry an American, not an Asian. In her view, if she married another Cambodian or Asian man, she would betray her dead husband, whom she loved, and who gave her the only happiness she ever knew.

Other refugees who were widowed by the Khmer Rouge have remarried, some without knowing whether or not their previous spouses are alive. As shown in other studies and in Pu Ma's narrative, such marriages tend to be unstable, and lonely refugee women often fall prey to unscrupulous men, with obvious repercussions for their emotional and physical well-being.

While marriage and having a family have provided some comfort and sense of belonging to Bopha, she still misses the comradeship of a "best friend" with whom she can share her joys, fears, hopes, and sorrows. Even though both she and Mum are friendly, outgoing women who speak English well and interact with mainstream Americans at work, neither feels she has been fully accepted by her co-workers.

Mum's bright academic future ended tragically both in Cambodia and here, as a consequence of Pol Pot's holocaust. Her marriage at seventeen ended in divorce. Although her ambition is to be a lawyer like her murdered father and she is obviously bright enough to achieve it, her traumatic experiences make her question whether she has sufficient emotional stability to do well in school. For this reason, she has not returned to school.

The abrupt ending of their traditional way of life by the Khmer Rouge has given the refugees a strong feeling of insecurity. Apsara, who is happily married, says: "Today I have a good marriage. Tomorrow my husband might not like me anymore. That is one of the reasons why I want to learn to be a secretary. If he left me, I think I could get a better job if I was a secretary."

Elderly and middle-aged refugees who came from rural backgrounds with little or no education or job skills suitable for a technologically advanced country such as this wish to return to Cambodia, but not while their historic enemies, the Vietnamese, remain in power. The Vietnamese presence in Cambodia is again a consequence of Khmer Rouge actions. While some younger refugees like Niseth have overcome the deep animosity that the Khmer feel toward the Vietnamese, others continue to mistrust them, and some are intimidated by them. Apsara, for instance, wishes to find new employment because she has been treated badly by a Vietnamese co-worker.

Like many other Khmer refugees, Nya Srey feels angry with herself because of her sense of inadequacy. She has so much anger for the Khmer Rouge "who killed their own people" that she tries to obliterate her memory of the past, but she is unable to do so. At the same time, she wishes her children to retain some of the Khmer cultural values, such as moderation in actions and consideration for others, that she cherishes. As already mentioned above, her tragic dilemma has had significant repercussions on her children's lives. Nya Srey expresses the hopelessness felt by many refugees when she says, "I just feel bad, sick, and tired, and it's not great to feel like that." To cope with their difficulties, Khmer refugees turn to their prerevolutionary cultural norms.

Buddhism as a Healing Mechanism

On the surface, Buddhist teachings about peaceful death and reincarnation might seem to contribute to the refugees' emotional problems. But the narrators in this book suggest otherwise. Look Tha and Nya Srey explain how Buddhist karmic theory and meditation techniques helped them to cope with and survive the holocaust, and now to cope with its aftermath. Nya Srey, who has enormous problems in coming to terms with the Khmer Rouge trauma, says:

> Although I have changed somewhat after coming to the United States, I still believe in kamma [karma]; that if I did something bad in my last birth, then I will suffer. This belief has helped me not to go crazy. . . It also depends on how far you can control your mind. When I was young, I tried meditation. My mom meditated, and she taught me to just stay still, and to put my mind on one thing. I think it helped me to control myself and to cope with what happened. Remember, Buddha said, "Always control yourself; don't be too happy or too sad." I try to follow his advice.

The karmic belief, which states that individuals will reap the consequences of their actions, further stopped survivors from committing wrongful or revengeful actions, which helped to save their own and their families' lives and prevented any subsequent remorse that would have resulted from such actions. Look Tha says: "Although I was angry with the Pol Pots, I never said or did anything to get revenge; if I did so, I would also be bad like them. The Buddha said, 'If someone does wrong to another person, and that person takes revenge, the result will never end.' "

Prince Sisowath Sirirath, Prince Sihanouk's ambassador to the United Nations, also turns to Buddhist teachings in searching for methods to cope with the holocaust: "All of us had sisters, brothers, and uncles who perished under the Khmer Rouge. But in Buddhism, one learns to forgive. We have learned to forgive" (*San Jose Mercury News*, May 27, 1990).

Such attitudes, which are based on the Buddhist ideals of extending loving compassion to all beings, may seem like passive acceptance of fate to non-Buddhists. On the contrary, a Theravada Buddhist monk who counsels Khmer refugees pointed out to me that the ability to forgive violations of such enormity requires one to be much more aggressive with oneself. One has to consciously control one's thoughts and actions, and not act deliberately or impulsively to avenge wrongdoings.

As can be seen from the narratives, Christian ideals of praying to a higher order for salvation and being forgiven after repentance are foreign to Cambodians. Bopha stated this well: "I believe all religions make people good. But what part of Christianity do you believe? In Buddhism sin can't be subtracted and become zero. But in Christianity, you do bad things, you tell God, and it's over. I don't think that's fair."

Khmer refugees are frequently intimidated and exploited by missionaries from various churches who not only try to coerce the adults to come to church but also forcibly take refugee children to church. This not only violates the refugees' constitutional right to practice their religion, it also deprives them of their means of healing the wounds inflicted by the Pol Pot holocaust, with obvious implications for their adjustment and mental health. While Cambodian coping techniques based on Buddhist teachings and beliefs may differ greatly from those practiced in the West, their significance for the survivors of the holocaust is recognized by specialists treating torture victims. Psychologist Barbara Chester, executive director of the Center for Victims of Torture in Minneapolis, notes:

> The Cambodians have no word for torture, but there is a phrase that vaguely means torture. It includes the word "karma." Torture is seen as the deserved consequence of some past life's experience. And that has a lot of treatment implications. I would avoid contradicting that. For a Cambodian who has a fairly spiritual background, I would take the approach that their debt has been paid, and I might enlist the help of a Buddhist monk. ("They Heal the Ravages of Torture," *INSIGHT*: Aug. 24, 1987)

While Bopha and others pretend to accommodate missionaries because it is against their social ethics to be inhospitable to visitors, these forced indoctrinations cause frustration and anger. Mum, for example, remarks: "Nobody ever forces you to get into the Buddhist religion. I hate it when people come to our door saying, 'You want to become such and such religion?' That really bugs me. I don't believe in that at all, because again, what is important is what is within you."

However spiritually pure one may be, the magnitude of the Khmer Rouge atrocities are such that Koun Srey and Bun Thab contemplate killing those who perpetrated such havoc in the victims' lives. Bun Thab says:

> I only know that Communists lied to people and destroyed our country. They took everything away from us—our monks, our temple, our culture. I hate the Pol Pot soldiers. If I meet those soldiers I will kill them. Although I believe in kamma, I don't think I would commit a sin if I killed Pol Pots; they did such bad things to people. Some say that Pol Pot soldiers killed only because the leaders told them to do so, but I don't know if that is so. I hate them all.

Bopha, Apsara, and many other victims of the Khmer Rouge do not want to kill, but they wish to inflict pain on the Khmer Rouge soldiers who killed their loved ones. While they entertain such thoughts, however, their narratives demonstrate that they have not destroyed their own, or other people's, lives or minds, either by actually acting out their threats or by continuously dwelling on such destructive thoughts, which might destroy their sanity.

On the contrary, the refugees cope with their grief and emotional trauma by projecting positive and constructive thoughts for the deceased, instead of hateful and destructive thoughts for the killers. This outlook is directly based on Buddhist teachings and activities. For instance, transferring merit to their dead relatives at almsgivings helps the deceased to attain better lives in the future. Such thoughts and actions give the refugees hope and lessen their guilt for having survived.

As described by Bun Thab, offerings to the monks need not be individual actions, but can also be a cooperative effort between family members as well as the larger community. Thus, if people are unable to participate in them owing to other commitments, they still benefit from the participation of family members or friends, since the offerings and contributions made to the monks are done in the memory of all those who died. Such collective actions in turn strengthen the solidarity of families and communities that were once torn apart by the Khmer Rouge.

Mum and Niseth demonstrate how they apply the positive approach stressed in Buddhism in their coping strategies. Instead of complaining about the Khmer Rouge experience, which robbed them of a happy childhood, and which may interfere with their lives as adults, these two narrators look upon this experience as a constructive agent on which to build their futures. Niseth, for example, reflected:

One cannot erase the past; it is part of your life. Under the Communists, we lost some of our family. We lost property. We never imagined that we'll ever become as poor as we did. Sometimes I get depressed when I think of all that happened. But as Dad says, you can learn from difficult experiences, and suffering under the Communists was a strong experience for me to go on to the future. I now see the future as brighter than the past.

CHAPTER FIFTEEN

Cambodian and American Views of Successful Adjustment

Americanization

In his narrative, Look Tha described his image of America before he arrived here: "I thought that in America, the government let refugees keep their natural cultures, because in this country there is freedom. Now I know it is not so."

Look Tha's observation reflects a widespread concern shared by many immigrants and refugees who confront pressures on them to Americanize. In fact, efforts to break down immigrant cultures can be traced as far back as the nineteenth century, when programs designed for immigrants advocated that in order to succeed in mainstream society, "they must adopt American attitudes, values and behaviors" (Tollefson 1989: 39).

The Refugee Act of 1980 has continued this policy of Americanization.

In this act, the primary goal of the federal resettlement program for refugees admitted to the United States is stated to be the "achievement of self-sufficiency as quickly as possible."

In order to achieve the "self-sufficiency" goal of the Refugee Act, the focus of refugee resettlement programs has been on the placement of adult refugees in regular employment (Rumbaut and Ima 1988: 2). Numerous sources describe how this process was initiated in the refugee camps themselves. Since the passage of this act, the vast majority of refugees arriving in the United States have been Southeast Asians. While regular immigrants as a rule have received no special aid from the federal government when settling in the United States, Congress has voted funds to voluntary agencies to resettle refugees. Once they have been resettled, refugees have received health care, education, and general assistance, although over the past decade, training and assistance programs have been shortened from three years to eight months.

Rumbaut and Ima, authors of the 1988 Southeast Asian Refugee Youth Study (hereafter referred to as the SARYS), observe that while the Vietnamese, who have been here longer, have been successful in establishing economic self-sufficiency, the Khmer have yet to match the same level of self-sufficiency. They also forecast that in the near future, strategies for economic self-sufficiency in Southeast Asian refugee communities will rest significantly with the generation born in Asia but educated in America.

An official of a refugee resettlement agency I interviewed in Santa Clara County, California, agreed with Rumbaut and Ima. She noted:

> When compared with other refugee groups both from Southeast Asia and from countries such as Iran and Ethiopia, many Cambodians in Santa Clara County have not mainstreamed successfully. They have not found jobs, not become citizens, and not learned English.

Those who perceive the Khmer as being less successful in their adjustment to the United States cite many reasons for their failure. These include historical and educational factors such as the Pol Pot trauma, the survivors' rural non-Western backgrounds, their relatively short length of stay in the United States, their limited, or lack of, literacy in their own language and in English, and their lack of transferable job skills. Researchers also claim that culture and worldview are other "key factors" that contribute to the Khmer refugees' lack of success. These include Khmer attitudes toward modernity and educational orientation; their methods of social interaction; their parenting techniques and family relations; the Theravada Buddhist worldview;

and the refugees' job expectations and views of economic success (Ima et al. 1983; Rumbaut and Ima 1988).

Some dissenting researchers argue that in examining the concept of assimilation, social scientists are imposing their own American values. After pointing out the power relations between the observer and the observed, they further argue that the choice of research topic itself is defined by those who wish to take some action on the refugees—who have no power to defend themselves—and that research models proposed by social scientists satisfy government and funding agencies, rather than the needs of Indochinese refugees. Because they claim that the success thesis can be used to make invidious comparisons among ethnic minority groups when carried to an extreme, they advocate a closer collaboration between researchers and social workers in order to better serve the needs of these refugees (Banks 1984; Bousquet 1988; Yu and Liu 1986).

The two opposing viewpoints mentioned above call attention to the need to understand different concepts of success and failure, as well as assimilation to a new society, from the points of view of the refugees themselves. In this chapter, I contrast the Khmer views of success and failure with American views of these concepts. In my view, many researchers and refugee service providers have imposed American images of success and failure on Cambodians, or have applied Vietnamese social and cultural values to evaluate the Khmer. In doing so they have misunderstood and misrepresented Cambodian refugee decisions about adapting to the United States.

Modernity, Education, and Social Interaction

Ima et al. (1983) suggest that refugee adjustment must be viewed in terms of modernity, in addition to being a move between different countries. By "modernity" the researchers mean a French bourgeois aggressive orientation. In their study, they use education and orientation toward education as keys to predicting success in adjustment. How do Western views of modernity and education coincide with those of Cambodians?

Emile Durkheim and Talcott Parsons, among others, have observed that in addition to teaching academic subjects, a major role of the school is to teach the values of society to students (Selakovich 1984). As seen in the narratives, in Cambodia, as in America, education was actively directed to socializing students, to producing the right types of citizens. While Kagan characterizes American public schools as "generally competitive, individualistic, and autocratic" (1986: 238), the narrators of this book, as well as other writers, describe how Cambodian schools promoted cooperation and obedience. In his story, Look Tha, a peasant and former monk, compares the social values of the two systems as they are taught in the schools: "In Cambodian culture, teachers tell students, 'When you go back home, you must never do anything that your parents dislike. You must always obey them.' But in America, teachers teach children about their freedom to do what they want, so they don't obey their parents."

Niseth, the daughter of urbanized parents, attended school first in Kratie town and then in Phnom Penh. She recalls that Cambodian parents told their children, "You always listen to the teachers and do whatever they ask you to do. When you go to another place you belong to someone else. When you go to school, you belong to the teachers, and you must not do anything bad or disrespectful to them."

The influence of this early socialization is such that even though she is now an American college student, Niseth does not feel comfortable in asserting her rights in her interactions with the teachers. In describing an incident when she believes a professor treated her unfairly, she says:

> I did not complain about this incident to anybody because I thought I may have been at fault; because of the way I was brought up, I think the teacher is always right. I have gone through high school and college in America, but I have never believed it is right to complain about the teacher, even if I may feel the teacher has done something wrong. I don't know if this is the right way to think, but I believe most Cambodian students are like me.

As Steinberg points out, Cambodians generally define social relationships such that each person involved has a distinct, prescribed role to play. The rules of etiquette between people of different status and rank are spelled out, with appropriate and circumscribed roles for every situation. Unlike Americans, for instance, a Cambodian who wants to assume a role that his current status does not permit him in particular situations cannot simply extend his role informally, but must first formally shift his status, and then assume the appropriate role.

> The Cambodian's greatest anxiety is that he will be unable to perceive the nature of the situation in which he is involved at the moment, and hence not know how to act or what to expect of others. He is therefore particularly sensitive to cues which will tell him what kind of a situation he is in and what he must and must not do. . . . A Cambodian to whom an assignment has been given will ask very detailed questions. . . . He

will not execute an order until he is sure that he knows precisely what he is to do. (Steinberg 1959: 274)

Because of such attitudes and behaviors, the Khmer are typically described as being "passive." Researchers as well as many teachers believe that such passivity inhibits the "successful" assimilation of Cambodians to mainstream American society. The refugee resettlement agency official represented this view in these remarks: "Peasant and tribal groups listen to their leaders, and Cambodians do not want to change their ways. They are quite unlike the Vietnamese, who are much more individualistic and Westernized, and are much more successful."

In her narrative, ethnic Cambodian Koun Srey perceives the aggressive style of communication she confronts in the United States as "modern" in the same manner that the researchers do. From her perspective, however, this style of communication reflects not success, but conflict. In her reflections about Vietnamese students in her class, she says: "Some Vietnamese students work quietly, but some people are modern. They have new ways; they are aggressive and say 'shut up.' I don't talk like that. At times I ask people to be quiet, but if they don't listen, I don't continue to ask them. I never fight with anybody, I just make friends."

Mum, the daughter of French-influenced, Chinese Cambodian parents, is a very able and articulate English speaker. She observes that her former junior high school friend who, along with herself, was one of the two best Cambodian students in school, is now so Americanized that

> If you see her, you would think she was born here. The way she talks, the way she eats, the way she acts, is so American. . . . She is a year older than me, but she acts like a kid. When we get together, she is always fighting with my friends. I can't recall getting into an argument with any friends. . . . I think everybody has different beliefs for themselves.

Vietnamese Cambodian Bopha, also the daughter of an educated civil servant, was a former medical student in Cambodia. She is now a gainfully employed college student here. She requires her four-year-old child born in America to obey rules of behavior based not on competition and aggression but on cooperation, and on demonstrating respect and consideration for others. The authors of the SARYS study speculate that the Khmer value harmony and cooperation because Buddhist teachings promote nonaggression and passivity. The narratives in this book, however, demonstrate that cooperation was important for other reasons as well. For instance, since Cambodia was an agrarian country with few technological advances in agriculture, mutual cooperation between family and community was essential, especially for cultivating irrigated rice. Cooperation also enabled landless families such as Pu Ma's to survive. While Buddhist teachings promoting social harmony and nonaggression certainly strengthened cooperative social values, Cambodians cooperated not because of passivity but because their adherence to these values ensured the welfare of the family and community. Such behavior is preferred by all the narrators because, as explained by Im (a man whose story does not appear in this book), "It fosters feelings of love, harmony, and goodwill toward others. When one speaks nicely, others do the same, and no one has to regret afterward."

The narratives further demonstrate that without cooperation the refugees could not have survived the holocaust, and that they would have had a much harder time coping with life in the United States.

While the refugees recognize that aggressive speech is acceptable here, they prefer not to employ it, even in their interactions with Americans. From their perspective, such speech and behavior create not success and social unity, but failure arising out of conflict. Such sentiments do not, however, mean that the Khmer refugees refuse to change their ways to suit their new environment. As Niseth points out, the refugees have changed many of their habits, including communication methods, but only to the degree that they feel comfortable. Mum, Bopha, Look Tha, and others point out that they are unable to transform their ways completely because they did not grow up in American society.

Parenting Techniques

Rumbaut and Ima view Khmer parents as "overprotective," and as exerting less discipline and influence on their children than do other Indochinese parents. Cambodians, on the other hand, believe that the assertion of individual rights and the legal prohibition on corporal punishment here lead to a lack of discipline among their children. From the Khmer perspective, beating a child does not constitute punishment; instead, it is a form of discipline that demonstrates a parent's love and concern for a child. Bopha, for instance, while criticizing her mother for switching her, recognizes that it was done as a means of teaching her proper behavior. She considers it "unfair" that she is not allowed to beat her child in America when her child talks back; such behavior by a child shows complete lack of respect for elders. Bun Thab says: "In our culture we believe that parents should be like teachers, and teach their children how to do things. In Cambodia parents controlled everything and children listened to their parents, and asked for permission before they did anything."

American "youth culture," including dating and sexual freedom, is perceived by Khmer refugees as a result of lack of caring for each other, on the parts of both parent and child, and as a loss of parental authority. This view is held both by twenty-two-year-old Mum and by sixteen-year-old Koun Srey, who are from different socioeconomic backgrounds. Both of them have attended public schools in the United States. Mum says:

> I respect Americans, but I'm embarrassed about some of the things they do. I think that here, kids have too much freedom. I think people have too much freedom. Parents can't tell the kids what to do. Kids don't care about parents. People around my age do practically everything they want to: drink, smoke, go out, and even move out.

Koun Srey echoes her view:

> In America, young girls can go anywhere without their parents. I think their religion says it's all right to go out. In the movies when eighteen- or nineteen-year-old American children go out with their boyfriends and girlfriends their mothers don't say anything. They don't seem to care about their children. They seem happy that their children have boyfriends and girlfriends. In my country it's not like that. Cambodian parents care about their children.

Niseth provides a slightly different view:

> Americans think Cambodians don't have independence. They believe that we should be on our own and have our own lives. . . . Americans believe that they are behind their children; but the first thing they want is for their children to be independent. They let the children have their own ways of thinking about life, and don't want to have a strong bond with their children. . . . I don't know whether the Cambodian way or the American way is better, but I think for the family to be one unit is good, and for me, I think the Cambodian way is the right one. But if the Americans think their way is better, then that is what is right for them.

Khmer refugees have such strong negative views about dating because it was never a part of Khmer culture. Until they arrived in the United States, they did not expect that unmarried men and women would socialize freely with each other, and Cambodian parents, like parents in many other Asian societies, consider it their duty to find socially and economically compatible partners for their children. Ebihara says that Khmer parents did not force their children into arranged marriages as a rule, and Pu Ma demonstrates that some indeed chose their own mates. Even then, they first sought parental permission out of respect and consideration for their parents, as shown by Bun Thab, who arranged his own marriage in the United States.

For Khmer refugees, not only dating but also explicit expressions of physical feelings are alien ways. While Pu Ma wishes her daughter to obtain a good education so she will find employment and also be in a position to choose a good husband, she worries about her children approaching adulthood here because she believes peer pressure might influence them to seek love and romance on their own. She also worries that her children might marry non-Cambodians, and that this would prevent her from helping her children if they experienced marital problems, because of cultural and language barriers.

Implicit in Pu Ma's concerns is the Khmer view of motherhood. Cambodians believe that a mother should take care of her unmarried and married children whenever the need arises. In fact, this sense of maternal responsibility is so great the Khmer believe that even after a mother dies, her spirit continues to take care of her children, and they appeal to her in times of distress. Koun Srey's story about the Human Birds shows the consequences of parental neglect.

Marriage and motherhood are such a natural part of womanhood for the Khmer that even Nya Srey and Bopha, who came from urban backgrounds and of Chinese and Vietnamese origins respectively, and who are now gainfully employed, still see their roles mainly as wives and mothers. The refugees continue to teach their daughters household duties and values that will enable them to be capable wives and mothers; they do not think highly of American girls who are incapable of managing households. Nya Srey says: "I don't care much for white girls because they don't know how to care for a family. But I don't blame them; we have different customs. I feel we are completely different. We like to take care of our families."

Apsara, who was married here and who is apparently aware of women's liberation, consciously chooses the changes that she wants to make as a wife. She says:

> If we lived in Cambodia I would have behaved differently toward my husband. Over there, we have to always try to be nice to the husband. Wives don't talk back, but sometimes I do that here a little bit, because I have more freedom to say what I think here. However, I am careful not to speak too disrespectfully to him, and in that way, I think I'm different

from the Americans. . . . I always look up to my husband as the person who takes care of the family. I want my husband to be in a higher position at work than myself. If the woman earns more money, she becomes stronger than her husband, and I don't think that's good because then she might always speak harshly to him and make him feel bad.

Khmer Attitudes About Family and Economic Success

Rumbaut and Ima rightly point out that two main reasons for the Khmer refugees' lack of significant economic success are that many older refugees are unemployed owing to lack of English and job skills; and, because of family disruptions created by the Khmer Rouge, refugee households usually consist of several unrelated nuclear families whose capacity to generate capital is less than that of Vietnamese refugees. They contend, however, that the primary reasons for the more immediate economic success of the Vietnamese are their "vertical and family-oriented" patterns and their "pooled income strategies," which they say are absent among the Khmer. They describe the Khmer as having "a looser sense of discipline and obligation that pervades all social life—not only outside the family, but within the family as well, including both parent/child and husband/wife relationships," and claim that individualistic feelings among the Khmer emphasize feelings of emotional fulfillment rather than commitment. The authors also believe that the Khmer have fewer filial piety norms and a weaker sense of obligation to parents.

In contrast to the views of these researchers, Ebihara, Ngor, and Yathay, among others, assert that in Cambodia, the most fundamental social group was the nuclear family, bound together by a variety of emotional, economic, and legal ties. It is hardly surprising, then, that all the narrators in this book describe how they contribute to the welfare of the family as a whole. Look Tha and Pu Ma, born into poverty and deprivation, did not choose to become individually wealthy once they began to earn incomes. Instead, they supported both their nuclear and extended families, financially and emotionally. Bopha and Apsara speak admiringly of their husbands' concern for the welfare of the family.

This focus on the family rather than the individual is particularly significant in the cases of Niseth, Mum, and Koun Srey, who have spent many of their formative years in the United States. All of them consider it more important to ensure the economic and emotional welfare of their families than to seek their own individual satisfaction. Twenty-two-year-old Mum earns a salary that enables her to buy an easily affordable and much-desired sports car, but she does not do so because it would make her mother unhappy. She does not believe that her economic independence gives her the right to acquire her individual independence if this causes problems for her mother. Koun Srey gave all of her earnings from her first summer job to her mother to help meet their living costs. Niseth says:

> In my family we save money together, and when we had $5,000 in the bank, Dad suggested we should invest it in a house. . . . We still owe money on this house and all of us work hard to pay it off, but it's the base that enables us to move on. I think this is our prize for all the effort we've put in together. . . . I don't save my money individually because I live with my family, and I know the family is needy. I think the family and I are one unit. When I'm wealthy, the family is wealthy; and when the family is wealthy I am also wealthy.

The narrators of this book also describe their efforts to provide economic and emotional help to other relatives and friends who are here, in Cambodia, or in refugee camps. Clearly, Khmer social values, reinforced by Theravada Buddhist values, and now by the Pol Pot tragedy, impart to them a deep moral obligation to do their duty for their people. However, it is an obligation not explicitly institutionalized by a hierarchical structure, as it is in Vietnamese society, but one that is taught implicitly by a way of life with deep roots, not immediately obvious to outside observers. In my view, Rumbaut and Ima missed this point because they paid no attention to Khmer cultural values; instead they judged the Khmer on the basis of Vietnamese values.

In assessing the economic achievements of the Khmer, it is essential to remember that the primary reason for the refugees' move to the United States was to save their families, and not to gain material wealth. Nya Srey and Mum, who were wealthy Chinese Cambodians before the Pol Pot revolution, are financially secure here too. But for both, a harmonious family is more important than wealth, as it is for Pu Ma, a mother on welfare. Although Bopha and her husband do not have as much money as she would like, she considers herself fortunate because her husband takes good care of the family.

While this outlook reflects Buddhist ideals, placing a higher value on life than on material wealth, it is also an outcome of the Pol Pot holocaust, which destroyed loved ones and the family lives of these refugees. While the Pol Pot experience shows that material wealth can be regained, it also tragically demonstrates that lost family and friends can never be regained. Mum articulates clearly how the Pol Pot tragedy strengthened the value of family for Khmer refugees:

> I don't take what I have for granted, the way American people do. There's more to life, more to families, than money and stuff. For me, money is no big deal. Of course it's something you always need living in this country, but it's not . . . the main thing in life. Money comes and goes. I think to me, the main thing is happiness. Happiness is to have a pretty close family.

Khmer Work Ethic and Academic Achievement

Rumbaut and Ima believe that because of their Theravada Buddhist values, the Khmer are more pragmatic, fatalistic, and oriented to recreational values than to an ethic of personal effort and hard work. They believe that the Buddhist karmic theory contributes to a lack of competitive aggressiveness, especially with regard to education and work. The authors also note that the refugees they observed were rural, with lower-class resources and socio-cultural elements that are less likely to produce "success" in a competitive American context, and that it is only the educated elite with French urban middle-class backgrounds who search for educational success.

In contrast to the above views, Look Tha, Pu Ma, and Bun Thab, narrators with rural origins, describe how they overcame severe hardships in attaining economic self-sufficiency in Cambodia, and it is clear that they have an independent work ethic and determination to succeed.

Similarly, Mum, who came from a French-influenced urban middle-class background, has demonstrated by her hard work and successful record at school and at work that the Khmer do have a work ethic. She now has a desire to become a lawyer, but hesitates to return to school simply because she feels she may not have the emotional strength, after all the tragic experiences of her life. Her inability to do very well in school is a direct result of the traumas she suffered both in Cambodia and in America, rather than Buddhist fatalism or the absence of an ethic of hard work. Both Bopha and Nya Srey are now gainfully employed, and Bopha still attends school for career advancement.

An alternative interpretation of the Khmer work ethic, and the one that I prefer, is that, as shown below, the Khmer worldview places a different emphasis on the importance of money as a measure of personal success.

It is the refugees' lack of transferable job skills and English-language skills that present problems in finding employment, as noted by many researchers. Although the refugee agency official I interviewed believes that some Khmer shun work because of a "welfare mentality," from my acquaintance with the Khmer, I believe that many who come from rural backgrounds have the desire to work, and what they need is the type of job and English-language training that suits *their* skills and needs, and not the needs of various agencies or educators.

In teaching a language, instructors present students with three tasks: acquiring a new syntax, a new lexis, and a new set of cultural concepts (Brick and Louie 1984). Success in achieving these three tasks is the first step to successful language acquisition. I take this idea one step further: the new cultural concepts, to be taught first, have to be those that are experienced by the students and not by the teachers (see Welaratna 1988: 23).

As a result of my teaching English to refugees in their own homes, I was able to observe their lifestyles, their needs and problems, their cultural values, and their methods of communication in a manner that a teacher in a classroom is unable to do. My observations gave me valuable insight into the language-learning problems of Khmer refugees, and convinced me that the main reason for the refugees' lack of success in language acquisition was not a lack of interest or an inability on their part, as claimed by some teachers, but the inappropriateness of the ESL lessons themselves, which do not address their needs as refugees. For instance, widespread use of money, banking systems, and credit cards were not part of village or urban life. Look Tha says that even in urban areas, only businessmen or "big people" (the very rich) used banks. Talking about another aspect of daily village life, Bun Thab recalls that villagers dined not seated at tables laid out with silverware, but seated on the floor on beautifully woven mats.

As refugees dependent on welfare, many of them do not have savings to deposit in banks. In their overcrowded houses, many do not have room for dining tables, and most refugees who came from village backgrounds continue to use floor mats at mealtimes. But ESL lessons are often about matters such as banking or setting the table, which reflect the practical needs of middle-class people, and not of refugees on welfare who come from rural lifestyles.

Since banking or setting tables is not part of their daily experience, lessons about these subjects have no immediate application or meaning to the refugees, and therefore do not provide stimulation for learning or retention. Although it is necessary to teach unfamiliar concepts such as bank-

ing to Khmer refugees since they now live here, I believe it is more important to teach them concepts that meet their survival needs first. While current ESL pedagogy and methodology recognize the importance of assessing
students' needs, the ESL lessons I observed being taught to Khmer refugees
appeared to address the needs and preferences of teachers from Western
middle-class backgrounds, rather than those of Cambodians. Citing thirteen assumptions on which refugee programs are based in American refu-
gee-processing centers in Southeast Asia, Tollefson echoes this view when
he says, "Though it is claimed that the curricula represent the refugees'
needs, the sources focus on *employers'* needs" (1989: 67).

A Cambodian community leader and a refugee health care provider I
interviewed mentioned the following as survival needs of Cambodian refugees: learning to deal with apartment managers, police officers, and personnel in institutions such as hospitals, schools, and housing and welfare
departments; learning to overcome the fear of using the telephone; awareness of smoking hazards and drug and alcohol abuse; awareness of health
problems such as parasites; an awareness of germ theory and other preven-
tive health measures; legalities regarding issues such as traffic violations
and child abuse; and learning more assertive communication methods,
particularly to minimize exploitation by unscrupulous salespeople and
missionaries.

The above subjects could well be incorporated into ESL courses to provide useful and meaningful lessons that meet the students' needs. To be effective and successful, language lessons must be developed initially with
consideration for Khmer cultural values. For example, I witnessed an en-
counter between Nya Srey and an unsolicited insurance agent who came to
her home. Nya Srey is more Westernized and has better English-speaking
skills than most other Khmer refugees. When confronted by the insurance
agent who requested information about her personal background, however, she did not know how to respond. She did not want to volunteer personal information, and she clearly did not want to divulge the fact that she
was a widow. Ultimately, she solved the problem by asking the man to
come later when her son was at home.

After the visitor left, I told Nya Srey that she does not have to entertain
or reveal information to any outsiders, and that she has the right to ask
them to leave. But from her expression, it was apparent that I had embarrassed her; the Khmer value hospitality, and would not ask a guest to leave.
I then told her that if she felt uncomfortable about asking unsolicited salespeople to leave, she could ask for their business cards and let them know

she will call them if she needs their services. That was an appropriate suggestion; it provided a solution without violating Nya Srey's cultural values.

Rumbaut and Ima claim that another reason for the Cambodians' failure to succeed is that even Khmer refugee children who have been educated here tend to choose jobs entailing human services, such as nursing and clerical assistance, that the researchers consider "low-status" jobs. They speculate that the Khmer are not yet acquainted with technologically advanced "high-status" jobs. They further observe that the need to serve others seems to be a central source of life satisfaction for the Khmer and believe it probably reflects the Buddhist concept of doing good deeds to earn merit for future life. A better understanding comes from looking at the Cambodian orientation to success.

It was an individual's good conduct rather than wealth that brought recognition in Cambodia. Therefore, what researchers perceive as low-status jobs entailing human services are the high-status ones from the Khmer perspective, because human life is the highest form of life one can attain. Therefore, rather than looking for merit for future lives by doing good deeds, I believe the Khmer are trying to find job satisfaction in their present lives.

The emphasis the Khmer place on "emotional fulfillment rather than commitment" is seen as another reason for their lack of success. Since Buddhist teachings deal with humanity and not divinity, they necessarily explore human feelings and fulfillment. From the perspective of the Khmer, to have commitment one must find emotional fulfillment; financial fulfillment alone does not suffice. For instance, Koun Srey says she would like to grow vegetables for a living even though it is hard work; since she will be happy doing that, it will not seem like hard work. Mum sums up this view, saying, "Money comes and goes. For me, the main thing is happiness. . . . It's what's within you that really counts."

The following quotation from Chhim points out the difference between the Khmer and American perspectives on success and freedom.

> Personal independence is given high value by Cambodians, but it is not conceived in the same way Americans do. For a Cambodian, independence would mean freedom from obligation or commitment beyond his defined role of his status in a given situation. . . . Cambodians rarely confuse their formal roles in society with their informal personal roles. They do not inject personal overtones into formal situations. . . . Cambodians have felt little compulsion to succeed in a material sense. Ac-

quisitiveness is not a dominant characteristic; adequacy is the objective in life. (Chhim 1987: 14)

Clearly, a lack of awareness of Khmer perspectives and the imposition of American and Vietnamese expectations and ideals on Khmer refugees have led to misinterpretations of their behavior and actions and to the view that Khmer refugees have not made a "successful adjustment." It should also be noted that in reality, not all Vietnamese adhere to their social ideals of family values and educational achievement (see Freeman 1989).

An important issue this book raises is the extent to which immigrants and refugees might be expected to conform to mainstream American values. Americans themselves have been divided about this for decades (Takaki 1989, Tollefson 1989, Bodnar 1985, Archdeacon 1983). As the narratives of this book show, it is unrealistic to expect people who are newcomers to America to erase their cultures and begin all over with a blank slate as Americans, because they are not native-born and no amount of posturing or pretending will change that, for, as Mum points out, "It's what's within you that really counts." The traditions of Cambodian refugees give them a sense of identity and self-worth that they are not likely to gain by abandoning their heritage.

Many Cambodians consciously choose their modes and degree of assimilation, and they consider their adjustment to be quite successful. The narratives in this book demonstrate that for the Khmer, particularly as Theravada Buddhist survivors of a holocaust, successful social adjustment does not necessarily mean the American dream of economic achievement and individual freedom, but success in personal and family interactions. The narratives also show that because the refugees are now influenced by a new socioeconomic environment, they have begun to change their views and ways. But the ways in which they adjust, and the degree to which they change, are based on their experiences and their particular worldview.

Furthermore, the narratives show that by selectively choosing American values and activities that are compatible with their own ways of life, Cambodians can achieve economic self-sufficiency while maintaining successful and fulfilling lives. Such sentiments are not unique to the Khmer. Early immigrants from European as well as Asian countries also "did not hesitate to exploit or draw upon past belief and practice if it in some way would facilitate and render intelligible their new life and condition" (Bodnar 1985: 185).

Thus enforced "Americanization" does not ensure successful adaptation to the United States, as I found out when I tried to persuade one of my ESL students to allow her talented daughter to attend free art lessons offered to her by a teacher. Speaking with both the mother and the daughter, I said they must not refuse this opportunity for the daughter to achieve the "American dream." Both responded by looking away, indicating that neither of them wished to continue the discussion. I changed the subject, but I was disconcerted.

I returned the next day, hoping to find out what mistake I had made. When I explained to the mother the reason for my visit, she was silent for a moment. Then she spoke gently, yet with certainty, searching for the right words both to express her views and to preserve my dignity. "Teacher, in my country girls do not become artists. It is not right. I want my daughter to go to school and learn a lot, and she can enjoy drawing for pleasure, but I don't like her to be an artist," she said. She also did not want her daughter to be alone with a man, and she could not chaperon her daughter since she had to care for the younger children. Cambodian girls are expected to get married and become an example for their children, and if a girl had a reputation of entertaining boyfriends, she would not be considered a suitable wife.

Later that year the daughter got a job in an electronics company, and I realized that like many in their community, this family wanted to become economically self-sufficient, and that they were making major changes in their lives in order to become productive participants in American society. But it was also clear that they wanted to preserve those aspects of life that they believed contributed to a person's self-worth, often more important than immediate economic success.

Looking back on this event, I realized that we should stop to question whether our interventions provide actual benefits or whether they are harmful from the refugees' points of view.

In addition, enforced "Americanization" may also reduce the diversity of adjustments and viewpoints that Cambodians and other newcomers bring with them, which could contribute to the cultural and social enrichment of this country. For example, when people live a routine existence, they may put aside ultimate values. Faced with annihilation not only of themselves but also of their families and their culture, Cambodians were forced to confront what was ultimately important to them. The refugees' experiences and the choices they make might prompt Americans to reconsider what they take to be ultimately important. From Cambodian survivors of the holocaust, Americans may learn valuable lessons about the powers of survival under extreme deprivation; consideration of such extreme circumstances might also prompt Americans to rethink the priorities they assign to various values. The distinctive view of humaneness that Cambodians have may also encourage Americans to reexamine that concept.

Cambodians have combined work and life in a way that enables many to be self-sufficient while maintaining cooperative family values and structures. Many have found economic niches that enable them to draw on their own strengths while learning new skills. In doing so, they have redefined the "American dream" to enable them to live well in America, and to become a productive part of the larger American community while retaining significant elements of their own heritage.

Bibliography

Bibliography

Allman, T. D. 1971. "Anatomy of a Coup." In J. Grant, ed., *Cambodia: The Widening War in Indochina*. New York: Washington Square Press.

Archdeacon, Thomas J. 1983. *Becoming American*. New York: Free Press.

Banks, James A. 1984. *Teaching Strategies for Ethnic Studies*. Boston: Allyn and Bacon.

Barron, John, and Anthony Paul. 1977. *Murder of a Gentle Land*. New York: Reader's Digest Press.

Becker, Elizabeth. 1986. *When the War Was Over*. New York: Simon and Schuster.

Bit, Seanglim. 1981. *The Study of the Effects of Reward Structures on Academic Achievement and Sociometric Status of Cambodian Students*. Ph.D. dissertation, Department of Education, University of California, San Francisco.

———. 1990. *The Warrior Heritage: A Psychological Perspective of Cambodian Trauma*. California.

Bodnar, John. 1985. *The Transplanted: A History of Immigrants in Urban America*. Bloomington: Indiana University Press.

Bousquet, Gisele. 1988. "The Refugees Next Door: A Critical Approach to the Studies on Indochinese Refugees in the United States." A paper delivered at the 87th Annual Meeting of the American Anthropological Association, Phoenix, November.

Brick, J., and G. Louie. 1984. *Background Notes for Teachers in the Adult Migrant Education Program. Language and Culture: Kampuchea*. Sydney: Australian Department of Immigration and Ethnic Affairs.

Burchett, Wilfred. 1981. *The China-Cambodia-Vietnam Triangle*. Chicago: Vanguard Books.

Caplan, Nathan, John K. Whitmore, and Marcella H. Choy. 1989. *The Boat People and Achievement in America*. Ann Arbor: University of Michigan Press.

Carrison, Muriel P. 1987. *Cambodian Folk Stories from the Gatiloke*. From a translation by the Venerable Kong Chhean. Rutland, Vermont: Charles E. Tuttle.

Chandler, David P. 1983. *A History of Cambodia*. Boulder, Colo.: Westview Press.

Chhim, Sun H. 1987. *Introduction to Cambodian Culture*. Sacramento: Bilingual Education Office, California State Department of Education.

Clifford, James, and George E. Marcus. 1986. *Writing Culture: The Poetics and Politics of Ethnography*. Berkeley: University of California Press.

Cooke, Patrick. 1991. "They Cried Until They Could Not See." *New York Times Magazine*. June 23.

Criddle, Joan D., and Teeda Butt Mam. 1987. *To Destroy You Is No Loss*. New York: Atlantic Monthly Press.

Cultural Survival Quarterly. 1990. Vol. 14, no. 3.

Dukakis, Kitty. 1988. Comments. Congressional Hearings on Cambodia.

Ebihara, May Mayko. 1971. *Svay, a Khmer Village in Cambodia*. Ph.D. dissertation, Department of Anthropology, Columbia University.

———. 1985. "The Khmer" In D. Haines, ed., *Refugees in the United States*. Westport, Conn.: Greenwood Press.

Edmonds, I. G. 1970. *The Khmers of Cambodia: The Story of a Mysterious People*. New York: Bobbs-Merrill.

Etcheson, Craig. 1984. *The Rise and Demise of Democratic Kampuchea*. Boulder, Colo.: Westview Press.

Freeman, James M. 1979. *Untouchable: An Indian Life History*. Stanford: Stanford University Press.

———. 1984. "Knowledge, Compassion, and Involvement." San Jose State University: President's Annual Scholar's Address, May.

———. 1989. *Hearts of Sorrow: Vietnamese-American Lives*. Stanford: Stanford University Press.

Grant, Jonathan S., ed. 1971. *Cambodia: The Widening War in Indochina*. New York: Washington Square Press.

Haines, David W. 1985. *Refugees in the United States*. Westport, Conn.: Greenwood Press.

Hall, D. G. E. 1955. *A History of South-East Asia*. New York: St. Martin's Press.

Holzman, David. 1987. "They Heal the Ravages of Torture." *INSIGHT*, August 24.

Huffman, Franklin E. 1970. *Modern Spoken Cambodian*. New Haven, Conn.: Yale University Press.

Ima, Kenji, et al. 1983. "Adjustment Strategies of the Khmer Refugees in San Diego, California: Six Ethnographic Case Studies." San Diego: Study sponsored by Union of Pan Asian Communities, San Diego, California.

Isajiw, Wsevolod. 1974. "Definitions of Ethnicity." In *Ethnicity*.

Johnson, Steve. 1991. "Laotian Converts Put Past to Torch." In *San Jose Mercury News*, August 18.

Kagan, S. 1986. "Cooperative Learning and Sociocultural Factors in Schooling." In *Beyond Language: Social and Cultural Factors in Schooling Language Minority Students*. Sacramento: Bilingual Education Office.

Kiernan, Ben. 1985. *How Pol Pot Came to Power*. London: Verso.

Kiernan, Ben, and Chanthou Boua. 1982. *Peasants and Politics in Kampuchea 1942–1981*. London: Zed Press.

Knoll, Tricia. 1982. *Becoming Americans: Asian Sojourners, Immigrants, and Refugees in the Western United States*. Oregon: Coast to Coast Books.

Langness, L. L. 1987. *The Study of Culture* (rev. ed.). Novato, California: Chandler and Sharp.

Lebar, Frank M., Gerald G. Hickey, and John K. Musgrave. 1964. *Ethnic Groups of Mainland Southeast Asia*. New Haven, Conn.: Human Relations Area Files.

Loescher, Gil, and John A. Scanlon. 1986. *Calculated Kindness: Refugees and America's Half-Open Door, 1945–Present*. New York: Free Press.

MacDonald, Malcolm. 1987. *Angkor and the Khmers*. Oxford: Oxford University Press.

Mandelbaum, David G. 1973. "The Study of Life History: Gandhi." *Current Anthropology*, vol. 14, no. 3 (June).

Marcus, George E., and Michael M. Fischer. 1986. *Anthropology as Cultural Critique*. Chicago: University of Chicago Press.

May, Someth. 1986. *Cambodian Witness*. New York: Random House.

Meinhardt, Kenneth, et al. 1984. *Asian Health Assessment Project*. Santa Clara County Health Department.

Ngor, Haing, with Roger Warner. 1987. *A Cambodian Odyssey*. New York: Macmillan.

Nguyen-Hong-Nhiem, Lucy, and Joel Martin Halpern, eds. 1989. *The Far East Comes Near: Autobiographical Accounts of Southeast Asian Students in America*. Amherst: University of Massachusetts Press.

Ouk, Mory, Franklin E. Huffman, and Judy Lewis. 1988. *Handbook for Teaching Khmer-Speaking Students*. California: Folsom Cordova Unified School District.

Owen, Tom Choken, ed. 1985. *Southeast Asian Mental Health: Treatment, Prevention, Services, Training, and Research*. Washington, D.C.: U.S. Government Printing Office.

Reimers, David M. 1986. *Still the Golden Door: The Third World Comes To America*. New York: Columbia University Press.

Ross, Russell, ed. 1990. *Cambodia: A Country Study*. Washington, D.C.: U.S. Government Printing Office.

Rumbaut, Ruben G., and Kenji Ima. 1988. *The Adaptation of Southeast Asian Refugee Youth: A Comparative Study*. Washington, D.C.: U.S. Government Printing Office.

Rumbaut, R. G., et al. *Indochina Health and Adaptation Research Project* (IHARP) 1982–85. San Diego County, California.

Selakovich, D. 1984. *Schooling in America*. New York: Longman.

Shawcross, William. 1979. *Sideshow: Kissinger, Nixon and the Destruction of Cambodia*. New York: Simon and Schuster.

————. 1984. *The Quality of Mercy*. New York: Simon and Schuster.

Sheehy, Gail. 1986. *Spirit of Survival*. New York: William Morrow.

Smith, Frank. 1989. "Interpretive Accounts of the Khmer Rouge Years: Personal Experience in Cambodian Peasant World View." Wisconsin Papers on Southeast Asia. Madison: University of Wisconsin.

Smith, Roger M. 1971. "The Politics of Sihanouk." In Jonathan S. Grant, ed. *Cambodia: The Widening War in Indochina*. New York: Washington Square Press.

Spradley, James P. 1979. *The Ethnographic Interview*. New York: Holt, Reinhart and Winston.

————. 1980. *Participant Observation*. New York: Holt, Reinhart and Winston.

Spradley, J., and M. Rynkiewich, eds. 1975. *The Nacirema: Readings on American Culture*. Boston: Little, Brown.

Steinberg, David J. 1959. *Cambodia: Its People, Its Society, Its Culture*. New Haven, Conn.: Human Relations Area Files.

Steinberg, David J., ed. 1987. *In Search of Southeast Asia*. Honolulu: University of Hawaii Press.

Stuart-Fox, Martin, and Bunheang Ung. 1985. *The Murderous Revolution*. Australia: Alternative Publishing Cooperative.

Szymusiak, Molyda. 1986. *The Stones Cry Out: A Cambodian Childhood, 1975–1980*. New York: Farrar, Straus and Giroux.

Takaki, Ronald. 1989. *Strangers from a Different Shore: A History of Asian Americans*. Boston: Little, Brown.

Tarr, Chou Meng. 1990. "A Talk with Prime Minister Hun Sen." *Cultural Survival Quarterly*, vol. 14, no. 3: 6–10.

Tenhula, J., ed. 1991. *Voices from Southeast Asia: The Refugee Experience in the United States*. New York: Holmes and Meier.

Tollefson, James W. 1989. *Alien Winds: The Reeducation of America's Indochinese Refugees*. New York: Praeger.

UNICEF Office of the Special Representative. 1990. *Cambodia: The Situation of Children and Women*. Phnom Penh.

Vickery, Michael. 1984. *Cambodia 1975–1982*. Boston: South End Press.

Welaratna, Usha. 1988. "Cambodian Refugees: Factors Affecting Their Assimilation and English Language Acquisition." *The CATESOL Journal*, vol. 1, no. 1 (November): 17–27.

————. 1989. "Cambodian Refugees in California: After the Holocaust." M.A. thesis, The Office of Graduate Studies and Research, San Jose State University, May.

————. 1990. "Visits with a Cambodian Refugee Family." *San Jose Studies*, vol. 16, no. 3: 86–96.

Wijayatilake, S. R. 1970. *The White Lotus: The Personality of the Buddha*. Sri Lanka: M. D. Gunasena.

Willmott, William E. 1967. *The Chinese in Cambodia*. Vancouver: University of British Columbia Press.

Yathay, Pin. 1987. *Stay Alive, My Son*. New York: Simon and Schuster.

Yu, E., and W. Liu. 1986. "Methodological Problems and Policy Implications in Vietnamese Refugee Research." *International Migration Review*, no. 2 (Summer).

Library of Congress Cataloging-in-Publication Data

Welaratna, Usha, 1948–
  Beyond the killing fields : voices of nine Cambodian survivors
in America / Usha Welaratna
      p. cm. — (Asian America)
Includes bibliographical references.
ISBN 0-8047-2139-4 (cloth)
1. Cambodia—History—1975–   2. Political atrocities—Cambodia.
3. Refugees, Political—Cambodia. 4. Refugees, Political—United
States.   I. Series.
DS554.8.W45   1993
959.604—dc20
92-28557   CIP
(rev.)

⊗ This book is printed on acid-free paper.
It has been typeset on a Macintosh IIci in Adobe Minion
at Stanford University Press.